Stress and Social Anxiety

STRESS AND SOCIAL ANXIETY:

PSYCHOBIOLOGICAL EFFECTS OF ACUTE STRESS ON SOCIAL INTERACTION IN SOCIAL ANXIETY DISORDER

Amalie Anna Trüg

Bibliografische Information der Deutschen Nationalbibliothek

Die Deutsche Nationalbibliothek verzeichnet diese Publikation in der Deutschen Nationalbibliografie; detaillierte bibliografische Daten sind im Internet über http://dnb.d-nb.de abrufbar.

1. Aufl. - Göttingen: Cuvillier, 2017

   Zugl.: Freiburg, Univ., Diss., 2017

Umschlaggestaltung: Amalie Anna Trüg

© CUVILLIER VERLAG, Göttingen 2017

   Nonnenstieg 8, 37075 Göttingen

   Telefon: 0551-54724-0

   Telefax: 0551-54724-21

   www.cuvillier.de

   ISBN 978-3-7369-9605-2

   eISBN 978-3-7369-8605-3

To Thilo,

Renate & Rainer

Acknowledgements

Over the last several years I have had the honor of working on this exciting and demanding project. It would not have been possible, and would not have been nearly as much fun, if it had not been for all of the people behind me, supporting me in so many ways.

First and foremost, I am deeply grateful to my mentor Bernadette von Dawans and my supervisor Markus Heinrichs for their guidance and support throughout this process. Bernadette, your enthusiasm and courageous manner inspired me. Thank you so much for always being so approachable for minor and major questions, and for your encouragement and faith in me. It means a lot.

To Markus Heinrichs, I am profoundly thankful for his support, motivation and expert guidance during the research process. He created a great working atmosphere, highly professional, with a friendly, sociable ambience and room for humor. I very much appreciated and enjoyed working in his team.

Moreover, I would like to thank Gregor Domes, who impressed me with his expertise and brainy ideas. Thank you for calmly answering all my sudden questions whenever I dropped in on you.

Sincere thanks also go to my fellow researchers and colleagues. I am thankful to Tobias Stächele who brought me back down to earth with his incomparable therapeutic skills just when I was about to take off in catastrophic Ph.D. worries (I'll keep in mind the Prinzenrolle!). I also thank Bastian Schiller, Ines Spenthof, Marion Schwaiger, Manuela Kanat, Petra Kamelger, Nicole Ower, Valentina Colonnello, and Ellen Rückert for our fruitful exchanges. Ines, our coffee breaks, and your Nordic serenity, were soothing in stressful moments during the past year. Thank you all for a great time, for discussing both research-related and private issues, and for - every now and then - blowing off steam together with me about the relative merits of simultaneous psychotherapy training in parallel to pursuing a Ph.D. You made sure I always looked forward to coming to work.

Furthermore, I would like to thank all my awesome students for their contribution to this project and their team spirit. I thank Marthe Rump who devotedly supported me in data collection until the late evenings. I also thank Lana Gawron, Emily Feldmann, Janina Zink, Rebecca Overmeyer, Annika Konrad, Katja Fröhlich and all the interns whose help was indispensable: Kristina Dworsky, Antonia Vehlen, Catrin Angst-Eckert, Laya Lehner, Lisa Marx, Lia York, Roxana Petri, Malin Stiene, Amelie Hörburger, Florian Scharpf, and Sebastién Nicolay. The experimental setup was a bit of a personnel challenge, and your commitment made its success possible.

Special thanks go to all the participants of the study, especially the social anxiety patients who courageously engaged in the experiment and were thus exposed to psychosocial stress. I owe them a deep debt of gratitude, and I want to thank them all for their commitment and their interest in our research.

Beyond that, thanks heaps to my amazing friends! Thank you for patiently listening to me, pondering over recruitment strategies, and simply for being there. I know I have been missing for a while, but I am looking forward to making up for it, and re-entering life beyond the desk again. Special thanks go to Brian for so patiently proofreading this thesis.

My most heartfelt thanks go to my parents, who always supported me. You taught me to pursue the things in life that are important to me, and that fascinate me. Your open-mindedness and critical thinking inspire me to this day. I also thank my brother. Basti, you have always believed in me, and have made me feel I can achieve anything. Finally, deepest thanks go to my one and only, Thilo.

Thanks a lot to you all, and let's keep on both thinking and joking, for "Nonsense wakes up the brain cells" (Theodor Seuss)[1].

---

[1](as quoted by Nel, 2003, p. 38)

Abstract

For people suffering from social anxiety disorder (SAD), social interactions imply severe distress. Nonetheless, little is known about the reaction to acute stress and the stress-related psychobiology of SAD. Moreover, there is accumulating evidence for increased affiliation and prosocial behavior in healthy individuals after stress. It is unclear, however, whether SAD patients exhibit a similar social behavioral response to stress, with fear of social interactions being a core symptom of this disorder. A crucial prerequisite for positive social interactions is the ability to infer other peoples' mental states, i.e. empathy. Thus, the aim of this thesis was to examine the stress reaction and its interactional consequences in SAD patients, taking into account individual empathic abilities.

In the empirical part of the thesis, the reaction to a standardized psychosocial stressor was investigated in SAD patients and matched healthy controls on several levels. Firstly, the endocrine, cardiovascular and subjective reaction to acute stress was examined. Patients with SAD exhibited an elevated subjective reactivity to stress, while the biological stress response did not differ from that of healthy controls. Secondly, we investigated the social behavioral response to stress. In contrast to healthy controls, SAD patients did not exhibit increased affiliation behavior under stress but rather showed reduced prosocial behavior. These adverse effects of stress in SAD were buffered by high cognitive empathic abilities. The findings suggest that people with SAD in general do not display affiliation behavior in reaction to stress, but that high cognitive empathy may be able to 'normalize' the behavioral reaction. The results extend previous data in the domain of stress reactivity and social behavior in SAD and provide leverage points for future studies.

The empirical part is embedded in a theoretical section and an enclosing discussion. The theoretical section addresses principal characteristics of the stress system, and elaborates on social behavior and social anxiety disorder. The general discussion summarizes the key findings and discusses methodological considerations and limitations. It closes by drawing clinical implications and highlighting new directions for future research.

Contents

I   GENERAL INTRODUCTION

Anxiety is one of the most fundamental sensations in humans and other mammals. Social contact is one of the most fundamental human needs. In social anxiety disorder (SAD), both aspects collide in a way that results in substantial suffering. That is, social interactions imply severe psychological stress for SAD patients. Despite this essential relation, little is known about the psychobiological mechanisms underlying SAD patients' social interaction behavior under stress. This includes one of its most basic aspects, the stress response in SAD. To date, the physiological stress reaction in patients with SAD is not completely understood. From neuroimaging studies, there is evidence that SAD patients exhibit elevated amygdala reactivity in response to social threat (Evans et al., 2008; Gentili et al., 2016; Straube, Mentzel, & Miltner, 2005; Yoon, Fitzgerald, Angstadt, McCarron, & Phan, 2007). As the amygdala plays a vital role in the detection of threat and the regulation of the subsequent endocrine and autonomous stress response (Forray & Gysling, 2004; Gray, 1993), an exaggerated response to stress in SAD might be expected. However, literature on the physiological stress response in SAD is ambiguous with findings of both elevated reactions (e.g. Condren, O'Neill, Ryan, Barrett, & Thakore, 2002; van West, Claes, Sulon, & Deboutte, 2008) and no differences to healthy controls (e.g. Klumbies, Braeuer, Hoyer, & Kirschbaum, 2014; Martel et al., 1999). A better understanding of the psychophysiological processes underlying the experience of stress in SAD may extend our knowledge of this disorder and help develop adapted treatments. Thus, one aim of this thesis was to investigate the stress response in patients with SAD and matched healthy controls in both major stress pathways, i.e. the hypothalamus-pituitary adrenal (HPA) axis and the sympatho-adrenal medullary (SAM) system, as well as on the subjective stress level. Acute psychosocial stress was induced through a standardized and well-established method, the *Trier Social Stress Test for Groups* (TSST-G; von Dawans, Kirschbaum, & Heinrichs, 2011).

As stress is an everyday phenomenon in our lives, we need reliable ways of regulating its psychological and physiological consequences in order to prevent health hazards, such as hypertension, type-2 diabetes mellitus or psychiatric disorders (Chrousos, 2009; McEwen & Stellar, 1993). Humans have a general need to affiliate with others and form stable relationships (Baumeister & Leary, 1995; Caporael, 1997). Belongingness and being in close relationships has a positive impact on health and well-being (Cacioppo, Cacioppo, Capitanio, & Cole, 2015; Holt-Lunstad, Smith, & Layton, 2010). Accordingly, a vital source of coping is social support (Ditzen & Heinrichs, 2014). While the classical view of the behavioral stress reaction in humans is the *fight-or-flight* response (W. B. Cannon, 1915), which describes aggressive or escaping behavior in response to stress, this view has been broadened by a concept that takes into account the social dimension of human stress. In their *tend-and-befriend* model, Taylor and colleagues (Taylor, 2006; Taylor et al., 2000) suggest that acute stress promotes affiliation to others, which in turn leads to stress reduction, resulting from social support through positive social contacts. This entails difficulties for people suffering from SAD, as key symptoms of this disorder are insecurity and uneasiness regarding social encounters and avoidance of social situations (e.g. Rapee & Heimberg, 1997). While there is accumulating empirical evidence for a *tend-and-befriend* response to stress in healthy individuals (Berger, Heinrichs, von Dawans, Way, & Chen, 2015; Buchanan & Preston, 2014; Takahashi, Ikeda, & Hasegawa, 2007; von Dawans, Fischbacher, Kirschbaum, Fehr, & Heinrichs, 2012), it is unclear whether this mechanism exists in SAD.

Moreover, social cognitive abilities, such as inferring the other's mind, form an important prerequisite for successful social contacts. Deficiencies in these abilities lead to miscommunication and impaired social functioning (Fett et al., 2011; Shanafelt et al., 2005). Taking into account these basic requirements and how they might influence patients' social response to stress enables us to derive conclusions about the social behavioral consequences of acute stress in SAD and its possible underlying mechanisms. Thus, to shed further light on the interactional consequences of stress in SAD, the second aim of this thesis was to examine the effects of stress on social interaction behavior in patients with SAD, taking into consideration the individual empathic abilities. This approach is in accord with the Research Domain Criteria project ("NIMH » Research Domain Criteria (RDoC)," n.d.), an initiative to promote psychopathology research that focuses on dimensional constructs rather than solely on hypothetical diagnosis categories.

The present thesis is based on two empirical chapters from an experimental study on stress reactivity and social interaction behavior after stress in SAD. The empirical section is preceded by a theoretical section that addresses principal characteristics of the stress system (chapter 1), social behavior (chapter 2), social behavior in light of stress (chapter 3) and social anxiety disorder with its psychopathology, etiology, and treatment (chapter 4). It is followed by an enclosing discussion (section IV), which summarizes the key findings and discusses methodological considerations and limitations. Finally, an integrative model of the effects of stress on social behavior in health and psychopathology is presented and clinical implications as well as new directions for fruitful future research are highlighted.

II   THEORETICAL BACKGROUND

1   Basic Knowledge on the Human Stress Response

Stress. We are constantly confronted with it throughout our lives, whether we experience it running to catch a bus, clashing with friends or colleagues, or from more severe, traumatic events.

As one of the pioneers of stress research, Walter Bradford Cannon developed the concept of 'fight or flight' to describe an organism's response to threat (W. B. Cannon, 1915). He found that in confrontation with a stressor, the sympathetic branch of the autonomous nerve system activates the secretion of catecholamines in the adrenal medulla ("sympathoadrenal" system), mobilizing the organism's reaction. Drawing on the idea of a 'milieu intérieur' by Bernard (1878), he later coined the expression *homeostasis* (1929) to describe the physiological adaptations of the organism to maintain a stable internal environment. In the title of his summarizing work "The Wisdom of the Body" (1932), Cannon already acknowledged that the stress reaction forms a vitally important mechanism.

Another pioneer in this area, Hans Selye, extended the work by Cannon by emphasizing the activation of the hypothalamic-pituitary-adrenal (HPA) axis and associated secretion of glucocorticoids (1936). He suggested that this response pattern to stress was nonspecific. That is, independent from the nature of the stressor, the body would react with specific changes such as secretion of cortisol and catecholamines. In his concept of a *general-adaption-syndrome,* he proposed that the organism reacts in a profile with three phases: an "alarm state", analogous to Cannon's fight-or-flight reaction, an "adaption state", associated with resistance, and eventually an "exhaustion state" (1950).

Selye's concept was later extended by Mason (1971), arguing that the concept of non-specificity is lacking psychological processes. He claimed that the psychological evaluation of the stressor initiated the stress response, thus framing the concept of stress as not primarily physiological, *"[...] but rather as a behavioral concept"* (Mason, 1971, p. 331).

McEwen (1998) integrated physiological aspects of the stress reaction and the individual perception of the stressor into his model of allostatic load. The model differentiates between a regular, moderate reaction to a stressor, and an aberrant reactivity. Normally, the physiological stress response is initiated, sustained for an appropriate time and then terminated, thus providing the organism with a flexible and advantageous reaction to the environment. However, due to multiple stressors or a lack of adaptation, for example, the stress response remains on a high level, resulting in 'allostatic load'. This state in turn results in adverse consequences for the organism. The model thereby underlines the dissociation of the physiological stress response, both as an important mechanism for the organism's survival, and as a potential health risk when endured chronically or when the system is unable to adapt sufficiently.

1.1 The physiological stress reaction

On the biological level, stress can be described as a state of imbalance, with the stress reaction attempting to regain balance and to "maintain physiologic integrity" (Ulrich-Lai & Herman, 2009, p. 397). Two distinct but interconnected systems are responsible for the execution of those adaptations: the sympathetic-adrenal-medullary system (SAM) and the hypothalamus-pituitary-adrenal axis (HPA-axis) (**Fig. 1.1**). A prompt response to the stressor is realized by the autonomic nervous system (ANS), more precisely via the SAM. Under resting conditions, the sympathetic and the parasympathetic parts of the ANS act in synergy; under stress, the activity of the sympathetic branch predominates and the influence of the parasympathetic branch is reduced. Due to their antagonistic functioning, an attenuation of the parasympathetic part can result in effects analogous to those of the sympathetic branch (Chrousos & Gold, 1992). That is, under stress, the hypothalamus addresses nuclei in the brainstem, which transmit the signal to the preganglionic sympathetic neurons of the spinal cord. These, in turn, project via pre- or paravertebral ganglia to the adrenal medulla. By this, secretion of epinephrine (esp. in the adrenal medulla) and norepinephrine (esp. in the postsynaptic sympathetic neurons) is triggered (Ulrich-Lai & Herman, 2009). This cascade results in immediate physiologic changes, such as accelerated heart rate, elevated blood pressure, and vasodilatation in muscles, preparing the body for action by ensuring blood sup-supply to the relevant structures. Moreover, glycogenolysis in the liver provides energy through increased glucose levels (Gunnar & Quevedo, 2007) and on the brain level, norepinephrine is released in the locus coeruleus in the brainstem, resulting in enhanced vigilance and arousal (Gunnar & Quevedo, 2007). These physiologic changes can be assessed as markers of ANS activity. In psychological research, one of the most prominent peripheral physiologic markers is the detection of heart rate (Birbaumer & Schmidt, 2002; Freeman, 2006) Alternatively, endocrine changes can be measured as direct products of ANS activity, such as level of catecholamines epinephrine or norepinephrine in blood or saliva (B. Kennedy, Dillon, Mills, & Ziegler, 2001; Okumura, Nakajima, Matsuoka, & Takamatsu, 1997).

The HPA axis is the slower of the two systems (de Kloet, Rots, & Cools, 1996). This is mainly due to the respectively faster and slower mechanisms of neural versus humoral information processing and synthesis of the end-effector glucocorticoids in the HPA system, which involves gene transcription (Gunnar & Quevedo, 2007; R. M. Sapolsky, Romero, & Munck, 2000). In the parvocellular division of the paraventricular nucleus (PVN) of the hypothalamus, corticotropin-releasing hormone (CRH) and arginine vasopressin (AVP) are secreted (Chrousos, 1992). Under circumstances of stress, CRH is released into hypophysial portal vessels and activates cyclic adenosine monophosphate (cAMP), which stimulates the release of adrenocorticotropic hormone (ACTH) in the anterior pituitary. The neuropeptide AVP potentiates these effects of CRH on ACTH release (Rivier & Vale, 1983). ACTH, in turn, binds on receptors in the adrenal cortex, where glucocorticoids (in humans esp. cortisol) are synthesized and released into the bloodstream. From here, they bind to receptors throughout body and brain (Charmandari, Tsigos, & Chrousos, 2005; S. M. Smith & Vale, 2006). The name *glucocorticoid* indicates its involvement in the glucose metabolism, its synthesis in the adrenal cortex, and its steroid structure. The initiated metabolic effects include glycogenolysis, gluconeogenesis, the allocation of lipids and amino acids through lipolysis in fat cells, and the inhibition of protein synthesis in muscle cells (Sapolsky et al., 2000). This results in increased blood glucose levels and modifies fat and protein metabolism (Stephens & Wand, 2012). Further, glucocorticoids have immunosuppressive and anti-inflammatory effects, namely through changes in leukocyte traffic and decreased cytokine production (Chrousos, 1995). Moreover, glucocorticoids are crucial for the termination of HPA axis activity, forming a negative feedback loop by inhibiting CRH and ACTH production in extrahypothalamic centers, in the hypothalamus and in the pituitary gland (Miller et al., 1992; S. M. Smith & Vale, 2006). Hence, the stress response constitutes a pivotal mechanism that allows the organism to adapt to challenging situations. On the downside, if stress has to be endured chronically, it is associated with structural changes in the brain (Arnsten, 2009) and impairs learning by inhibiting long-term-potentiation (de Kloet, Oitzl, & Joëls, 1999). Moreover, stress-related immunosuppression means that stress is one of the most significant risk factors for diseases associated with insufficient immune response, such as tuberculosis or certain kinds of tumors (Elenkov & Chrousos, 1999). On top of that, chronic stress is associated with increased risk for heart attack, and with mental diseases like depression and anxiety disorders (for reviews, see Chrousos, 2009; Kalia, 2002).

Regarding the investigation of stress-related HPA-axis activity, cortisol has been considered the best characterized marker (Foley & Kirschbaum, 2010). Only a small proportion (2-15%) of cortisol remains unbound and "free". However, it is this unbound cortisol that yields the glucocorticoid effects in tissue and brain. Due to its small size and lipid-soluble structure, unbound cortisol can easily pass cell membranes and thus occurs in all body fluids, including blood and saliva. In blood, both bound and unbound cortisol is measurable. Assessment of saliva does not imply an additional stressor for participants the way that venipuncture for blood sampling does. Thus, salivary cortisol depicts a valid and useful measure of HPA-axis activity (Kirschbaum & Hellhammer, 1989).

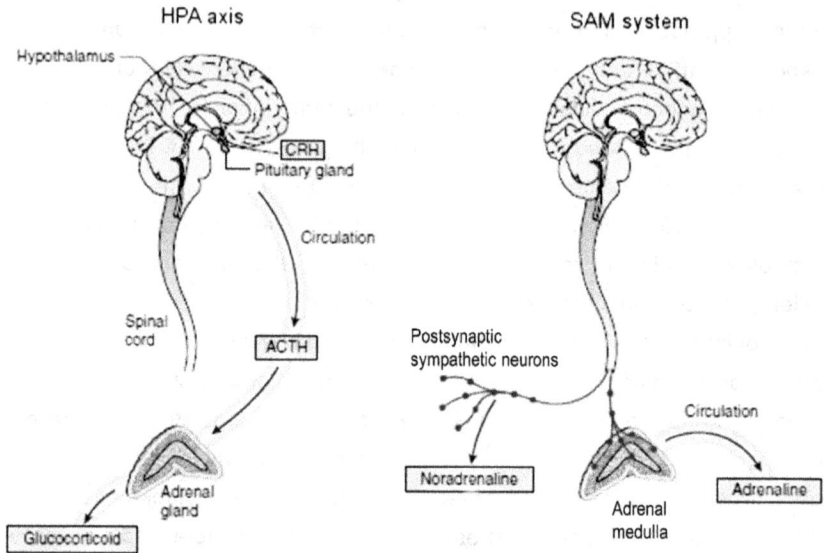

Figure 1.1. Reactions to stress. The hypothalamus-pituitary-adrenal (HPA) axis (left) and the sympatho- adrenal-medullary (SAM) system (right). Adapted from Eisenberger & Cole (2012).

1.1   The psychological stress reaction

Confrontation with a stressor not only induces symptoms on the physiological level but also affects emotion and cognition. The work by Lazarus and his colleagues (1984; Richard S Lazarus, 1966) has highlighted the psychological aspects of stress. According to his transactional model of stress, it is the subjective evaluation of a situation that is crucial for the occurrence of a stress reaction, not the objective stressor alone. In other words, through this evaluation and subsequent coping processes, a reciprocal interaction or 'transaction' between the environment and the self emerges. Lazarus postulated two phases of subjective evaluation that influence the stress reaction: *primary appraisal* and *secondary appraisal*. In primary appraisal, the person estimates the threat potential of the stimulus and what might be possible outcomes, resulting in an evaluation of the personal relevance. In secondary appraisal, one's own resources to deal with the stressor are reconciled. If one's own resources are considered insufficient to overcome the threat, the situation is perceived as stressful. The two phases are thought to happen simultaneously, influencing each other. The model contributes to the explanation of why the same stressor may evoke very divergent reactions in different individuals. Moreover, along with its extension by Folkman (1997), it provides a basis for the explanation of different coping strategies, such as reappraisal, reordering priorities or referral to spiritual beliefs (for a review, see Folkman, 2008). On the downside, due to a more complex view of the stress process and the inclusion of interacting internal factors, clear empirical evidence for the model is missing.

The subjective stress response is typically assessed using questionnaires or visual analogue scales (VAS), where the participant has to indicate the intensity of the criterion by indicating a position along a continuous line. This type of assessment has been shown to be sensitive and suited for repeated measures (S. Grant et al., 1999; Luria, 1975).

2   Behavior among Others: Social Interaction

Human beings exhibit a general desire to affiliate with others and form social groups (Baumeister & Leary, 1995; Caporael, 1997). Social relationships form a substantial evolutionary advantage through, for example, facilitating food supply and providing safety or care for the offspring. Maintenance of social contacts requires performance according to certain rules and conventions and adapting successfully to a given social situation (Ackerman, Huang, & Bargh, 2012). Violations of these rules can result in social rejection. The concept of social performance is discussed in chapter 2.1. In order to perceive social signs and attune one's own behavior to that of one's interaction partner, social cognitive abilities are necessary, i.e. cognitive processes that underlie social interactions. Chapter 2.2 addresses those processes.

2.1   Social performance

Social situations, such as talking to colleagues at work, require people to interact in a way that follows certain social rules, such as joining in a conversation at a suitable time, reacting to what the other person says and revealing some, at some times more and other times less, personal information about oneself. Possessing such competencies and implementing them in an adaptive way in social situations outlines the concept of *social performance*. The literature provides multiple terms in this regard, including 'social competence', 'social skills' or 'communication competence', which are also used interchangeably (Segrin, 2000). Also, different models have been proposed, with some defining social competencies as a personality trait (e.g. Riggio, 1986, 1992) and some conceptualizing them on a molecular level, focusing on situation-specific behavior (e.g. Arkowitz, Lichtenstein, McGovern, & Hines, 1975).

Social performance requires nonverbal, verbal and paralinguistic abilities (Romanczyk, White, & Gillis, 2005). Nonverbal behavior involves aspects such as eye-contact, facial expressions, and gestures. Verbal behavior refers to talking on-topic, answering questions, making self-disclosure etc., while paralinguistic behaviors comprise formal aspects of speech, including, for example, fluency, volume of speech and understood prosody (e.g. Argyle & Kendon, 1967; Sheffer, Penn, & Cassisi, 2001).

2.2   Cognitive and emotional processes underlying social behavior

Social interactions are influenced by the way our mind processes the information it receives in a given situation. Do we recognize what the other person is feeling? Do we understand his or her intent and can we resonate with this? The cognitive and emotional processes that underlie our behavior in social contexts can be subsumed under the field of *social cognition* (Moskowitz, 2005). Those processes form a crucial prerequisite for successful social interactions. If we do not detect social signals from others and thus fail to integrate them into our perception of the situation, we are not able to adjust our reaction properly, leading to miscommunication or attracting social conflict. Accordingly, social cognitive deficiencies entail impairments in social functioning and well-being (Fett et al., 2011; Shanafelt et al., 2005). Social cognition comprises a large number of different but interrelated processes, including emotion recognition, social perception, emotion regulation or self-other-distinction (Green et al., 2008). One of the most fundamental mechanisms is the ability of understanding the other's emotional and mental state, i.e. empathy.

Much has been written about the definition of empathy and it has been defined in numerous ways. In general, it is defined as the ability to understand other people's emotional and mental state and to resonate with it (for an extensive overview on the different concepts of empathy, see Bateson, 2011). A predominant conceptualization, underpinned by neuroanatomical evidence (for a review, see Dvash & Shamay-Tsoory, 2014), depicts the dissociation between *cognitive* and *emotional* empathy. While *cognitive empathy* refers to mental perspective-taking, *emotional empathy* is concerned with one's own emotional response to another person's affective state (for a review, see Singer, 2006).

In a conversation, for example, a person has to decode another person's emotional and mental state in order to arrive at an adequate reaction. This requires the perception of cues from the other person's face, voice and posture and the identification of emotions, desires or intentions (Achim, Guitton, Jack-Jackson, Boutin, & Monetta, 2013; Baron-Cohen, Wheelwright, Hill, Raste, & Plumb, 2001; Sabbagh, 2004). This ability refers to cognitive empathy, but it has also been called theory of mind (ToM) or mentalizing (for reviews, see Eslinger, 1998; Frith & Frith, 2007). The terms cognitive empathy, ToM, and mentalizing conceptually overlap and are used with a certain degree of synonymy (e.g. A. Smith, 2010; Straub, 1990). Perspective-taking and ToM have been suggested to be subcategories of cognitive empathy (Eslinger, 1998; S. G. Shamay-Tsoory, Tomer, Goldsher, Berger, & Aharon-Peretz, 2004). At the same time, cognitive empathy has been suggested to depict a subcategory of ToM, relating to inferring other people's affective states in contrast to cognitive states (Walter, 2012). In the present study, we distinguish between the cognitive process of intellectually understanding the thoughts and feelings of others ('cognitive empathy') and the affective reaction to another person's emotional state ('emotional empathy').

Other aspects have been subsumed under social cognition, too, including social knowledge or attributional style (Pinkham et al., 2014). In contrast to the basal process of identifying another person's mental state, they depict higher order processes, referring to the awareness about social norms and to the typical way of explaining the causes of events, respectively (e.g. Green et al., 2008).

2.2.1 Neural correlates of empathy

Across different social cognitive tasks, social cognitive functions have in general been associated with a relatively constant neuronal pattern, the so called 'social brain network' (Blakemore, 2008; Brothers, 1990; Frith, 2007; D. P. Kennedy & Adolphs, 2012). This network includes prefrontal areas, such as the dorsolateral prefrontal cortex (dlPFC), medial prefrontal (mPFC) and orbitofrontal (OFC) regions as well as temporal areas (Fett, Shergill, & Krabbendam, 2015).

For the two aspects of empathy, *cognitive* empathy, i.e. inferring another person's mental state, and *emotional* empathy, i.e. sharing another person's feelings, distinct patterns of activation have been found (for a review, see

Dvash & Shamay-Tsoory, 2014). Research has mainly focused on *cognitive* empathy, commonly referred to as theory of mind (ToM). For the investigation of ToM, several methods have been implemented. They range from simple tasks such as assigning a mental state to a person by looking at pictures of their eye region *(mind in the eyes)* to more complex tasks such as false belief paradigms or strategic games. In their meta-analysis, Schurz and colleagues (2014) categorized imaging studies according to their methodological approach and analyzed them separately as well as together. They found the medial prefrontal cortex and the temporo-parietal junction bilateral as overlapping areas for the different tasks, suggesting a 'core network' of theory of mind, as claimed by previous studies (Frith & Frith, 2006; Gallagher & Frith, 2003; Van Overwalle, 2009). This has been cross-validated by a recent meta-analysis on ToM (Molenberghs, Johnson, Henry, & Mattingley, 2016). Evidence for an involvement of frontal regions also comes from lesion studies, with impairments in ToM following frontal lobe damage (for a review, see Sabbagh, 2004).

Regarding research on *emotional* empathy, empathy for several feelings (happiness, anger, disgust) has been investigated. A commonly used method is 'pain for others' (e.g. de Vignemont & Singer, 2006; Decety & Lamm, 2009; Singer et al., 2004), where the participant observes others receiving a painful stimulus. Those studies showed that watching another person feel pain elicits activation in similar regions as perceiving the painful stimulus oneself, supporting the hypothesis of a shared representation network for empathy (Preston & De Waal, 2002). Other approaches use simple observation of stimulus material (Blakemore, Bristow, Bird, Frith, & Ward, 2005; Grosbras & Paus, 2006) or imagination (e.g. Jackson, Brunet, Meltzoff, & Decety, 2006). A consistent pattern of activation in response to those tasks has been found in the anterior insula, medial/anterior cingulate cortex and, regarding empathy for pain, somatosensory areas (Decety, 2011; Lamm, Decety, & Singer, 2011). A meta-analysis on empathy that used a whole-brain approach (Fan, Duncan, de Greck, & Northoff, 2011) found the bilateral anterior insula and dorsal anterior mid-cingulate cortex to be engaged in empathy, independent of task and stimulus material. This suggests that activation in those regions seems to be related to emotional empathy per se, independent of any specific emotion.

2.2.2   Empathy and prosocial behavior

When we see an injured child that fell off his or her bike, we instantly have the impulse to help. It is only through understanding how the person is feeling that this type of reaction is triggered. Accordingly, empathy is thought to motivate prosocial behavior and inhibit antisocial behaviors (e.g. Batson & Coke, 1981; Krebs, 1975; Stocks, Lishner, & Decker, 2009). For example, individuals are more likely to help others if they feel empathy for them (Eisenberg, 2007; Hoffmann, 2008; Lockwood, Seara-Cardoso, & Viding, 2014; for a review, see Bateson, 2002). More precisely, the perception of the other person's emotional state evokes a vicarious response, resulting in empathic concern, which is associated with the wish to reduce the other person's affliction and in turn fosters prosocial behavior (Eisenberg & Miller, 1987). Instead of empathic concern, one might as well primarily react with negative feelings such as anxiety or discomfort, also called personal distress. Bateson (1998) proposed that experiencing empathic concern promotes other-oriented motivation, whilst personal distress leads to a rather self-focused state. Moreover, while personal distress is thought to be based on lower-order processes, such as contagion, empathic concern is thought to arise from the comprehension of another's mental or emotional state and thus to require higher-order cognitive process of mentalizing/cognitive empathy (Eisenberg, 2000; Lamm, Batson, & Decety, 2007). Accordingly, a recent longitudinal study found perspective-taking abilities to predict later prosocial behavior in children (Kuhnert, Begeer, Fink, & de Rosnay, 2016). Taken together, there is evidence for cognitive as well as emotional empathic abilities to promote prosocial behavior.

3   Stress and Social Behavior

How do we behave under stress? A few years ago, the answer would have been either that we face the stressor, maybe becoming aggressive; or we withdraw from it, following the classical *fight-or-flight* response established by Cannon (1932). Accordingly, aggressive and antisocial behavior in response to stress has been observed both in primates and humans (I. W. Craig, 2007; Honess & Marin, 2006; Sandi & Haller, 2015). In recent years, this view has been extended by an alternative behavioral response to stress, i.e. increased affiliation behavior, conceptualized as *tend-and-befriend* behavior (Taylor et al., 2000, 2006).

3.1   The *tend-and-befriend* concept and its biological basis

Shelly E. Taylor postulates an additional model for the reaction to stress, the *tend-and-befriend* concept (2006; Taylor et al., 2000). This model provides an alternative perspective on the response to stress, focusing on social behavioral aspects. It submits that, from an evolutionary perspective, under circumstances of threat, fighting or fleeing would result in endangering the offspring by direct harm or separation from the social group. Rather, in order to maximize survival, behaviors that protect oneself and one's offspring might have evolved. Thus, under stress, the impetus to nurture and protect the offspring *(tending)* and to affiliate with social groups *(befriending)* may be strengthened. Thereby, possible risks can be reduced by obtaining support and protection, which in turn helps to regulate distress. The model suggests that in times of stress, affiliative behavior is promoted, mediated by a biological signaling system, including the oxytocin system (**Fig. 3.1**).

Oxytocin is a neuropeptide that, synthesized in the hypothalamic paraventricular and supraoptic nuclei, is released via the pituitary in the blood stream (Brownstein, Russell, & Gainer, 1980; Swaab, Nijveldt, & Pool, 1975). The oxytocin system has been suggested as a crucial factor in the modulation of social behavior under stress (Heinrichs, Chen, & Domes, 2013; Heinrichs, von Dawans, & Domes, 2009). Intracerebral oxytocin has anxiolytic effects by dampening the responsiveness of the HPA-axis. This has been shown in animal (Neumann, Krömer, Toschi, & Ebner, 2000; Uvnäs-Moberg, Ahlenius, Hillegaart, & Alster, 1994; Windle, Shanks, Lightman, & Ingram, 1997) as well as human research (Heinrichs, Baumgartner, Kirschbaum, & Ehlert, 2003; Koch et al., 2016). Further, evidence from neuroimaging studies suggests that this effect is mediated by a downregulation of amygdala activity (Baumgartner, Heinrichs, Vonlanthen, Fischbacher, & Fehr, 2008; Domes, Heinrichs, Gläscher, et al., 2007; Kanat, Heinrichs, Mader, van Elst, & Domes, 2015; Petrovic, Kalisch, Singer, & Dolan, 2008). This is underpinned by findings on the cellular level in rats (Huber, Veinante, & Stoop, 2005). Moreover, the oxytocin system has been shown to be crucial for social affiliation behavior (Heinrichs & Domes, 2008). This has been demonstrated for several aspects of social interaction. For example, there is evidence that oxytocin increases eye-contact (B. Auyeung et al., 2015; Guastella, Mitchell, & Dadds, 2008), promotes the processing of positive social cues (Di Simplicio, Massey-Chase, Cowen, & Harmer, 2009; Domes et al., 2013; Marsh, Yu, Pine, & Blair, 2010), improves emotion recognition and theory of mind (Domes, Heinrichs, Michel, Berger, & Herpertz, 2007; Lischke et al., 2012; Schulze et al., 2011), increases trust (Baumgartner et al., 2008; Kosfeld, Heinrichs, Zak, Fischbacher, & Fehr, 2005), generosity (Barraza & Zak, 2009; Zak, Stanton, & Ahmadi, 2007) and positive communication (Ditzen et al., 2009), hence facilitating social approach behavior.

Originally developed with particular respect to women, the *tend-and-befriend* model has been broadened to men's stress response as well (Geary & Flinn, 2002). It is in line with the work by Baumeister and Leary (1995), who described the general human motivation to affiliate with others and form stable relationships, a motive they called *need to belong*.

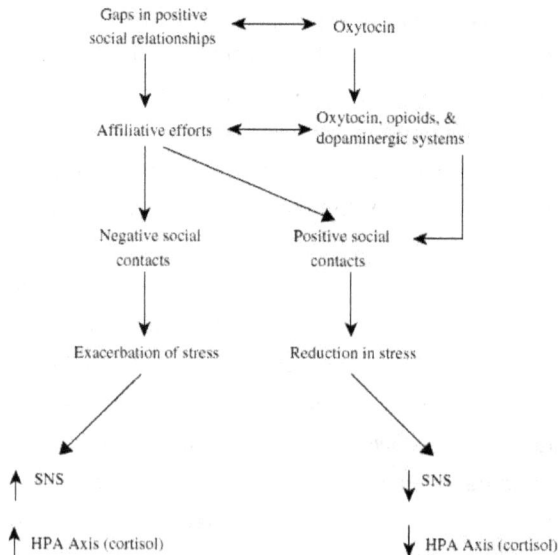

Figure 3.1. Model of *tend-and-befriend* behavior (Taylor, 2006).

3.2   Effects of stress on social behavior: Empirical findings

A growing body of research provides underpinnings for affiliative behavior in response to stress (Buchanan, Bagley, Stansfield, & Preston, 2012; Margittai et al., 2015; Takahashi et al., 2007; von Dawans et al., 2012). In a study by von Dawans and colleagues (2012), for example, healthy men who had been stressed showed more prosocial behaviors like trust, trustworthiness and sharing than those who hadn't been stressed. Furthermore, several studies indicate that it might be the individual cortisol response in reaction to stress, rather than the exposure to stress per se, that contributes to subsequent social behavior (Berger et al., 2015; Smeets, Dziobek, & Wolf, 2009). Berger and colleagues (2015) asked their participants to rate the psychological closeness to an interaction partner after undergoing the TSST-G and the Fast Friends procedure (Aron, Melinat, Aron, Vallone, & Bator, 1997). While there was no difference between subjects in the stress and the control condition of the TSST-G, subjects with high cortisol responses reported a stronger feeling of closeness to their interaction partner than subjects with low cortisol responses. Additionally, in a study on social cognition under stress, men with higher cortisol reactions in response to stress showed better social-cognitive abilities than those with lower reactions (Smeets et al., 2009). Those findings suggest that the magnitude of HPA-axis reactivity might modulate social behavior in response to stress. Moreover, specifically individual stress-induced cortisol responses have been associated with approach-avoidance behavior in animals (Kalin, Shelton, Rickman, & Davidson, 1998; R. M. Sapolsky, 1990) and humans (Roelofs, Elzinga, & Rotteveel, 2005).

Those studies on the relation of stress and affiliative behavior are in line with findings from animal research. In primates, affiliation behavior in terms of reconciliation and consolation has been observed after stressful events such as conflicts (Aureli, Van Schaik, & Van Hooff, 1989; Fraser, Stahl, & Aureli, 2008; Koski, Koops, & Sterck, 2007). Such behavior may help preserve group coherence and thus provide an evolutionary advantage over breakup of the group, for example through protection against predators and improved capabilities for foraging. Furthermore, stress has been shown to activate pair bonding in prairie voles (DeVries, Guptaa, Cardillo, Cho, & Carter, 2002).

There are also a few studies that report contrary findings. They found a positive association of the cortisol response to stress with egoistic decision-making (Starcke, Polzer, Wolf, & Brand, 2011), and with fewer utilitarian judgements (Youssef et al., 2012), respectively. Both studies used moral dilemmas that require reflection on an abstract problem instead of measuring social behavior per se. Because of the cognitive character of those tasks, biases such as social desirability might have had a greater influence compared to behavioral tasks. A recent study on social decision-making (Steinbeis, Engert, Linz, & Singer, 2015) found participants experiencing anticipatory stress to trust less than participants who were not stressed. However, the study used solely anticipation as a stressor, and cortisol reaction was rather low (increase under 1.5 nmol/l in 66% of stressed participants). Moreover, the authors argued that the affiliative tendencies in the design by von Dawans and colleagues (2012), which equals that of the present study, arose from in-group favoritism due to the shared stress experience in the TSST-G, rather than from stress per se. Notably, the interaction partners in the decision paradigm by von Dawans and colleagues were additional participants and not the same as those in the TSST-G. Apart from that, Steinbeis and colleagues did not find differential effects after formation of in- and out-groups.

4   Social Anxiety Disorder

As has been pointed out, the formation of social contacts and relationships is a general human need (Baumeister & Leary, 1995; Caporael, 1997) and its success is dependent on a certain social behavior. In people with social anxiety disorder (SAD), severe worry about their behavior and appearance in social situations leads to clinically relevant suffering. Despite being one of the most common mental disorders (Fehm, Pelissolo, Furmark, & Wittchen, 2005; Kessler et al., 2005), SAD had been widely ignored in psychological and clinical research until 1985. In that year, Liebowitz, Gorman, Fyer and Klein (1985) published their article *"Social Phobia. Review of a neglected anxiety disorder"*, where they turned the spotlight on precisely that deficiency. Thirty-two years later, many insights into this disorder have been gained, but still a lot of ques-questions remain.

Social anxiety disorder is characterized by a "marked and persistent fear of one or more social or performance situations in which the person is exposed to unfamiliar people or to possible scrutiny by others. The individual fears that he or she will act in a way (or show anxiety symptoms) that will be embarrassing and humiliating" (DSM V, American Psychiatric Association, 2013, p. 202). Thus, social encounters trigger distress and often also bodily symptoms such as sweating, trembling or blushing. As a consequence, people suffering from SAD avoid social situations or endure them with intense distress (APA; American Psychiatric Association, 2013).

4.1   Brief history of social anxiety disorder

Social anxiety disorder was first named "social phobia" and was not included as an official disorder until 1980, in the DSM-III. The DSM-III restricted the diagnosis to few situations, while lacking empirical support for this restriction. Diagnosis of social phobia was precluded when that person had been diagnosed with an avoidant personality disorder (APD). Thus, the diagnosis social phobia was limited to people suffering from social fears in very circumscribed situations, such as performance anxiety (Heimberg et al., 2014). This view was refuted by Liebowitz and colleagues (1985). As a result, in the revision of the DSM-III, a 'generalized subtype' was introduced and the exclusion of comorbid avoidant-personality disorder was removed. Due to this broader concept of social fears, the label was later changed to 'social anxiety disorder' in the DSM-IV. With the introduction of the DSM-V in 2013, small changes were made such that patients no longer had to recognize that their fear was excessive or unreasonable. Instead, it had to be rated as out of proportion by the clinician. Moreover, the requirement of the 6-month duration was extended from patients younger than 18 to adults as well.

The DSM-IV and -V distinguish two subtypes of SAD, the *generalized* type and the *non-generalized* type. The former encompasses cases where the anxiety occurs in a wide range of social situations, the latter refers to cases with only one or two feared situations, often performance situations, such as delivering a speech. The existence of those two subtypes has been subject to substantial criticism, as the aspect "in most situations" is not clearly operationalized. With focus on a qualitative rather than quantitative distinction, differentiation into "performance" and "interactional" subtypes has been proposed by some authors (e.g. Mannuzza et al., 1995; Turner, Beidel, & Townsley, 1992). However, the subtypes have been called into question by recent research that found little evidence for such a distinction (Ruscio et al., 2008). As such, the classification of different social anxiety subgroups is still not satisfying. More research is needed. Moreover, in order to develop empirically-grounded subtypes, the diagnostic system could benefit from data-driven categorization rather than settling for arbitrary definitions based on theoretical assumptions. A deeper knowledge about differential subtypes could be advantageous for allocating fine-grained treatment.

Furthermore, the distinction of SAD and APD has been the focus of much discussion. While some suggest they form a continuum (severity-continuum hypothesis), with APD representing a higher degree of symptom severity than SAD (Carter & Wu, 2010; Chambless, Fydrich, & Rodebaugh, 2008; Ralevski et al., 2005; Reich, 2009), others suggest that SAD and APD share a severe amount of symptomatology but may be two qualitatively distinct diagnostic entities, with APD comprising qualities of a personality disorder, thus dissociating itself from SAD (Bögels et al., 2010; Eikenaes, Hummelen, Abrahamsen, Andrea, & Wilberg, 2013; Rettew, 2000). Thus far, more knowledge is needed regarding personality disorders in general (i.e. stability versus plasticity of symptoms over time), and the distinction between SAD and APD in particular, before this question can be answered satisfactorily. Accordingly, the Anxiety Sub-Workgroup for the DSM V concluded that there was insufficient evidence for SAD and APD to be considered as one disorder (Heimberg et al., 2014). The difficulty of a conceptual delineation is also reflected in comorbidity rates: In about 50-90% of individuals with SAD, avoidant personality disorder is additionally diagnosed (B. F. Grant, Hasin, Stinson, et al., 2005; Shea et al., 2004).

With impairments in social contexts, the cultural aspect of a disorder may be of relevance. In eastern cultures, there is a disorder called *taijin-kyo-fusho,* which shares a lot of symptoms with SAD, but the anxiety refers to the other person. That is, instead of fearing to embarrass oneself, people suffering from taijin-kyo-fusho are afraid of offending or hurting others (Stein, 2009; Hofmann & Hinton, 2014). As more research is needed to discover to what extent SAD and taijin-kyo-fusho are overlapping, the present study focuses on social anxiety disorder only.

4.2 Epidemiology

For social anxiety disorder, a 12-month prevalence of 7.1% and a lifetime prevalence of 12.1% have been reported for the U.S. (Kessler, Chiu, Demler, Merikangas, & Walters, 2005; Ruscio et al., 2008). Prevalence rates from European studies are in accordance with this (for a review, see Wittchen & Fehm, 2003). Women are more likely than men to suffer from SAD (gender ratio of 3:2). However, the sex difference is less skewed than in other anxiety disorders (Wittchen & Fehm, 2003). Social anxiety disorder has an early age of onset, with the majority of cases beginning in childhood or adolescence. A review by Chavira and Stein (2005) found onset rates of 50% by the age of 11 and 80% by the age of 20 years. Typically, SAD is considered a chronic disorder. Symptom duration in clinical samples is 10-25 years on average. Looking at the natural course, remission rates from retrospective studies are rather low and vary between 11% and 48% (e.g. Chartier, Walker, & Stein, 2001; DeWit, Ogborne, Offord, & MacDonald, 1999). Prospective studies retrench this extent of chronicity to some degree. While some report similar remission rates of about 35%, including the Harvard Brown Anxiety Research Project, the longest prospective study on SAD to date with a run-time of 12 years (Beard, Moitra, Weisberg, & Keller, 2010; Bruce et al., 2005), other longitudinal studies find higher rates of 48-66% (Beesdo-Baum et al., 2012; Blanco et al., 2011; Karlsson et al., 2010). Those variations might be explained by the following factors: first, methodological reasons might contribute to the varying rates, such as differences in definition criteria for *remission* and the length of follow-up; second, the results highlight the heterogeneity of this disorder and suggest that it may not only differ in behavioral aspects but also in course (e.g. fluctuating or chronic) (cf. Vriends, Bolt, & Kunz, 2014); finally, results from wait-list control groups of treatment studies suggest no substantial symptom reduction without therapy, at least in those patients who seek treatment (e.g. Acarturk, Cuijpers, van Straten, & de Graaf, 2009).

4.3   Severeness and comorbidity

Social anxiety disorder is associated with functional impairment, especially in social life and relationships, and consequently with reduced quality of life (Aderka et al., 2012; Kessler, Berglund, et al., 2005; Mendlowicz & Stein, 2000; Ruscio et al., 2008). In adults, it is associated with heightened rates of unemployment (Beesdo et al., 2007; Wittchen, Fuetsch, Sonntag, Müller, & Liebowitz, 2000), and in children and adolescents with a raised likelihood of early school leaving (Stein & Kean, 2000). Moreover, SAD is linked with suicidal ideation and attempts (Cougle, Keough, Riccardi, & Sachs-Ericsson, 2009; Sareen et al., 2005; Schneier, Johnson, Hornig, Liebowitz, & Weissman, 1992). Many people suffering from SAD also meet criteria for another mental disorder. A study on a large US sample by Grant and colleagues (2005) found high comorbidity rates for other anxiety disorders (49%), major depression (20%), and alcohol abuse (13%). Comparable rates were found in a European sample (Ohayon & Schatzberg, 2010).

4.4   Etiology and psychobiology

As with most psychiatric disorders, a multi-causal etiological framework is considered for SAD. The vulnerability-stress model describes the development of psychopathology as a result of predisposed factors interacting with the perceived stress due to environmental influences (Hankin & Abela, 2005; but see also Kendler, Myers, & Prescott, 2002). Genetic predispositions such as temperament might increase susceptibility to certain environmental risk factors and thus lead to the formation of the pathology. To date, there is no comprehensive etiological theory about the pathogenic mechanisms for the development of social anxiety disorder (for reviews, see Brook & Schmidt, 2008; Hudson & Rapee, 2000), but several contributing factors have been pointed out. The following sections give an overview of the predominant ones. Compared to risk factors, little attention has been drawn to potentially protective factors. So far, several candidates have been reported, like crowd affiliation, romantic relationships or quality of best friendships (La Greca & Harrison, 2005). With more knowledge about protecting factors, more profound preventive interventions might be designed and thus help lowering the risk for developing SAD.

4.4.1 Heritability and genetic influence

Several familial studies have shown an aggregation of social anxiety disorder in first-degree relatives of patients with SAD compared to relatives of non-socially-anxious controls (Fyer, Mannuzza, Chapman, Liebowitz, & Klein, 1993; Hettema, Neale, & Kendler, 2001; Merikangas, Lieb, Wittchen, & Avenevoli, 2003). In familial studies, however, genetics and environmental factors are intertwined. From twin-studies, which help disentangle the genetic contribution, there is some evidence for a specific genetic heritability, with higher concordance rates in monozygotic twins than in dizygotic twins (e.g. Kendler, Neale, Kessler, Heath, & Eaves, 1992). In those studies, the variance explained by genetic factors, however, varies between 0.13 - 0.60 (Hallett, Ronald, Rijsdijk, & Happé, 2012; Hettema, Neale, Myers, Prescott, & Kendler, 2006; Kendler et al., 1992). A recent meta-analysis of 13 twin-studies on social anxiety and SAD reports estimates of 0.42 for genetic contribution and 0.54 for non-shared environmental factors, such as peer relationships (Scaini, Belotti, & Ogliari, 2014). The influence of shared environmental factors, such as socioeconomic status or parenting style, was low, emphasizing genetic factors as the basis for familial transmission of social anxiety. Moreover, the impact of genetic factors on social anxiety symptoms varied with age. Genetic factors explained more variance in socially anxious children than in socially anxious adults (54% in respect to 27%), where individual non-shared environmental factors became more relevant. The authors explain this by the notion that adults have been exposed to more social situations in their lives, thus having more opportunities to experience social fears or develop social skills, which could explain more of the phenotypic variance. Additionally, a genome-wide study on social anxiety (Gelernter, Page, Stein, & Woods, 2004) found chromo-chromosome 16 to be implicated, proximate to the norepinephrine transporter, a possible candidate gene (see chapter 4.4.3). Findings like this suggest that the detection of susceptibility genes for social fears and related phenotypes may be possible. Genome-wide pooling studies would thereby provide an unbiased investigation of the whole genome (Stein & Stein, 2008).

Further, anxiety disorders frequently co-occur (Hettema et al., 2001). Thus, it has been proposed that heritability in SAD might depict a predisposition for general anxiety rather than a particular genetic strain for social anxiety disorder (for a review, see Hudson & Rapee, 2000). Studies on this topic, however, primarily found associations between SAD patients and their relatives but not with other anxiety disorders, i.e. specific familial aggregation (Fyer, Mannuzza, Chapman, Martin, & Klein, 1995; Merikangas et al., 2003).

In conclusion, research on social anxiety and SAD report familial clusters of occurrence, with a moderate role of genetic influence (Hettema et al., 2001; Scaini et al., 2014). In order to paint a clearer picture of the heritability of SAD, more research is needed to differentiate any genetic predisposition either toward general anxiousness or toward specific social anxiety.

4.4.2   Neural correlates

Eighty years ago, Papez (1937) proposed a model on the neuroanatomical mechanisms underlying emotion processing. Since then, much research on the neural correlates of emotions in general and anxiety in particular has been conducted (for a review, see LeDoux, 2000). The following section gives an overview of the brain regions that have been associated with social anxiety and SAD.

Being an indicator for saliency of stimuli, the amygdala plays a key role in the processing of fear (e.g. LeDoux, 2000; Zald, 2003). For example, it is involved in regular fear conditioning. Accordingly, it has repeatedly been suggested that amygdala activity is exaggerated in anxiety disorders (for reviews, see Rauch, Shin, & Wright, 2003; Kent & Rauch, 2003). In addition, the insular cortex, among other regions, has been implicated in the processing of negative emotions like disgust and fear (e.g. Calder, Lawrence, & Young, 2001; Damasio et al., 2000; Ibañez, Gleichgerrcht, & Manes, 2010), as well as salience (e.g. A. D. B. Craig, 2009).

In SAD, hyperactivity of the amygdala and insula has been reported for threat-related cues such as emotional faces (Evans et al., 2008; Straube et al., 2005; Yoon et al., 2007) or public speaking (Lorberbaum et al., 2004; Tillfors, Furmark, Marteinsdottir, & Fredrikson, 2002). These findings are strengthened by a meta-analysis on negative emotion processing in anxiety disorders by Etkin & Wagner (2007). They report hyperactivation in the bilateral amygdala and insula for patients with SAD, specific phobias and PTSD. No regions of hypoactivation compared to healthy controls were found in SAD. Furthermore, in response to threatening faces, positive correlations were reported between symptom severity of SAD (and not general trait or state anxiety) and activity in the amygdala (Ball et al., 2012; e.g. Frick, Howner, Fischer, Kristiansson, & Furmark, 2013; Goldin, Manber, Hakimi, Canli, & Gross, 2009; Phan, Fitzgerald, Nathan, & Tancer, 2006) and in the insula (Ball et al., 2012; Carré et al., 2014). The findings of Etkin and Wagner (2007) have been confirmed by a recent meta-analysis on the neural correlates of fear-related cue processing in SAD (Brühl, Delsignore, Komossa, & Weidt, 2014). Here, increased activation compared to healthy controls was consistently found in the amygdalae and the insular cortices. Additionally, increased activation was also found in the bilateral medial and ventrolateral prefrontal cortices; in the anterior cingulate cortex (ACC); in the bilateral parietal cortex; and, in some of the studies, in the bilateral hippocampus as well as in the fusiform gyrus. The fusiform gyrus is associated with face recognition (Weiner & Zilles, 2016). Frick and colleagues (2013) found increased activity in this structure in SAD in response to fearful faces. While connectivity between the fusiform gyrus and amygdala was enhanced, it was reduced between the fusiform gyrus and ventromedial PFC. Moreover, increased connectivity between amygdala and pre- and orbitofrontal regions has been found in SAD patients (Danti et al., 2010; Ding et al., 2011), but also reduced connectivity (Hahn et al., 2011; Liao et al., 2010; Prater, Hosanagar, Klumpp, Angstadt, & Phan, 2013; Sladky et al., 2015). Further, increased connectivity of medial prefrontal cortex and subcortical regions such as thalamus and striatum have been reported (Giménez et al., 2012; Liao et al., 2010). The prefrontal cortex (PFC) as well as the ACC, among others, have repeatedly been associated with emotion regulation, e.g. reappraisal. It is assumed that these regions influence activity in structures like the amygdala and insula and thereby play an important role in the regulation of stress (Ochsner & Gross, 2005).

In order to extend functional neuroimaging, studies using diffusion tensor imaging (DTI) focus on structural connectivity by investigating white matter. A review on structural alterations in SAD reports reduced connectivity in the right uncinate fasciculus (UF) (Phan et al., 2009), a major fiber tract, connecting frontal regions such as the orbitofrontal cortex (OFC) with limbic regions such as the amygdala. As the OFC has been implicated in the control and reduction of emotions (Ochsner & Gross, 2005) the authors interpret this such that decreased top-down control leads to hyperactivation of the amygdala. This finding was partially replicated by Baur and colleagues (2011), who found reduced fractional anisotropy near the UF and a negative correlation of the UF with trait anxiety in SAD. In line with the findings of reduced connectivity between the amygdala and prefrontal regions (Hahn et al., 2011; Liao et al., 2010; Prater et al., 2013; Sladky et al., 2015), these findings could explain why in SAD, enhanced prefrontal activation co-occurs with decreased emotional control. Top-down processes like reappraisal or suppression could be initiated but not transmitted to the limbic regions properly, due to insufficient connectivity (Brühl et al., 2014).

Moreover, volume reductions have been found for SAD patients in amygdala/hippocampus (Irle et al., 2010; Meng et al., 2013) and insula (Kawaguchi et al., 2016). Other studies, however found an increase in amygdalar/hippocampal volume in SAD patients (Machado-de-Sousa et al., 2014; Talati, Pantazatos, Schneier, Weissman, & Hirsch, 2013).

Taken together, compared to healthy controls, SAD has been associated with increased neural activity in limbic and cortical areas, more precisely in the amygdala, insula, ACC and prefrontal cortex, describing the typical fear circuit (e.g. Etkin, 2012; LeDoux, 2000). Connectivity studies report somewhat inconsistent results but nonetheless point towards an impaired emotion regula-regulation network in SAD (Baur et al., 2011; Brühl et al., 2014; Phan et al., 2009). It should be noted that imaging research in SAD has thus far mainly been concentrated on the amygdala. The exploration of other critical regions, cortical and subcortical, as well as research on the question of how they are interconnected has begun, but findings are still in their infancy. The integration of findings derived from those analyses could account for the heterogeneity in the phenotype of social anxiety disorder (see Miskovic & Schmidt, 2012). As Stein concluded, "It is clear that we have a long way to go before we can speak with authority about the 'neurobiology of social phobia'." (1998; p. 128).

4.4.3   Neurotransmitter systems

Several neurotransmitters have been associated with anxiety in general and social anxiety in particular, including monoamines such as serotonin (Charney, Woods, Krystal, & Heninger, 1990), glutamate (Phan et al., 2005), gamma-aminobutyric acid (GABA) (Pollack, Jensen, Simon, Kaufman, & Renshaw, 2008), as well as dopamine and norepinephrine (Mathew, Coplan, & Gorman, 2001) To date, alterations in serotonergic and dopaminergic transmission systems have received the most attention in the research on SAD.

Association between serotonergic functioning and anxiety is suggested by the effectiveness of selective serotonin reuptake inhibitors (SSRIs) in many anxiety disorders including SAD (for reviews, see Koen & Stein, 2011; van der Linden, Stein, & van Balkom, 2000). This is underpinned by a PET-study that found reduced serotonin receptor ($5-HT_{1A}$) binding potential in SAD (Lanzenberger et al., 2007). Moreover, in recent years, there has been research on the functional polymorphism of the serotonin transporter (5-HTT) gene. It mediates the reuptake of serotonin in the synapse, with the short allele accounting for decreased serotonin transporter expression (Heils et al., 1996; Lesch et al., 1996). The amygdala is densely innervated by serotonergic fibers (Bauman & Amaral, 2005). Accordingly, variations in the alleles of the 5-HTT polymorphism have been associated with amygdala reactivity (Furmark et al., 2009; Hariri et al., 2002). As social anxiety is associated with increased amygdala responsiveness, variation in this polymorphism appears to be a promising candidate in the etiological research on SAD. The literature, however, is mixed, with some studies reporting higher manifestations of social anxiety in carriers of the short allele (Blom et al., 2011; Domschke et al., 2008; Furmark et al., 2004), and others finding associations between the long allele and social anxiety (Arbelle et al., 2003; Reinelt et al., 2013), or no linkage whatsoever (Stein, Chartier, Kozak, King, & Kennedy, 1998).

Further, dopamine has been suggested as another factor involved in the psychopathobiology of SAD. Patients with SAD exhibit lower densities of striatal dopamine reuptake sites compared to healthy controls (Cervenka et al., 2012; Schneier et al., 2000; Tiihonen et al., 1997; but see also Schneier et al., 2009). Moreover, relatively high manifestations of social anxiety have been reported for patients suffering from Parkinson's disease (Stein, Heuser, Juncos, & Uhde, 1990), a disorder caused by the degeneration of dopaminergic cells in the substantia nigra. A recent genome-wide study suggested the norepinephrine transporter as a possible candidate gene for SAD (Gelernter et al., 2004). This protein plays a crucial role in reuptake of norepinephrine and dopamine, and is a target for medication in the treatment of SAD with substances such as venlafaxine (Gorman & Kent, 1999).

4.4.4   Interactional aspects

Behavioral inhibition

Behavioral inhibition (BI) describes a tendency in infancy and early childhood to react with wariness, fear and withdrawal to novel situations and unfamiliar persons (Coll, Kagan, & Reznick, 1984; Kagan, Reznick, & Gibbons, 1989). Behaviorally inhibited children are less likely to initiate social interactions and show less approach behavior than their uninhibited contemporaries (Coplan, Rubin, Fox, Calkins, & Stewart, 1994). Moreover, they exhibit increased physiological activity at rest, including heart-rate, pupil-dilation and cortisol level (Kagan, Reznick, & Snidman, 1987; for a review, see Fox, Henderson, Marshall, Nichols, & Ghera, 2005), and greater sensitivity to novelty in terms of physiological responsivity and behavioral response (for a review, see Helfinstein, Fox, & Pine, 2012). Hence, behavioral inhibition is considered a temperamental precursor to anxiety disorders. Evidence from prospective stud-studies links BI and the risk for developing SAD (for a meta-analysis, see Clauss et al., 2014).

Parental style and modeling

Most studies regarding parenting practices in SAD are retrospective, and use socially phobic childrens' reports of their parents' behavior rather than observations of the actual parental interaction. In an observation paradigm, Hudson and Rapee (2001) found a more controlling parental style in mothers of clinically anxious children (separation anxiety disorder, generalized anxiety disorder, social phobia, and specific phobia) than in mothers of non-anxious children. Parental rejection and overprotection in particular seem to be critical factors in the development of social anxiety (Bögels, van Oosten, Muris, & Smulders, 2001; Lieb et al., 2000). Further, socially anxious parents may transmit their behavior and cognitive style to their children via modeling. This includes talking about their own social anxiety, expressing themselves as visibly anxious or embarrassed, and avoidance behavior (Aktar, Majdandžić, de Vente, & Bögels, 2014; de Rosnay, Cooper, Tsigaras, & Murray, 2006; Murray, Cooper, Creswell, Schofield, & Sack, 2007). Moreover, familial isolation and showing concern for the opinion of others might also be adopted through modeling/ and thus contribute to social fears in children (for a review, see Fisak & Grills-Taquechel, 2007).

4.4.5   Attention & perception in SAD

Cognitive theories postulate an attentional bias for threat in SAD (e.g. Beck, 1979; Clark & Wells, 1995; Rapee & Heimberg, 1997). In particular, it is assumed that information processing in SAD is biased to the effect that they are hypervigilant to negative or threatening stimuli. There is a growing body of empirical studies supporting this claim (for a meta-analysis, see Bar-Haim, Lamy, Pergamin, Bakermans-Kranenburg, & van IJzendoorn, 2007; for a review on neuroimaging data, see Schulz, Mothes-Lasch, & Straube, 2013).

Furthermore, Miskovic and Schmidt (2012) showed that highly socially anxious individuals exhibit heightened vigilance toward angry faces compared to controls, and even toward ambiguous faces (50% threat, 50% neutral). In accordance with this, Klumpp and colleagues (2010) reported exaggerated amygdala reactivity to moderately threatening morphed faces (50-60% intensity) in SAD compared to healthy controls.

Moreover, people with SAD are assumed to exhibit an interpretation bias for social information, that is, they show a tendency to interpret ambiguous social situations as negative. Evidence comes from several studies in which people with SAD saw negative outcomes as more likely than positive outcomes (Amin, Foa, & Coles, 1998; Foa, Franklin, Perry, & Herbert, 1996; Stopa & Clark, 2000). Further, Voncken, Bögels and de Vries (2003) report an interpretation bias for SAD irrespective of valence; that is, not only were ambiguous situations judged as more negative and threatening, but positive and negative ones as well. In addition, in contrast to socially non-anxious individuals, socially anxious people seem to lack a positivity bias, i.e. the tendency to expect positive outcomes from ambiguous information. For example, while non-anxious participants were faster to complete inconclusive sentences with words that led to a positive outcome, socially anxious participants were not (Hirsch & Mathews, 2000). Moreover, in an EEG-study, Moser and colleagues (2008) investigated the P600, an event-related potential that indexes violations of expectation. They found the P600 to be increased after negative sentence endings in socially low-anxious individuals. In contrast, this positivity bias was not apparent in socially high-anxious individuals. Finally, in a study by Joormann and Gotlieb (2006) regarding facial recognition, participants with SAD needed lesser intensity of emotion to correctly identify anger than either participants with depression or healthy controls.

4.5   Cognitive theories and models

One of the most prominent cognitive models of social anxiety disorder is the one by Clark and Wells (1995), see **Fig. 4.1 (A).** It has its roots i.a. in the work of Beck and colleagues (1985), who were among the first to state that people suffering from SAD have dysfunctional cognitions about themselves and about how they are perceived by others. Clark and Wells' model goes beyond that by submitting an explanation for the maintenance of social anxiety: The model suggests that people with SAD have certain assumptions about social contacts. When entering a social situation, one is exposed to the danger of behaving in an unacceptable manner. Such behavior would have devastating consequences such as loss of reputation and, finally, rejection. This causes an "anxiety program" (Clark & Wells, 1995, p. 70) to start, i.e. the typical stress reaction with changes on the physiological, cognitive, affective and behavioral level. Patients recognize the relevant symptoms, such as accelerated heartbeat, sweating, trembling, blushing etc. and interpret them as evidence of inappropriate behavior, which in turn leads to an increase in physiological and affective symptoms and eventually results in a vicious cycle. Based on their own feelings, patients build a mental image of themselves that is thought to reflect how they are viewed by others. On top of this, the heightened attention towards one's own symptoms and thoughts in a social situation ('self as a social object') leaves less capacity to process relevant social cues. This interference is recognized and again is interpreted as proof of one's own shortcomings. Moreover, another important aspect of the model is the use of *safety behaviors*, that is, idiosyncratic cognitive and behavioral strategies to reduce signs of anxiety. For example, such strategies may include wearing thin clothes in order to avoid sweating and blushing, memorizing possible answers beforehand or speaking in a low voice in order to avoid attention being drawn to oneself. The authors further consider rumination as a maintaining factor (see below). In short, the core elements of the model by Clark and Wells include dysfunctional assumptions about oneself and about evaluation by others, in combination with heightened self-focused attention and use of safety behaviors.

A similar model is that by Rapee and Heimberg (1997), shown in **Figure 4.1 (B)**. Here, too, it is assumed that patients with SAD form a mental representation of their appearance and how they are presumably seen by others. Attentional resources are being drawn to that mental representation as well as to external cues of potential threat, such as frowning etc. Additionally, patients define a standard for performance and compare the mental representation of themselves to that standard. Deviations lead patients to expect negative evaluation by others. The expected negative evaluation trig-triggers anxiety symptoms on the physiological, cognitive and behavioral level, which in turn influence the mental representation of the self, fueling the vicious cycle. The main difference to the model by Clark and Wells is the assumed focus of attention. While Clark and Wells (1995) stress that the critical maintaining factor for SAD is self-focused attention, Rapee and Heimberg (1997) assume that scrutinizing other people's behavior for indications of negative evaluation is the most relevant factor.

Rumination

Anticipatory and post event processing are additional cognitive aspects that contribute to the maintenance of the symptomatology (e.g. Clark & Wells, 1995). Patients envision upcoming social situations and what might happen and what could go wrong. Thoughts about the past are likely to focus on memories of alleged failures and misbehaviors. This triggers anticipatory anxiety and increases self-focused attention and expectation of new failures. Thus, the person enters the situation with an already-dysfunctional mind-set or he or she may avoid the situation in question altogether. After social interactions, post-processing can occur, i.e. the situation is recapitulated repeatedly and in detail, with focus on potential social lapses and indications of rejection by others. Thus, painful feelings like shame are likely to persist even after cessation of the social situation. Moreover, the interaction is memorized with a negative bias, reinforcing the vicious circle.

4.6   Treatment of social anxiety disorder

Despite the high prevalence and significant personal impairments, social anxiety disorder is highly underdiagnosed (Katzelnick et al., 2001) and fewer than half of the diagnosed patients receive treatment (Gross et al., 2005).

4.6.1   Pharmacotherapy

In a Cochrane review on pharmacotherapy of social anxiety disorder (Stein, Ipser, & Balkom, 2004), medication proved to be effective in the treatment of

SAD. Selective serotonin reuptake inhibitors (SSRIs) in particular showed ef-
effects with respect to the reduction of core symptom severity, depressive
symptoms, and associated disabilities at work and in social contexts. Further,
monoamine-oxidase inhibitors (MAOIs) and benzodiazepines have been shown
to reduce anxiety. Shortcomings are the food and drug interaction liabilities of
MAOIs and a high potential for addiction in benzodiazepines. These findings
were confirmed by a more recent meta-analysis (Canton, Scott, & Glue, 2012).
In addition, this study reported efficacy for venlafaxine, a serotonin
norepinephrine reuptake inhibitor (SNRI). Hence, SSRIs and SNRIs are the
first-line choice in the pharmacological treatment of SAD, as also recommended
by the World Federation of Biological Psychiatry guidelines (Bandelow et al.,
2012). Pooled odds ratios [95% confidence interval] for response to SSRIs
range between 1.98 [1.07, 3.67] and 3.41 [2.51, 4.69] (Canton et al., 2012).

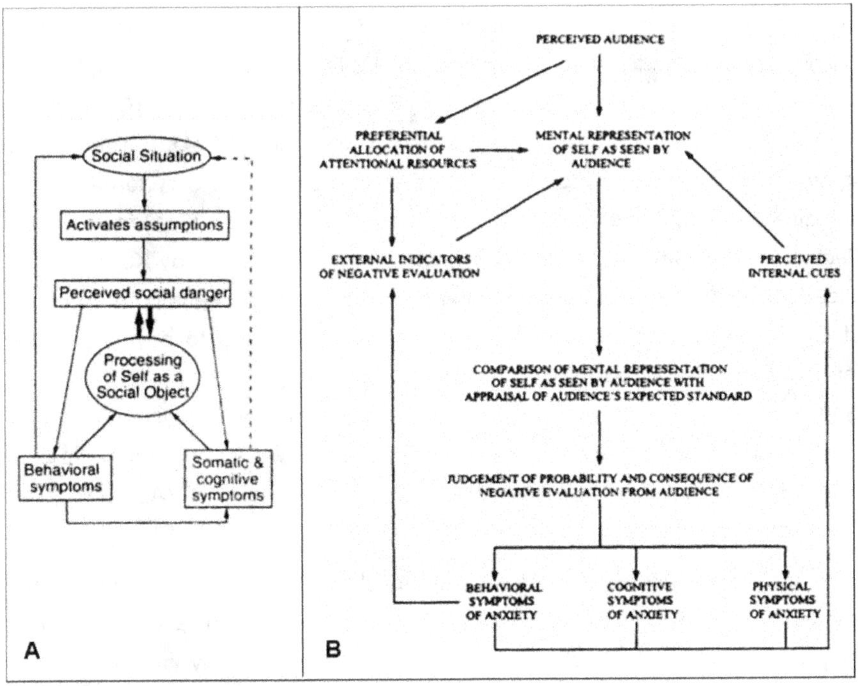

Figure 4.1. A: Cognitive model of social anxiety disorder by Clark and Wells (1995).
B: Cognitive-behavioral model of social anxiety disorder by Rapee & Heimberg (1997).

4.6.2 Psychotherapy

Two recent meta-analyses on individual and group-therapy concluded that psychological interventions for SAD are effective, albeit, with the effect sizes largely depending on the control condition (Acarturk et al., 2009; Wersebe, Sijbrandij, & Cuijpers, 2013). That is, compared to waitlist, psychotherapy exhibited large effects sizes (d = 0.80), whereas compared to placebo or treatment as usual, effects were moderate (d = 0.36 - 0.38). Most randomized trials on treatment effects of psychotherapy in SAD were concerned with cognitive behavioral therapy (CBT), though some used exposure therapy, social skills training or relaxation techniques. As many of the studies applied a mixture of several of those treatments, no satisfying conclusions can be drawn regarding differential effects (Acarturk et al., 2009). Earlier studies that compared exposure therapy directly to CBT found no differences (Fedoroff & Taylor, 2001; for a meta-analyses, see Feske & Chambless, 1995; Gould, Buckminster, Pollack, Otto, & Massachusetts, 1997; S. Taylor, 1996). In more recent studies, however, CBT was superior to exposure therapy in terms of effect size (Clark et al., 2006) and maintenance of treatment success (Hofmann, 2004). Further, there are some randomized-controlled trial studies that compared CBT to other psychological therapeutic approaches. Stangier and colleagues (2011) found larger effects for CBT compared to interpersonal therapy. In a study by Koszycki and colleagues (2007), CBT and mindfulness-stress reduction were both effective, but CBT was superior. Further, CBT has been compared to psychodynamic therapy, with comparable effects (Bögels, Wijts, Oort, & Sallaerts, 2014; Leichsenring et al., 2013). In general, effect-sizes for psychotherapy for SAD vary between large (Cohen's d = 0.86) when compared to waitlist and rather small (d = 0.36 - 0.38), when compared to placebo or treatment as usual (Acarturk et al., 2009; Canton et al., 2012).

There are some studies that directly compared psychotherapy to medication treatment and that included follow-ups of several months (Clark et al., 2003; Haug et al., 2003; Liebowitz et al., 1999). Psychotherapy showed longer maintenance of effects in all of those studies. Moreover, there is little systematic research on the effects of combined pharmacologic and psychotherapeutic treatment for SAD. There are trends in favor of a combination therapy (Canton et al., 2012; Kuzma & Black, 2004) and it is recommended by most practitioners and guidelines (Bandelow et al., 2012; Ganasen, Ipser, & Stein, 2010). However, irrespective of treatment approach, a rather large number of patients do not benefit sufficiently from therapy but continue to experience severe social impairments (Davidson et al., 2004).

4.6.3   Other approaches

Derived from the knowledge of neurobiology underlying SAD (see chapter 4.4.2), other approaches seek directly to influence brain areas that have been associated with social anxiety. Mainly used for treatment of depression (for a review, see Loo & Mitchell, 2005), transcranial magnetic stimulation (TMS) was used in two studies on SAD (Paes, Baczynski, et al., 2013; Paes, Machado, Arias-Carrión, Silva, & Nardi, 2013). They report reductions in social anxiety symptoms after one session of TMS over the medial prefrontal cortex. However, those studies are case reports and implemented no control condition. Hence, randomized sham-controlled trials are needed to corroborate their findings. Internet-based treatment approaches report promising first results (for a review, see Olthuis, Watt, Bailey, Hayden, & Stewart, 2015). This form could lower the threshold to undergo treatment. Accessibility of treatment needs to be facilitated, as, despite the severe impairments and reduced quality of life (e.g. Kessler, Chiu, et al., 2005), only a small number of people suffering from SAD seek treatment (Masia, Klein, Storch, & Corda, 2001; Wells et al., 2006; Wittchen, Stein, & Kessler, 1999).

Taken together, CBT has the broadest empirical foundation and seems to be the most effective psychotherapeutic approach. Compared to medication, CBT has been shown to be superior, especially in the long-term. First-line pharmacotherapeutic choices are SSRIs or SNRIs. Regarding other psychological approaches and combination therapy, further research is needed.

4.7   Social performance in social anxiety disorder

Several cognitive models of social anxiety disorder (SAD) foreground dysfunctional cognitions and biased perception of the self as central maintaining factors

(Clark & Wells, 1995; Rapee & Heimberg, 1997). Some models also mention impeded social performance as one factor (e.g. Clark, 2005; Clark & Wells, 1995). In those models, performance deficits are mostly seen as a consequence of the anxiety as well as a way to handle it via safety behaviors such as avoiding eye-contact (Clark & Beck, 2011).

The possibility of actual deficits in social interactions in SAD has already emerged in the discussion of the lack of social skills in those patients (Hofmann & Barlow, 2002). While early researchers in the seventies and eighties held the opinion that social skill deficits were the central factor in the psychopathology of SAD and resulted in a fear of negative evaluation (Stravynski & Greenberg, 1989; Trower, Bryant, & Argyle, 1978), other studies called such deficits into question (Clark & Arkowitz, 1975; Hofmann, Gerlach, Wender, & Roth, 1997; Rapee & Lim, 1992; Stopa & Clark, 1993). Moreover, unsatisfying outcomes from pure social skill trainings (for a review, see Ponniah & Hollon, 2008) suggested that this thesis falls short and calls for a more elaborate framework. More recent conceptualizations suggest that patients with SAD may possess social skills after all, but that they are unable to draw on those skills in times of distress and anxiety, resulting in social *performance* deficits (Hopko, McNeil, Zvolensky, & Eifert, 2001). A clearer picture, however, has evolved regarding a biased self-perception, with patients underestimating their own behavior in social interactions (Rapee & Lim, 1992; Stopa & Clark, 1993; Voncken & Bögels, 2008). But there may be a core of truth to the negative viewpoint of SAD.

A growing body of evidence shows actual deficits in social performance for socially anxious non-clinical samples (Beidel, Turner, & Dancu, 1985; Bögels, Rijsemus, & Jong, 2002; Thompson & Rapee, 2002; Twentyman & McFall, 1975) as well as for patients with SAD (Baker & Edelmann, 2002; Fydrich, Chambless, Perry, Buergener, & Beazley, 1998; Stopa & Clark, 1993; Voncken & Bögels, 2008). Moreover, socially anxious individuals are less liked than healthy controls in short interactions with strangers (Alden & Wallace, 1995; Creed & Funder, 1998; Meleshko & Alden, 1993; Voncken & Bögels, 2008; Voncken & Dijk, 2013).

4.8   Social cognition in social anxiety disorder

The ability to identify other people's emotions and infer their mental states varies across individuals. An examination of this ability is especially relevant in disorders where the main problem area regards social interaction, such as social anxiety disorder. Deficits in social interactive functioning have been observed in social anxiety disorder (see 4.7). Those deficits not only depict a disabling clinical characteristic but also contribute to maintenance of the disorder (Clark & Wells, 1995; Rapee & Heimberg, 1997). Thus, the investigation of cognitive processes underlying social interaction behavior is of special interest in disorders like SAD.

Social cognitive deficits have been reported for psychiatric disorders that show impairments in social functioning, such as autism (Baron-Cohen, 2000), or schizophrenia (Couture, Penn, & Roberts, 2006; Green, Horan, & Lee, 2015). In SAD, literature regarding emotion recognition is ambiguous, with some studies reporting deficits and others finding no differences in SAD compared to healthy controls. A meta-analysis comes to the conclusion that emotion recognition is not severely impaired in SAD, if at all. By contrast, attributional biases (see chapter 4.4.5) were markedly apparent in SAD (d = -1.15; Plana, Lavoie, Battaglia, & Achim, 2014). Another meta-analysis reviewed studies regarding emotion recognition (O'Toole, Hougaard, & Mennin, 2013). They found social anxiety to be strongly associated with diminished understanding of one's own emotions, but only weakly associated with diminished recognition of the feelings of others. Further, there are few studies that investigated cognitive empathy/theory of mind in SAD. Some report deficits in SAD (Buhlmann, Wacker, & Dziobek, 2015; Hezel & McNally, 2014; Washburn, Wilson, Roes, Rnic, & Harkness, 2016), while others found no differences to healthy controls (Jacobs et al., 2008). Moreover, one study found economic exchange games leading to reduced activation in the medial prefrontal cortex in SAD compared to healthy controls, a region that has been associated with theory of mind (Sripada et al., 2009). However, contrary results have been reported, too. One study found highly socially anxious individuals to exhibit increased scores for cognitive empathy in a self-rating compared to lower socially anxious participants (Tibi-

Elhanany & Shamay-Tsoory, 2011). In another study, social anxiety was associated with increased cognitive empathy under social threat (Auyeung & Alden,
2016). Even less is known about emotional empathy in SAD. In a healthy sample, there was a small association between social anxiety and self-reported
emotional empathy (Davis, 1983). A recent study that compared empathy in
SAD and healthy controls found no differences in cognitive empathy and found
reductions in emotional empathy only for positive emotions (Morrison et al.,
2016).

In conclusion, the literature on social cognition in SAD has hitherto provided a
rather ambiguous picture, with several studies reporting no differences to
healthy controls, as well as scattered indices of an impaired social cognitive
functioning, especially for complex emotions (O'Toole et al., 2013). As social
cognitive abilities are an important prerequisite for successful social interactions, deficiencies in this domain would have considerable consequences for
people with SAD. Moreover, the ambiguity of findings may indicate that people
suffering from social anxiety disorder represent a rather heterogeneous group
and that the consideration of further discriminating aspects may be necessary.
Thus, for the investigation of social interaction behavior in SAD, the present
thesis took empathic abilities into account as a crucial prerequisite for social
interactions.

4.9   Stress in social anxiety disorder

In primates, social stress as constituted by a subordinate status is associated
with elevated HPA-axis functioning (R. M. Sapolsky, Alberts, & Altmann, 1997;
Sassenrath, 1970). This could lead to the assumption of a general overactive
HPA-axis in SAD. In a study measuring 24-hour cortisol and postdexamethasone cortisol levels, however, no deviations were found for SAD
compared to healthy controls (Uhde, Tancer, Gelernter, & Vittone, 1994). Furthermore, several studies found no differences in baseline cortisol between
SAD and healthy controls, either (Condren et al., 2002; Martel et al., 1999;
Potts, Davidson, Krishnan, Doraiswamy, & Ritchie, 1991). Others even reported
reduced basal cortisol levels in SAD (Beaton et al., 2006) and associated this
with a blunted HPA-axis reactivity, as hypothesized for post-traumatic stress

disorder (Heim, Ehlert, & Hellhammer, 2000; Yehuda, Giller, Southwick, Lowy, & Mason, 1991).

In addition to the examinations of baseline cortisol levels, there are several studies on the stress reaction in SAD. The literature, however, is mixed (see table 2.1). Klumbies and colleagues (2014), for example, used the TSST to induce stress and examined the stress reaction in SAD and healthy controls on the endocrine, autonomic and subjective level. Differences between groups were only observed in the subjective stress response. Another study reported finding two subgroups of SAD patients: One subgroup (n = 9) showed a stronger cortisol increase compared to the control group, while the other subgroup (n = 11) did not respond to the stress and showed a stronger decrease in cortisol compared to the non-responder controls (Furlan, DeMartinis, Schweizer, Rickels, & Lucki, 2001). In short, previous findings have failed to generate a clear picture of the physiological stress response in individuals with social anxiety disorder.

Inconsistency in findings might be due to the different stress induction methods used (e.g. speech, conversation, watching an embarrassing movie). Besides this, differences in sample characteristics might also contribute to the equivocal results. Some studies used clinical samples of SAD (e.g. Furlan et al., 2001; Klumbies et al., 2014), while others applied social anxiety screenings in non-clinical samples (e.g. Beidel et al., 1985). Further, comorbidity status and medication can have an influence on stress measures, which was not accounted for in all of the studies. Thus, patients with SAD often suffer from comorbid depression, which has been associated with dampened cortisol responses (Burke, Davis, Otte, & Mohr, 2005; for reviews, see Kudielka & Wüst, 2010). Medication, such as antidepressants (Barden, Reul, & Holsboer, 1995; Pariante et al., 2004), and even short-term drugs have been shown to affect HPA-activity (Kudielka, Hellhammer, & Wüst, 2009). In addition, three studies investigated stress reaction in children with SAD (Krämer et al., 2012; Martel et al., 1999; van West et al., 2008) and therefore have to be interpreted with caution when focusing on the stress reaction in adults, as age has been related to variations in the physiological stress response (Kudielka, Buske-Kirschbaum, Hellhammer, & Kirschbaum, 2004a, 2004b; for a meta-analysis, see Otte et al., 2005).

Kirschbaum, Hellhammer, & Kirschbaum, 2004a, 2004b; for a meta-analysis, see Otte et al., 2005).

In addition, there is evidence that patients suffering from SAD experience social stress more frequently (Beidel, Turner, & Morris, 1999; Farmer & Kashdan, 2015; Yeganeh, 2005). As a biological function that prepares the individual to respond to threat, the stress response temporarily suppresses long-term functions that are not immediately needed, such as growth and immune system function (Johnson, Kamilaris, Chrousos, & Gold, 1992; Segerstrom & Miller, 2004). While this is adaptive for facing current challenges, cumulated activation of the stress system promotes a state of allostatic load, as described by McEwen (1998), thereby leading to elevated risk for stress-related disorders (Chrousos, 2009). Accordingly, SAD has been, among other anxiety disorders, associated with an increased risk for coronary heart disease (Kawachi, Sparrow, Vokonas, & Weiss, 1994; Shen, Wachowiak, & Brooks, 2005).

Taken together, the literature on the physiological stress reaction in SAD is ambiguous and limited by inconsistent and partly unstandardized stress induction methods. In the present study we investigated stress reaction in SAD and healthy controls using a standardized and well-established method to induce psychosocial stress, the *Trier Social Stress Test for Groups* (TSST-G; von Dawans et al., 2011). Stress responses were assessed on both the physiological level, i.e. in the hypothalamus-pituitary adrenal (HPA) axis and the sympathoadrenal medullary (SAM) system, and on the subjective level.

Table 4.1. Summary of studies on physiological stress reactivity in social anxiety.

Authors	Total sample	Classification of social anxiety	Stress-induction method	Stress-parameters	Effects (reactivity to stress)
Beidel et al. (1985)	13 m; 13 f	social anxiety (questionnaires)	5-min. impromptu speech	heart rate; systolic/diastolic blood pressure	*HR*: high SA = low SA *SBP*: high SA ↑ (p < .01) *DBP*: high SA = low SA
Levin et al. (1993)	31 m; 21 f	SAD diagnosis (generalized and discrete)	10-min. speech	salivary cortisol; heart rate	*cortisol*: GSAD; DSAD = HC *HR*: GSAD = HC DSAD ↑ (p < .05)
Martel et al. (1999)	42 f (adolescents)	SAD diagnosis	modified TSST	salivary cortisol	*cortisol*: SAD = HC
Furlan et al. (2001)	38 (no indications for gender)	SAD diagnosis	7.5-min. speech	salivary cortisol	*cortisol*: SAD ↑ & ↓
Gerlach et al. (2001)	20 m; 24 f	SAD diagnosis (with and without fear of blushing)	video-recorded singing & 5-min. talk	heart rate; skin conductance level	*HR*: SAD (fear of blushing) ↑ (p < .01) SAD (no fear of blushing) = HC *SCL*: SAD = HC
Grossmann (2001)	42 m; 18 f (age 47 - 83 yeas)	SAD diagnosis	4-min. speech	heart rate; systolic/diastolic blood pressure	*HR*: SAD = HC *SBP*: SAD (m) = HC *DBP*: SAD (m) = HC *SBP*: SAD (f) ↑ (p < .01) *DBP*: SAD (f) ↑ (p < .01)
Condren et al. (2002)	20 m; 10 f	SAD diagnosis	15 min. mental arithmetic	plasma cortisol; ACTH	*cortisol*: SAD ↑ (p < .05) *ACTH*: SAD = HC

(Continued)

Authors	Total sample	Classification of social anxiety	Stress-induction method	Stress-parameters	Effects (reactivity to stress)
Edelman & Baker (2002)	5 m; 31 f	SAD diagnosis	5-min. mental arithmetic & 2-min. imagination of anxiety provoking scene	heart rate; skin conductance level; neck/face temperature	*all measures:* SAD = HC
Mauss et al. (2004)	97 f	social anxiety (questionnaires)	speech	heart rate; blood pressure; skin conductance; respiratory rate	*all measures:* high SA = low SA
Beaton et al. (2006)	5 m; 14 f	SAD diagnosis	self-presentation speech	salivary cortisol; heart rate	*cortisol:* SAD = HC *HR:* SAD = HC
van West et al. (2008)	34 m; 16 f (children)	SAD diagnosis	public speaking task	salivary cortisol	*cortisol:* SAD ↑ ($p < .001$; $f^2 = 0.20$)
Anderson & Hope (2009)	174 m; 196 f (adolescents)	SAD diagnosis	10-min. impromptu speech	heart rate; systolic/diastolic blood pressure	*HR:* SAD = HC *SBP:* SAD = HC *DBP:* SAD = HC
Roelofs et al. (2009)	18 m; 22 f	SAD diagnosis	TSST with modifications	salivary cortisol; diastolic blood pressure	*cortisol:* SAD ↑ ($p < .05$; $\eta_p^2 = 0.11$) *DBP:* SAD = HC
Krämer et al. (2012)	40 m; 41 f (children)	SAD diagnosis	speech & mental arithmetic	heart rate; salivary cortisol; alpha-amylase	*HR:* SAD ↓ ($p < .05$; $\eta_p^2 = 0.07$) *cortisol:* SAD = HC *alpha amylase:* SAD = HC
Yoon & Joormann (2012)	22 m; 17 f	SAD diagnosis	5-min. speech & working memory	salivary cortisol	*cortisol:* SAD ↑ ($p < .05$; $\eta_p^2 = 0.08$)

(Continued)

Authors	Total sample	Classification of social anxiety	Stress-induction method	Stress-parameters	Effects (reactivity to stress)
Klumbies et al. (2014)	85 m; 81 f	SAD diagnosis	TSST	heart rate; plasma cortisol; salivary cortisol; salivary alpha-amylase; prolactin	*all measures:* SAD = HC
Losiak et al. (2016)	10 m; 34 f	social anxiety (questionnaires)	impromptu speech	salivary cortisol	*cortisol:* high SA = low SA

Note: m = male; f = female. *HR* = heart rate. *SBP* = systolic blood pressure. *DBP* = diastolic blood pressure. *SCL* = skin conductance level. SA = socially anxious. SAD = social anxiety disorder. GSAD = generalized social anxiety disorder. DSAD = discrete social anxiety disorder. HC = healthy controls. TSST = Trier Social Stress Test. CA = childhood abuse. Arrows mark direction of effect in comparison to healthy controls. Effect size is presented when reported.

5   Summary and Objectives of the Thesis

To date, little is known about the consequences of acute stress in patients with social anxiety disorder. The literature on the physiological stress reactivity in SAD is highly inconsistent. Moreover, a growing body of research describes increased affiliation behavior in healthy participants after stress. However, with key symptoms of this disorder being fear of social interactions and avoidance of such situations, it is unclear, whether people suffering from SAD exhibit similar social behavioral reaction to stress. A better understanding of the effects of acute stress on social behavior in SAD as well as its underlying psychophysiological mechanisms may extend our understanding of this and related disorders and furthermore may promote the development of individually adapted and more effective treatments.

For this reason, we conducted a study to shed further light on the effects of stress in social anxiety disorder. The results are presented in two empirical chapters. The objective of the first chapter was the examination of the stress response in patients with social anxiety disorder compared to healthy controls. Stress manipulation was realized using a standardized well-established stress induction method, the *TSST-G* (von Dawans et al., 2011), and stress reactivity was assessed on an endocrine, cardiovascular and subjective level. The aim of the second chapter was to gain more insight into the effects of acute stress on social interaction behavior and possible modulating influences of individual empathic abilities in patients with SAD compared to healthy controls. Therefore, empathic abilities were examined using the *Multifaceted Empathy Test* (Dziobek et al., 2007), and social interaction behavior in response to stress was assessed by applying both a naturalistic conversation paradigm as well as a laboratory task on social decision-making. In section IV of this thesis, the insights from both research questions will be summarized and critically discussed in consideration of methodological limitations. Finally, open questions and goals for future research will be delineated.

III EMPIRICAL RESEARCH SECTION

6 Study Overview

The results presented in this section derive from an experimental study on the effects of stress on social interaction behavior in social anxiety disorder (SAD) and healthy controls (HC). The present study is the first one to use the TSST-G in SAD patients. This section gives an overview of the general study design, participants, procedure and stress induction method. Instruments specific to one of the two individual empirical chapters will be described in the relevant chapter.

6.1 Study design

In order to examine the effects of acute stress in social anxiety disorder, SAD patients and matched healthy controls were assigned to the stress or no-stress condition of the *Trier Social Stress Test for Groups* (TSST-G; von Dawans et al., 2011). The study was a single-blind randomized controlled trial with a 2x2 between-subjects design with the factors group (SAD vs. HC) and stress (stress vs. no-stress). Participants came to the laboratory twice, first for a diagnostic session and then for the actual experiments.

6.2 Participants

Male participants were recruited via advertising in local newsletters, informational talks on social anxiety, notices and flyer dissemination, as well as via our University research register. Due to influences of female menstruation cycle on cortisol levels (Gordon & Girdler, 2014) and marked sex differences in social experiments (for a review, see Eagly, 2009), the study focused on men only. An online questionnaire was used to screen out participants who were female, younger than 18 years or older than 55 years of age, or who smoked more than five cigarettes per day, as smoking has been shown to influence HPA-axis functioning (Rohleder & Kirschbaum, 2006). The questionnaire also included the Social Interaction Anxiety Scale (SIAS) and the Social Phobia Scale (SPS). Depending on their score in the SIAS, participants were included as potential participants for the SAD (> 30) or HC group (0 - 30). Following the online questionnaire, telephone interviews were conducted to apply further exclusion criteria (see below).

A total of 182 men participated in the study. In the SAD group, exclusion criteria were any other current mental disorder except SAD or avoidant personality disorder. In the control group, participants were excluded if they had any current or past diagnosis of a mental disorder. Further exclusion criteria for both groups were: neurological disorders, shiftwork, current use of medication, drug or alcohol abuse. Additionally, participants were excluded if they were students of psychology or economics and if they were not naïve to the TSST procedure or decision paradigm. Healthy controls were matched by age, education and intelligence (verbal IQ test; Schmidt & Metzler, 1992). The study was approved by the local ethics committee of the University Freiburg and participants gave written informed consent on both study days.

For the first appointment, 100 participants were recruited for the SAD-group and 82 for the HC group. From these, $n = 55$ had to be excluded and were not invited for the second appointment due to the following reasons: did not meet full criteria for diagnosis of SAD ($n = 22$), took HPA-axis relevant medication ($n = 3$), met criteria for current or lifetime mental disorder other than SAD or in the HC-group ($n = 13$), marihuana consumption ($n = 3$), had moved ($n = 2$), insufficient language abilities ($n = 2$), not naïve to the decision paradigm ($n = 2$), working night shifts ($n = 1$), decided against participation ($n = 6$), not available via telephone and email ($n = 1$). In total, 127 subjects (64 SAD; 63 HC) were invited to the second appointment and underwent the experiment. From the experimental sample, four subjects with SAD and ten healthy controls had to be excluded due to the following reasons: BMI > 30 ($n = 2$), current use of antidepressant ($n = 1$), current use of HPA-axis relevant medication ($n = 1$), LSAS score of 63 in healthy control ($n = 1$), critically elevated global BSI score (T-value > 63; Derogatis & Melisaratos, 1983) in healthy control ($n = 2$), use of painkillers ($n = 3$), shifted circadian rhythm ($n = 1$), verbal IQ more than two SD under mean ($n = 3$).

Thus, the final sample consisted of $N = 113$ subjects, with $n = 60$ SAD, age 28.23 ± 8.98 years (mean ± SD) and $n = 53$ healthy controls, age 27.38 ± 6.51. Participants were divided into 6-person groups which were randomly assigned to the two conditions of the TSST-G. Subjects received a flat fee of 40 Euros and could earn additional money in the social-interaction paradigm € 5.68 ± € 0.92 (mean ± SD). A second group of 127 participants was recruited as interaction partners for the target participants. This second group did not participate in the TSST-G or any of the other measures and was only involved in the interaction games.

6.3   Procedure

On the first appointment, participants conducted a computer experiment testing social cognition, the *Multifaceted Empathy Test* (MET; Dziobek et al., 2007). The MET is a test for the assessment of cognitive and emotional empathy (for details, see chapter 8.2.6). Afterwards, diagnostics was carried out using the *SKID I and SKID II* (German version of the Structural Clinical Interview for DSM IV; Wittchen, Zaudig, & Fydrich, 1997). If participants met inclusion criteria, they were invited to the second day of study.

For the second day of study, participants were asked not to do physical exercise and to abstain from caffeine, nicotine, alcohol and medication for 24 hours prior to the experiment. On the day itself, they were asked to have a regular meal and abstain from any food and drinks besides water for two hours before the start of the experiment. Sessions started between 5 and 6 p.m. to control for diurnal variation in cortisol secretion. Duration was 2.5 hours. Groups of four to six subjects were tested simultaneously. In a randomized controlled between-subjects design, patients and healthy controls were assigned either to the stress or to the control condition of the TSST-G, with each session containing subjects of both groups. After instructions and baseline questionnaires, participants underwent the TSST-G. Results from the stress reaction are presented in the first empirical chapter of this thesis, (Chapter 7). Following each of the two parts (speech/reading and mental arithmetic/counting), participants had to make their decisions for the social decision paradigm. Subsequently, participants were informed that the next task would be a conversation with a stranger. Participants were guided into separate rooms where a confederate was waiting and the conversation task took place. Results from the decision paradigm and the conversation task are presented in the second empirical chapter (Chapter 8). After the conversation, participants came back into the computer lab for further questionnaires and saliva sampling. See **Fig. 6.1** for time course of study day two. All participants received monetary compensation.

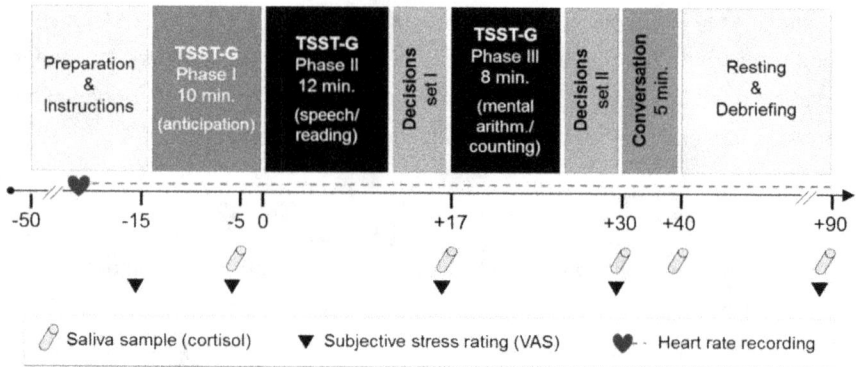

Figure 6.1. Experimental course (adapted from von Dawans et al., 2011). TSST-G = Trier Social Stress Test for Groups. VAS = visual analogue scale.

6.3.1 Stress induction

Stress was induced using the *Trier Social Stress Test for Groups* (TSST-G; von Dawans et al., 2011), a standardized laboratory protocol for the induction of psychological stress in groups. During the protocol, subjects are separated by dividing walls to prevent interaction between them. The TSST-G comprises two conditions, a stress and a control (no-stress) condition. In the stress condition, participants have to give a two-minute free speech for a mock job interview and do a mental arithmetic task, both in front of two evaluators and two cameras. In the no-stress condition, all parameters are kept constant except for the stress inducing components, particularly socio-evaluative threat and uncontrollability. That is, participants in the no-stress condition have to read a text in a low voice and recite number series instead of giving a free speech and doing mental arithmetic. Also, they are not videotaped. The TSST-G provides a moderate psychosocial stress induction and has been proven reliably to result in activation of the pituitary-adrenal axis with elevated cortisol levels, as well as significant cardiovascular and subjective stress responses (e.g. Boesch et al., 2014; Buckert, Kudielka, Reuter, & Fiebach, 2012; Hostinar, McQuillan, Mirous, Grant, & Adam, 2014; Kumsta, Chen, Pape, & Heinrichs, 2013; Smyth et al., 2015; von Dawans et al., 2012, 2011).

6.3.1   Additional psychometric measures

For the assessment of social anxiety as a continuous variable, the self-report measures *Social Interaction Anxiety Scale* (SIAS; Mattick & Clarke, 1998; German version by Stangier, Heidenreich, Berardi, Golbs, & Hoyer, 1999) and the *Liebowitz Social Anxiety Scale* (LSAS; Liebowitz, 1987; German version by Stangier & Heidenreich, 2005) were used. The SIAS consists of 20 items that describe the participant's reaction to social interactions in dyads and groups. The SIAS has been shown to be a valid and reliable measure of social anxiety (Mattick & Clarke, 1998). This has been confirmed for the German version of the SIAS (Stangier et al., 1999). The LSAS assesses magnitude of anxiety and frequency of avoidance in a wide range of social situations with 24 items. Reliability (Cronbach's $\alpha = 0.96$) and validity have been demonstrated (Heimberg et al., 1999). For the German version, internal consistency and convergent validity are satisfying (Stangier & Heidenreich, 2005). In order to assess general burden of psychological symptoms, the *Brief Symptom Inventory* (BSI; Derogatis & Melisaratos, 1983; German version by Franke, 2000) was administered and for the assessment of depressive symptoms, the *Beck Depression Inventory* (BDI-II; Beck, Steer, & Brown, 1996; German version by Hautzinger, Keller, & Kühner, 2006) was used. For the assessment of the verbal intelligence, the *Wortschatztest* (Schmidt & Metzler, 1992) was administered. It's validity and reliability (Cronbachs $\alpha = .94$) have been demonstrated (Schmidt & Metzler, 1992).

7   Empirical Chapter I:
Stress Reaction in Social Anxiety Disorder

7.1   Introduction

Social anxiety disorder (SAD) is the third most common mental disorder in Western societies after depression and alcohol addiction, displaying a lifetime prevalence of 7-13% (Fehm et al., 2005; Kessler, Berglund, et al., 2005). People suffering from SAD exhibit a distinct and persistent fear of social situations that could involve scrutiny by others (APA, 2013). Physiological arousal is a main part in SAD's diagnostic criteria *("[...] anxiety, which may take the form of a situationally bound or situationally pre-disposed panic attack"* (APA, 2013), as well as in its explanatory models (Clark & Wells, 1995; Rapee & Heimberg, 1997). In these models, it is assumed that the perception of symptoms such as accelerated heartbeat, sweating or trembling encourages dysfunctional cognitions about one's own appearance. This in turn amplifies the physiological reactions, thus triggering a vicious circle. Nonetheless, it is unclear whether the physiological arousal in response to stress is actually elevated in SAD. Further knowledge of the stress reaction in SAD would deepen our understanding of the psychopathophysiology of this disorder, thereby building the groundwork for the further development of adapted therapeutic approaches.

Neuroimaging studies have yielded evidence that SAD patients exhibit elevated amygdala reactivity in response to social threat cues like faces (Evans et al., 2008; Straube et al., 2005; Yoon et al., 2007) or public speaking (Lorberbaum et al., 2004; Tillfors et al., 2002). The amygdala plays a vital role in the detection of threat and, via projections to the hypothalamus and brainstem, in the regulation of the subsequent endocrine and autonomous stress response (Forray & Gysling, 2004; Gray, 1993). Thus an exaggerated physiological response to stress might be expected in patients with SAD. However, the literature on the endocrine and cardiovascular stress response in SAD is mixed. Some studies report hyperactivity in SAD as measured by salivary cortisol response (Roelofs et al., 2009; van West et al., 2008; Yoon & Joormann, 2012), plasma cortisol response (Condren et al., 2002) or heart rate (Beidel et al., 1985; Gerlach et al., 2001). Others detected no differences compared to healthy controls in salivary cortisol (Klumbies et al., 2014; Krämer et al., 2012; Martel et al., 1999), plasma cortisol (Levin et al., 1993) or heart rate (Beaton et al., 2006; Edelmann & Baker, 2002; Grossman, 2001). Klumbies and colleagues (2014) for example, used the TSST to induce stress and examined the stress reaction in SAD and healthy controls on the endocrine, autonomic and subjective level. Differences between groups were only observed in the subjective stress response. Another study reported finding two subgroups of SAD patients: One subgroup (*n* = 9) showed a stronger cortisol increase than the control group, while the other subgroup (*n* = 11) did not respond to the stress and revealed a stronger decrease in cortisol than the non-responder controls (Furlan et al., 2001). In short, these findings have failed to generate a clear picture of the physiological stress response in individuals with social anxiety disorder.

Inconsistent findings might be due to the different stress induction methods used (e.g., speech, conversation, watching an embarrassing movie). Moreover, differences in sample characteristics might also contribute to mixed results. Some studies used clinical samples of SAD (e.g., Furlan et al., 2001; Klumbies et al., 2014), while others applied social anxiety screenings in non-clinical samples e.g.,. Beidel et al., 1985). Three other studies investigated stress reaction in children with SAD (Krämer et al., 2012; Martel et al., 1999; van West et al., 2008) and must therefore be interpreted with caution when focusing on the stress reaction in adults, as age is known to influence the physiological stress response (Kudielka et al., 2004a, 2004b).

Taken together, the physiological stress reaction in SAD is not entirely understood and the literature is limited by inconsistent and partly unstandardized stress induction methods. In the present study we investigated stress reaction in SAD and healthy controls using a standardized and well-established method to induce psychosocial stress, the *Trier Social Stress Test for Groups* (TSST-G; von Dawans et al., 2011). Stress responses were assessed on both a physiological level, ie, in the hypothalamus-pituitary adrenal (HPA) axis and the sympatho-andrenalmedullary (SAM) system, and on a subjective level. HPA-axis and SAM system responses are considered the most important biomarkers of psychosocial stress (Foley & Kirschbaum, 2010). Cortisol is considered the best characterized marker of HPA-axis activity (Foley & Kirschbaum, 2010). Salivary cortisol has been shown to be closely correlated with unbound cortisol in plasma (Kirschbaum & Hellhammer, 1989; Teruhisa et al., 1981), thus qualifying as a valid and practical parameter for investigating HPA-axis activity (see chapter 2.1.3 for details). Systematic investigation of the stress reaction in SAD in the two major stress pathways may enhance our understanding of the fundamental processes in this disorder when subjects are confronted with social situations.

Therefore, the aim of this study was to examine the acute stress reaction in SAD on the subjective, autonomic and endocrine level. To compare the stress reaction to the response of healthy individuals, a group of matched healthy controls was included. Our hypothesis was that the subjective stress response would be higher in SAD than HC. Regarding SAD patients' endocrine and autonomic stress response, inconsistent results from prior studies did not enable us to formulate directional hypotheses, which is why we explored potential differences between those groups.

7.2   Methods

7.2.1   Study design and procedure

The study was a single-blind randomized controlled trial with a 2x2 between-subjects design with the factors group (SAD vs. HC) and stress (stress vs. no-stress). See chapter 6 for a detailed description of the experimental procedure.

7.2.2   Participants

For details on subject recruitment, sample description and procedure, see chapter 6.2. The final sample consisted of N = 113 subjects, with n = 60 SAD, age 28.23 ± 8.98 years (mean ± SD) and n = 53 healthy controls, age 27.38 ± 6.51. Patients with SAD and healthy controls were randomly assigned to the stress and no-stress condition of the TSST-G resulting in the following distribution: n = 30 SAD stress; n = 30 SAD no-stress; n = 26 HC stress; n = 27 HC no-stress.

7.2.3 Stress induction

Stress was induced by the *Trier Social Stress Test for Groups* (TSST-G; von Dawans et al., 2011), a well-established standardized laboratory protocol for the induction of psychological stress in groups. For detailed description, see chapter 6.3.1.

7.2.3.1 Endocrine and cardiovascular stress response

Free cortisol was repeatedly assessed via saliva sampling using cotton rolls (Salivette; Sarstedt, Nümbrecht-Rommelsdorf, Germany). Saliva was sampled before (-5 min.), during (+17 min.) and after cessation of stress induction (+30 min.), as well as at the end of the session after recovery (+90 min.). As is well known, cortisol gradually increases and peaks with a delay of 10-30 min. (Kirschbaum & Hellhammer, 1989). Consequently, we assessed salivary cortisol at an additional 10 min. after stress cessation (+40 min.) in order to depict the peak of the cortisol reaction.

Saliva samples were stored at -20° C. For biochemical analyses of free cortisol concentration, saliva samples were thawed and spun at 3.000 revolutions per minute for 10 min to obtain 0.5 to 1.0 ml of clear saliva with low viscosity. Salivary cortisol concentrations were determined by a commercially available chemiluminescence immunoassay (CLIA; IBL, Hamburg, Germany). Inter- and intra-assay coefficients of variation were below 8%. For one participant of the HC-stress group, saliva samples of the first four time points were empty due to inaccurate usage of the sampling device. Cortisol analysis were therefore conducted with $n =$ 52 healthy controls. For the identification of responders and nonresponders, a sound physiological stress response was defined as a cortisol increase by at least 1.5 nmol/l (Miller, Plessow, Kirschbaum, & Stalder, 2013). Within the SAD-stress group, 22 out of 30 subjects (73.3%) showed a cortisol response of 1.5 nmol/l or more. Mean increase was 9.73 (±8.33 *SD*) nmol/l. Within the HC-stress group, 23 out of 27 subjects (85.2%) showed a cortisol response of 1.5 nmol/l or more. Mean increase here was 9.23 (±9.95 SD) nmol/l. Percentage of responders did not differ between groups, $U = -1.09$, $p = .277$. In the no-stress condition, mean increase was -1.04 (±2.80 *SD*) nmol/l for healthy controls and -1.31 (±3.20 *SD*) nmol/l for SAD. In the SAD group, three subjects in the no-stress condition showed an increase above 1.5 nmol/l. One healthy participant showed a cortisol increase by 9 nmol/l in the no-stress condition. It was abstained from separate analyses of nonresponders, as sample size was too small and the study had not been designed for this specific comparison.

For the autonomic stress response, beat-to-beat intervals of heart rate (aggregated to mean levels per minute) were recorded throughout the experiment. A chest strap transmitter with wrist monitor recorder served as a heart rate device (800CX, Polar Electro, Oy, Kempele, Finland). For the baseline phase of the TSST-G, an aggregated measure (mean of 5 min.) was calculated. Heart rate analyses included 36 one-minute intervals (1 min. aggregated baseline, 5 min. anticipation, 12 min. speech/reading, 5 min. decisions set I, 8 minutes mental arithmetic/counting, 5 min. decisions set II). Due to technical problems, heart rate measures were not completely available for $n = 12$ participants (1 SAD-no stress, 3 SAD-stress, 4 HC-stress, 4 HC-no stress). Analyses of heart rate therefore were conducted with $n = 101$ subjects.

7.2.3.2 Psychological stress response

Psychological stress was repeatedly measured before, during and after stress induction, using visual analogue scales (VAS), assessing subjectively perceived *stress* and *tension*. Moreover, VAS were used to assess *anxiety, physical discomfort, avoidance (desire to leave the situation)* and *feeling of control over the situation* in order to capture stress symptoms specific to social anxiety. Points of measurement were at baseline (-15 min.), during anticipation (-5 min.), in the middle of stress induction (+17 min.), after cessation of stress induction (+30 min.), and at the end of the session after recovery (+90 min.). Visual analogue scales ranged from "not at all" to "very strong". Additionally, the state anxiety scale of the *State Trait Anxiety Inventory* (STAI; Spielberger, Gorsuch, & Lushene, 1970; German version by Laux, Glanzmann, Schaffner, & Spielberger, 1981), assessing participants' state anxiety, was given at four points: at baseline (-15 min.), after reading the instructions for the TSST-G (anticipation phase, -5 min.), right after the TSST-G (+30 min.) and during the recovery phase (+75 min.). The STAI includes 20 items that can be rated on a 4-point Likert scale. It has been demonstrated to be a reliable measure, with internal consistency ranging between 0.83 and 0.92 (Barnes, Harp, & Jung, 2002; Spielberger et al., 1970).

7.2.4   Statistical analysis

For cortisol, heart rate and each of the subjective stress measures, three-factorial mixed analyses of variance (ANOVA) were conducted, with group (HC/SAD) and condition (stress/non-stress) as between-factors and time as repeated factor (5 for cortisol and subjective rating, respectively and 36 for heart rate). In cases of heterogeneity of covariance (indicated by a significant Mauchly test of sphericity), Greenhouse Geisser corrections are reported. When necessary, significant interactions were further examined by means of simple effects. In order to examine the increase of the stress parameters more detailed, delta measures (maximum value in the TSST-G minus baseline) were calculated when necessary. Effect sizes are reported in η_p^2. All tests were conducted two-sided, with level of significance at .05. Data analysis was run by SPSS Version 22.0.

7.3   Results

7.3.1   Sample characteristics

The four subgroups (SAD stress/no stress; HC stress/no stress) did not differ in intelligence or educational status, see Table 7.1. There was a trend for an effect of condition in age, $F(1, 109) = 3.56$, $p = .062$. A significant group × condition interaction for body mass index (BMI) emerged, $F(1, 109) = 5.28$, $p < .05$, $\eta_p^2 = .05$. Post-hoc t-tests revealed that SAD in the stress condition had a higher BMI than SAD in the no-stress condition, $t(58) = -2.61$, $p < .025$. As BMI is associated with physical fitness, status of training was compared for the SAD group. Status of training did not differ between conditions, $t(51) = -1.05$, $p = .300$. Moreover, SAD and HC differed in BMI for neither stress-condition, $t(55) = -1.52$, $p = .134$ nor no-stress condition, $t(54) = 1.80$, $p = .078$. Expectedly, subjects in the SAD group reported significantly higher levels for social anxiety and depression and were currently less frequently involved in a serious relationship compared to the control group (Table 7.1).

Table 7.1. General characteristics of participants with SAD (n = 60) and healthy controls (n = 53) in the stress and no-stress condition.

	Condition				coeff.	p
	No-stress		Stress			
	SAD	HC	SAD	HC		
Age	25.83 (6.54)	27.00 (4.54)	30.63 (10.45)	27.74 (8.04)	n.s.	n.s.
Education	4.13 (0.77)	4.12 (0.86)	4.24 (0.74)	4.26 (0.66)	n.s.	n.s.
IQ	108.40 (11.31)	107.54 (8.30)	111.67 (6.93)	113.04 (9.12)	n.s.	n.s.
BMI (kg/m^2)	22.32 (2.19)	23.24 (1.50)	23.84 (2.31)	22.85 (2.60)	F = 5.28[b]	.023
Training status (min./week)	151.55 (127.60)	176.40 (155.15)	190.66 (224.53)	226.11 (213.99)	n.s.	n.s.
Partnership	43.3%	69.2%	36.7%	55.6%	χ^2 =5.53[a]	.019
SIAS	38.18 (10.73)	12.76 (3.23)	33.48 (9.09)	13.81 (6.18)	F = 174.02 [a]	.000
LSAS (total score)	67.76 (22.75)	18.28 (9.98)	63.93 (22.00)	20.96 (15.71)	F = 166.29 [a]	.000
Avoidant personality disorder	16.7% (n=5)	N/A	23.3% (n=7)	N/A	n.s.	n.s.
BDI	13.53 (7.04)	4.15 (4.53)	12.77 (10.21)	2.37 (2.82)	F = 58.23[a]	.000
BL Cortisol (nmol/l)	5.43 (4.69)	4.38 (3.53)	6.08 (7.52)	4.38 (3.14)	n.s.	n.s.
BL HR_agg (beats/min)	85.04 (12.06)	78.83 (9.67)	82.01 (14.41)	80.87 (11.35)	n.s.	n.s.

Note: SAD = social anxiety disorder. HC = healthy control. coeff. = coefficient. N/A = not applicable. Education: 1 = no graduation, 2 = main school graduation, 3 = middle school graduation, 4 = high school degree, 5 = university/college degree. BMI = Body Mass Index. Partnership = being in a serious relationship. SIAS = Social Interaction Anxiety Scale. LSAS = Liebowitz Social Anxiety Scale. BDI = Beck Depression Inventar. BL = baseline. HR_agg = heart rate, aggregated mean of 5 min. Data are expressed as mean *(SD)*.
In cases of significance, results of two-way (group × condition) analyses of variance or Kruskal Wallis test, respectively are depicted. n.s. = not significant.
[a] Group effect.
[b] Group by condition effect.

7.3.2 Endocrine stress response

For the analysis of the endocrine stress reaction, salivary cortisol was collected at five points (-5, +17, +30, +40, +90 min.). There were differences in baseline cortisol levels for neither GROUP, $F(1, 109) = 1.09$, $p = .30$ nor CONDITION, $F(1, 109) = .03$, $p = .87$ nor their interaction, $F(1, 109) = .26$, $p = .31$.

A three-way mixed 2×2×5 GROUP (SAD/HC) × CONDITION (stress/no stress) × TIME (-5, +17, +30, +40, +90 min.) ANOVA revealed a main effect for time, $F(2.23, 240.68) = 30.33$, $p < .001$, $\eta_p^2 = .22$ and a TIME × CONDITION interaction, $F(2.23, 240.68) = 43.10$, $p < .001$, $\eta_p^2 = .29$, indicating that participants in the stress condition showed an increase in cortisol over time, whereas those in the no-stress condition did not show any such increase (**Fig. 7.1**). Patients with SAD and HC did not differ regarding cortisol increase, as depicted by non-significant effects for TIME × GROUP, $F(2.23, 240.68) = .20$, $p = .85$ and TIME × GROUP × CONDITION, $F(2.23, 240.68) = .73$, $p = .50$. Concurrently, there was a main effect for CONDITION, $F(1, 108) = 26.88$, $p < .001$, $\eta_p^2 = .20$, but no main effect for GROUP, $F(1, 108) = .93$, $p = .34$.

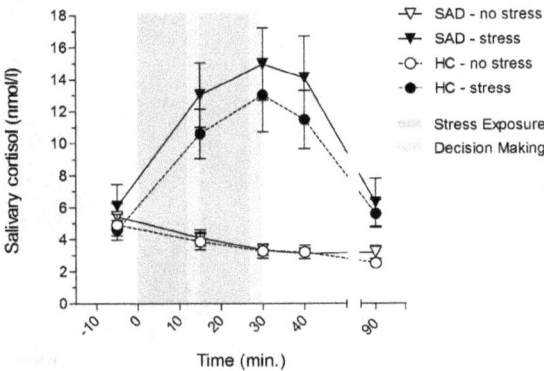

Figure 7.1. Mean salivary cortisol levels (± SEM) before and after the two conditions of the stress test (TSST-G) for subjects with SAD and for healthy controls.
SAD = social anxiety disorder, HC = healthy control. TSST-G = Trier Social Stress Test for Groups

7.3.3   Cardiovascular stress response

There were no differences in aggregated baseline heart rate, for neither GROUP, $F(1, 97) = 2.29$, $p = .13$, CONDITION, $F(1, 97) = .04$, $p = .84$ nor their interaction, $F(1, 97) = 1.09$, $p = .30$.

The three-way mixed 2×2×36 GROUP × CONDITION × TIME ANOVA showed a main effect for TIME, $F(7.85, 761.10) = 36.27$, $p < .001$, $\eta_p^2 = .27$ and a TIME × CONDITION interaction, $F(7.85, 761.10) = 2.57$, $p < .05$, $\eta_p^2 = .03$, but no TIME × GROUP, $F(7.85, 761.10) = 1.20$, $p = .294$ or TIME × GROUP × CONDITION interaction, $F(7.85, 761.10) = 1.10$, $p = .361$, indicating that heart rate in both groups showed a significant higher increase over time in the stress condition than in the no-stress condition **Figure 7.2**. There was neither a main effect for GROUP, $F(1, 97) = 0.83$, $p = .366$, nor for CONDITION, $F(1, 97) = 0.35$, $p = .557$ nor for their interaction, $F(1, 97) = 0.15$, $p = .698$, Accordingly, increase in terms of heart rate delta showed a significant effect for CONDITION, $F(1, 97) = 29.17$, $p < .001$, $\eta_p^2 = .23$ and no effect for GROUP or GROUP × CONDITION, all $ps > .393$. That is, heart rate increases for SAD patients (27.47 bmp ± 17.31) and HC (27.66 bmp ± 10.67) in the stress condition were similar and higher compared to participants in the no-stress condition (SAD = 12.67 bmp ± 6.90; HC = 16.59 bmp ±1 0.34).

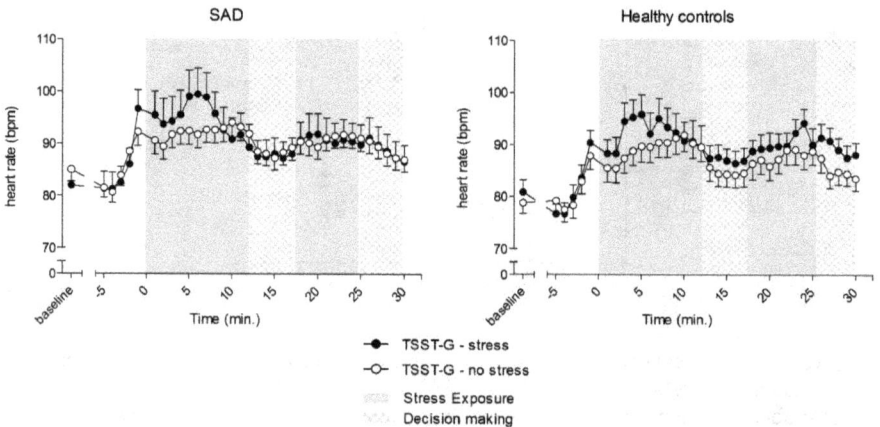

Figure 7.2. Mean heart rate in beats per minute (bpm) (with SEM bars) during the two conditions of the stress test (TSST-G), for subjects with SAD and for healthy controls, respectively.
SAD = social anxiety disorder. TSST-G = Trier Social Stress Test for Groups.

As BMI of the SAD group was higher in the stress condition than in the no-stress condition, and changes in heart rate are associated with BMI, analyses were conducted additionally with BMI as a covariate. Although groups differed in the covariate, which technically prohibits the usage of ANCOVA, as covariate and group share variance (G. A. Miller & Chapman, 2001), conduction of ANCOVA was considered justifiable as BMI measures can be considered to have differed in conditions by chance rather than reflecting meaningful differences, attributed to allocation of condition, as Miller and Chapman (2001) state: *"If [...] group differences on Cov [Covariate] truly arose by chance, ANCOVA is appropriate"* (p. 6). Results did not change with inclusion of BMI: The three-way mixed 2×2×36 GROUP × CONDITION × TIME with BMI as COVARIATE ANCOVA showed a main effect for TIME, $F(8.21, 787.91) = 4.70$, $p < .001$, $\eta_p^2 = .05$ and a TIME × CONDITION interaction, $F(8.21, 787.91) = 2.91$, $p < .05$, $\eta_p^2 = .03$. There was no TIME × GROUP interaction, $F(8.21, 787.91) = 1.23$, $p = .275$ or TIME × GROUP × CONDITION interaction, $F(8.21, 787.91) = 1.25$, $p = .268$, no main effect for GROUP, $F(1, 96) = 0.82$, $p = .367$, CONDITION, $F(1, 96) = 0.37$, $p = .403$ or their interaction, $F(1, 96) = 0.00$, $p = .966$. Furthermore, there was no effect of the COVARIATE (BMI) on heart rate, $F(1, 96) = 2.72$, $p = .103$. Additionally, correlations between BMI of SAD patients and heart rate increase (delta) were conducted to test for possible associations. In both conditions, BMI was not correlated with heart rate increase, all $ps > .544$.

7.3.4   Psychological stress response

SAD exhibited higher baseline measures of subjective stress, $F(1, 109) = 15.56$, $p < .001$, $\eta_p^2 = .13$, tension, $F(1, 109) = 20.44$, $p < .001$, $\eta_p^2 = .16$, anxiety, $F(1, 109) = 20.77$, $p < .001$, $\eta_p^2 = .16$, physical discomfort, $F(1, 109) = 22.97$, $p < .001$, $\eta_p^2 = .17$, wish to leave the situation, $F(1, 109) = 20.62$, $p < .001$, $\eta_p^2 = .16$, perceived control, $F(1, 109) = 6.01$, $p < .05$, $\eta_p^2 = .05$ and state anxiety, $F(1, 109) = 58.00$, $p < .001$,

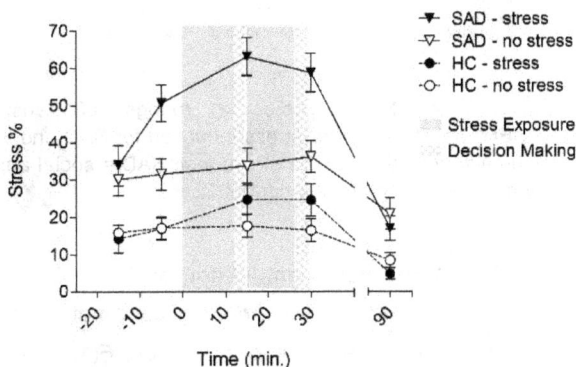

Figure 7.3. Mean subjective ratings of stress (± SEM) before and after stress induction for SAD and HC in the two conditions of the stress test. SAD = social anxiety disorder, HC = healthy control.

$\eta_p^2 = .35$. Regarding condition, baseline measures did not differ, all $ps > .190$.

Regarding subjectively perceived *stress*, the repeated ANOVA showed a main effect for TIME, $F(4, 420) = 44.72$, $p < .001$, $\eta_p^2 = .30$ and a TIME × CONDITION interaction, $F(4, 420) = 11.76$, $p < .001$, $\eta_p^2 = .10$, indicating higher increase in subjective stress in the stress- than in the no-stress condition (**Fig. 7.3**). Furthermore, significant effects for TIME × GROUP, $F(4, 420) = 5.58$, $p < .01$, $\eta_p^2 = .05$ and TIME × CONDITION × GROUP, $F(4, 420) = 2.80$, $p < .05$, $\eta_p^2 = .03$ emerged. Moreover, there were significant between-subjects effects for CONDITION, $F(1, 105) = 6.10$, $p < .05$, $\eta_p^2 = .06$, GROUP, $F(1, 105) = 45.04$, $p < .001$, $\eta_p^2 = .30$ and CONDITION × GROUP, $F(1, 105) = 4.32$, $p < .05$, $\eta_p^2 = .04$. That is, subjects with SAD had higher overall levels of subjective stress and also showed a stronger increase in the stress condition compared to the no-stress condition than HC.

Regarding subjective *tension*, there was a main effect for TIME, $F(4, 420) = 47.51$, $p < .001$, $\eta_p^2 = .31$ and a TIME × CONDITION interaction, $F(4, 420) = 10.28$, $p < .001$, $\eta_p^2 = .09$, indicating a higher increase in tension for the stress condition than for the no-stress condition. Further, there was a significant TIME × GROUP interaction, $F(4, 420) = 8.57$, $p < .001$, $\eta_p^2 = .08$, while the TIME × CON-

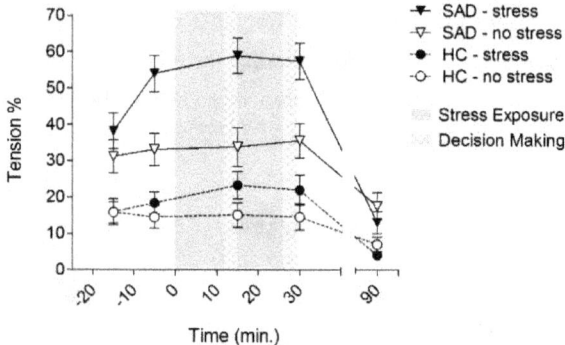

Figure 7.4. Mean subjective ratings of tension (± SEM) before and after stress induction for SAD and HC in the two conditions of the stress test. SAD = social anxiety disorder, HC = healthy control.

DITION × GROUP interaction did not reach significance, $F(4, 420) = 2.84$, $p = .073$, $\eta_p^2 = .02$. Further, there were significant main effects for CONDITION, $F(1, 105) = 7.71$, $p < .01$, $\eta_p^2 = .71$ and for GROUP, $F(1, 105) = 49.03$, $p < .001$, $\eta_p^2 = .32$, while the CONDITION × GROUP interaction did not reach significance, $F(1, 105) = 3.70$, $p = .057$, $\eta_p^2 = .03$, indicating that the SAD group in general showed more tension and a stronger increase over time compared to the HC group (**Fig. 7.4**).

Regarding subjectively perceived *anxiety*, again there was a significant effect for TIME $F(4, 420) = 33.83$, $p < .001$, $\eta_p^2 = .24$ and for TIME × CONDITION $F(4, 420) = 5.62$, $p < .001$, $\eta_p^2 = .05$. Moreover, significant interactions for TIME × GROUP $F(4, 420) = 10.68$, $p < .001$, $\eta_p^2 = .09$ and TIME × CONDITION × GROUP, $F(4, 420) = 2.48$, $p < .05$, $\eta_p^2 = .02$, as well as between-subjects effects for

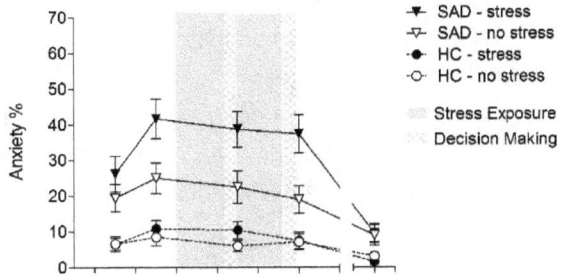

Figure 7.6. Mean subjective ratings of anxiety (± SEM) before and after stress induction for SAD and HC in the two conditions of the stress test. SAD = social anxiety disorder, HC = healthy control.

GROUP, $F(1, 105) = 39.08$, $p < .001$, $\eta_p^2 = .27$ and for CONDITION × GROUP, $F(1, 105) = 5.07$, $p < .05$, $\eta_p^2 = .04$ revealed that SAD felt more anxiety over the whole experiment, irrespective of condition, and showed an increase in anxiety in response to the stress manipulation, while the HC group did not. Accordingly, simple effects revealed that the TIME × CONDITION effect was driven by the SAD group, $F(1, 105) = 9.61$, $p < .01$ and was not apparent for HC, $F(1, 105) = 0.02$, $p = .880$ (**Fig. 7.5**).

For the feeling of *physical discomfort*, there was a main effect for TIME $F(4, 420) = 17.28$, $p < .001$, $\eta_p^2 = .14$ and a TIME × CONDITION interaction $F(4, 420) = 8.06$, $p < .001$, $\eta_p^2 = .07$, indicating a stronger increase under stress than under no-stress condi-

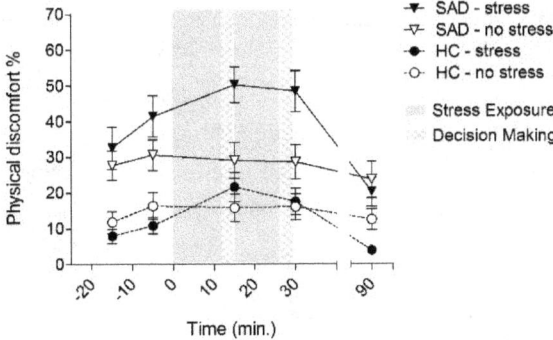

Figure 7.5. Mean subjective ratings of physical discomfort (± SEM) before and after stress induction for SAD and HC in the two conditions of the stress test. SAD = social anxiety disorder, HC = healthy control.

tion. A significant main effect for GROUP, $F(1, 105) = 32.52$, $p < .001$, $\eta_p^2 = .24$ and a significant CONDITION × GROUP interaction, $F(1, 105) = 4.00$, $p < .05$, $\eta_p^2 = .04$ revealed that SAD in general felt more physically uneasy than HC and showed a stronger reaction to stress in that respect. The absence of significant effects for TIME × GROUP and TIME × CONDITION × GROUP (all ps > .116), as well as simple effects confirmed that, nonetheless, the TIME × CONDITION interaction was apparent for both SAD, $F(4, 220) = 4.90$, $p < .01$, $\eta_p^2 = .08$ and HC, $F(4, 200) = 4.85$, $p < .01$, $\eta_p^2 = .09$ (**Fig. 7.6**).

The analysis of *avoidance* showed a an effect for TIME $F(4, 420) = 5.51$, $p < .01$, $\eta_p^2 = .05$, a TIME × CONDITION interaction $F(4, 420) = 6.88$, $p < .001$, $\eta_p^2 = .06$, as well as a TIME × GROUP interaction $F(4, 420) = 2.45$, $p < .05$, $\eta_p^2 = .02$. Again, SAD in general had a stronger desire to leave the situation than HC, indicated by a main effect of GROUP, $F(1, 105) = 33.70$, $p < .001$, $\eta_p^2 = .24$. Moreover, stress affected avoidance in the SAD group, but not in the HC

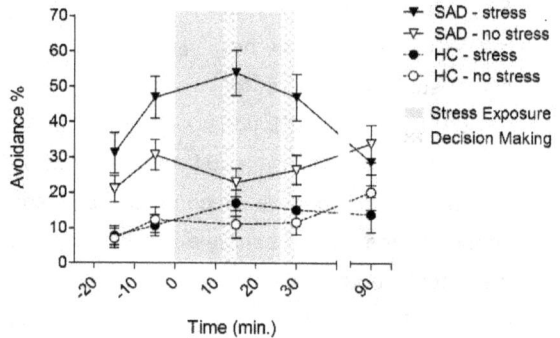

Figure 7.7. Mean subjective ratings of avoidance (± SEM) before and after stress induction for SAD and HC in the two conditions of the stress test. SAD = social anxiety disorder, HC = healthy control.

group, as indicated by a CONDITION × GROUP interaction, $F(1, 105) = 4.24$, $p < .05$, $\eta_p^2 = .04$, as well as by simple effects, which revealed that the TIME × CONDITION effect was apparent for SAD, $F(4, 220) = 5.59$, $p < .001$, $\eta_p^2 = .09$, but not HC, $F(4, 200) = 1.75$, $p = .140$ (**Fig. 7.7**).

For the subjectively perceived *control over the situation*, there was a main effect of TIME $F(4, 420) = 14.53$, $p < .001$, $\eta_p^2 = .12$, a TIME × CONDITION interaction $F(4, 420) = 7.64$, $p < .001$, $\eta_p^2 = .07$ as well as a TIME × GROUP interaction $F(4, 420) = 5.91$, $p < .01$, $\eta_p^2 = .05$, indicating less perceived control over time in the stress condition than in the no-stress condition for both groups and a stronger variation of perceived control over time in SAD compared to HC (**Fig. 7.8**). The main effect for GROUP did not reach significance, $F(1, 105) = 3.56$, $p = .062$, $\eta_p^2 = .03$.

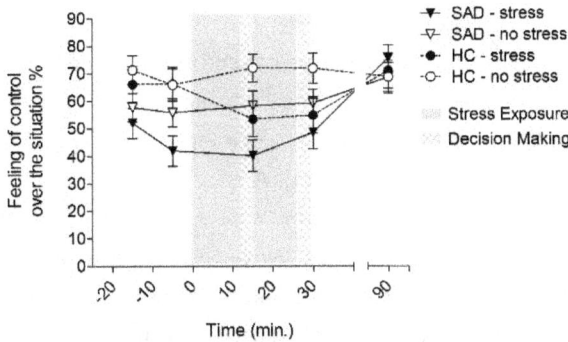

Figure 7.9. Mean subjective ratings of control over the situation (± SEM) before and after stress induction for SAD and HC in the two conditions of stress test. SAD = social anxiety disorder, HC = healthy control.

Additionally, *state anxiety* was measured using the STAI at four points. The three-way mixed (GROUP × CONDITION × TIME) ANOVA showed a main effect of TIME $F(4, 408) = 31.79$, $p < .001$, $\eta_p^2 = .24$ and a TIME × CONDITION interaction $F(4, 408) = 9.54$, $p < .001$, $\eta_p^2 = .09$, indicating a higher increase in anxiety in the stress condition compared to the no-stress condition. Furthermore, there was a TIME × GROUP interaction $F(4, 408) = 6.66$, $p < .001$, $\eta_p^2 = .06$, as well as a strong main effect for GROUP, $F(1, 102) = 73.54$, $p < .001$, $\eta_p^2 = .42$, indicating a higher anxiety increase in SAD and more anxiety in SAD in general than in HC (**Fig. 7.9**).

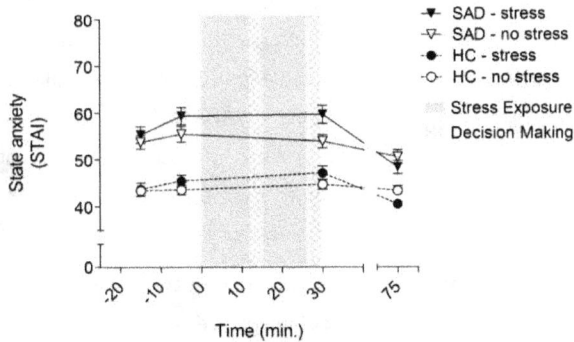

Figure 7.8. Mean subjective state anxiety (± SEM) before and after stress induction for SAD and HC in the two conditions of the stress test. SAD = social anxiety disorder, HC = healthy control.

7.4   Discussion

In the preceding section we investigated the physiological and subjective reaction to acute psychosocial stress in patients with SAD and matched healthy controls, using a standardized laboratory protocol for the induction of acute stress in groups, namely the TSST-G (von Dawans et al., 2011). A clear pattern of dissociated reactivity between subjective and physiological stress response in patients with SAD emerged, as compared to healthy controls. While SAD patients exhibited an elevated subjective response in all of the measures (stress, tension, discomfort, anxiety, avoidance, feeling of control), their reaction did not differ from that of healthy controls with respect to the physiological parameters (salivary cortisol and heart rate).

The stress induction was successful across all parameters measured (endocrine, autonomous, subjective). There was a significant and similar increase in salivary cortisol for SAD and HC in the stress condition, whereas neither group exhibited any increase in the no-stress condition. Heart rate measures revealed the same effect for both groups. That is, on a physiological level, there were no differences in the stress reaction of participants with SAD and healthy controls. A different pattern emerged regarding subjectively perceived stress: Here, in the stress condition, both HC and SAD perceived the TSST-G as more stressful than the participants in the control condition, i.e. they presented higher increases in subjectively perceived stress, tension, physical discomfort, state anxiety, and felt less control over the situation. In subjects with SAD, however, stress led to stronger increases in subjective stress and anxiety compared to HC and intensified the desire to leave the situation. Moreover, before, during, and after the TSST-G, SAD patients exhibited markedly higher levels of stress than HC in all subjective parameters.

This dissociation between subjective and physiological stress responses in SAD compared to HC is in concordance with previous studies (Anderson & Hope, 2009; Beaton et al., 2006; Edelmann & Baker, 2002; Grossman, 2001; Klumbies et al., 2014; Losiak et al., 2016; Martel et al., 1999; Mauss et al., 2004). Klumbies and colleagues (2014), for example, found higher subjective stress responses in SAD than in HC, as well as no differences to HC in salivary cortisol and heart rate. Furthermore, they found no differences in plasma cortisol, salivary alpha-amylase, prolactin, heart rate variability or long-term cortisol production (cortisol in hair), which corroborates the finding of the present study, namely that people with SAD demonstrate the same physiological stress response as healthy subjects.

The present results regarding the endocrine and cardiovascular stress response stand, however, in contrast to previous studies that report elevated physiological stress response in conjunction with SAD compared to HC (Condren et al., 2002; Furlan et al., 2001; Gerlach et al., 2001; Roelofs et al., 2009; van West et al., 2008; Yoon & Joormann, 2012). This inconsistency might be due to insufficient standardization of stress induction methods in previous studies. The only studies that also employed an established stress-induction method, namely the TSST (Kirschbaum, Pirke, & Hellhammer, 1993), and that had a sufficient sample size (Klumbies et al., 2014; Martel et al., 1999), report the same physiological stress response in conjunction with SAD as with HC and are well in line with the present study's findings. Furthermore, investigation of different age groups might account for discrepancies. Van West and colleagues (2008) examined socially anxious children, who may not be comparable to adults, as age is known to influence the stress reaction via an age-related decrease in responsiveness in the HPA-axis (Kudielka et al., 2004a; Otte et al., 2005; Strahler, Mueller, Rosenloecher, Kirschbaum, & Rohleder, 2010) and heart rate (Kudielka et al., 2004b; Strahler et al., 2010). Further, other accompanying psychiatric disorders might have led to different findings. For example, Roelofs and colleagues (2009) allowed for any comorbidity in the SAD-group except for psychotic disorders. The present study and that by Klumbies and colleagues (2014) employed stricter inclusion criteria regarding comorbidity and are thus more likely to depict the characteristics of the stress response specific to social anxiety disorder. There is also evidence that patients with performance-only SAD in particular exhibit a heightened heart rate in reaction to stress compared to generalized SAD (Boone et al., 1999; Heimberg, Hope, Dodge, & Becker, 1990; Levin et al., 1993)[2]. With the reaction to a circumscribed

---

[2] The study of Boone and colleagues (1999) is not included in the overview on stress reaction in SAD in chapter 2.4.8, as they did not recruit a healthy control group.

situation, the psychopathology of performance-only social anxiety might be related to a specific phobia, which could explain the different cardiovascular stress response pattern, as specific phobia has been associated with sympathetic hyper-responsiveness (Dieleman et al., 2015). Moreover, most of the studies examined both male and female participants. However, gender and, notably, the menstrual cycle as well as oral contraceptives influence HPA-axis functioning (Kudielka et al., 2009). For example, men consistently exhibit stronger cortisol reactions in response to psychosocial stress than women (Earle, Linden, & Weinberg, 1999; Lovallo, Farag, Vincent, Thomas, & Wilson, 2006; Seeman, Singer, Wilkinson, & McEwen, 2001), and women in their follicular phase and those taking oral contraceptives exhibit lower cortisol reactivity than women in the luteal phase (Kirschbaum, Kudielka, Gaab, Schommer, & Hellhammer, 1999; Rohleder, Schommer, Hellhammer, Engel, & Kirschbaum, 2001; Rohleder, Wolf, Piel, & Kirschbaum, 2003). For example, in the samples of Roelofs and colleagues (2009) and Yoon and Joormann (2012), the ratio of women to men was higher in the healthy control group than in the SAD-group, possibly dampening the healthy group's cortisol response compared to the social anxiety group's. Furthermore, medications such as antidepressants (Barden et al., 1995; Pariante et al., 2004) and even short-term drugs (Kudielka et al., 2009) can affect stress measures, a factor unaccounted for in most of the studies. Furthermore, two studies (Beidel et al., 1985; Gerlach et al., 2001) found accelerated heart-rate only in a group of socially anxious participants with a specific fear of blushing, presumably forming a subgroup that may react physiologically more strongly to challenges (Öst, Jerremalm, & Johansson, 1981; Voncken & Bögels, 2009). Finally, some of the studies comprised a small sample size (Condren et al., 2002; Roelofs et al., 2009), which is problematic as the associated low statistical power lowers the likelihood that a statistically significant result reflects a genuine effect (Button et al., 2013; Ioannidis, 2005). Despite those methodological limitations, there is a pool of studies that corroborate the idea of an exaggerated physiological stress response in SAD. Thus, additional research is needed in order to better understand the circumstances under which patients suffering from social anxiety disorder might exhibit increased HPA-axis and SAM reactivity, and in order to identify possible subtypes of SAD in this regard.

In the present study, SAD patients exhibited a higher BMI in the stress condition than in the no-stress condition. As a measure of adiposity, a high BMI means that the heart has to supply more mass with oxygen and is associated with hypertension (for a review, see Malnick & Knobler, 2006). Heart rate reactivity, however, has been shown to be reduced in people with high BMI (Carroll, Phillips, & Der, 2008; Phillips, Roseboom, Carroll, & de Rooij, 2012; Steptoe & Wardle, 2005). In those studies, however, BMI values were critically elevated, while in the present study, participants had normal weight. In a large sample (N = 200) of participants with normal weight, Steptoe and Wardle (2005) did find an association of BMI with impaired cardiovascular recovery but no association between cardiovascular stress reactivity and BMI. In accordance, in the present study, BMI values and overall heart rate as well as heart rate increase were not correlated and the inclusion of BMI as covariate did not change results. Thus, it can be assumed that BMI did not account for the findings of the present study.

How does the normal physiological stress reaction in SAD fit in with the well documented amygdala hyperactivity in this patient group (for meta-analyses, see Brühl et al., 2014; Etkin & Wager, 2007)? Heightened amygdala activity in response to social stimuli in SAD does not necessarily call for an increased physiological stress reaction. The amygdala has been shown to regulate glucocorticoid-secretion in animals (Jankord & Herman, 2008). In humans, there is less evidence for a direct relation, but in a study by Root and colleagues (2009), amygdala activity has been associated with increased cortisol secretion. However, the amygdala entails several connections to regions that are associated with the processing of visual, auditory, olfactory, gustatory and somatosensory information (McDonald, 1998). Thereby, an important role of the amygdala is modulation of vigilance (Davis & Whalen, 2001; Herman et al., 2003). Therefore, it has been suggested that increased amygdala activity in social anxiety reflects hypervigilance rather than the magnitude of anxiety (Davis & Whalen, 2001). Under stress, SAD patients may exhibit increased vigilance in order to detect signs of threat. Due to the possibility of rejection, people suffering from SAD are thought to alertly scan their environment for potential signs of negative evaluation. There is ample evidence for such hypervigilance for threat-relevant information in SAD (e.g.

Mogg, Philippot, & Bradley, 2004; Seefeldt, Krämer, Tuschen-Caffier, & Heinrichs, 2014; Vassilopoulos, 2005).

In line with previous studies (e.g. Klumbies et al., 2014; Mauss et al., 2004), patients exhibited a markedly elevated psychological reaction to stress compared to HC. Psychological response to a stressor also depends on the capacity to regulate emotions. Healthy individuals might possess more effective coping strategies, or have an easier time using them. For example, SAD patients have been found to frequently suppress negative (Erwin, Heimberg, Schneier, & Liebowitz, 2003; Spokas, Luterek, & Heimberg, 2009) and positive emotions (Farmer & Kashdan, 2012). Accordingly, patients with SAD have been shown to exhibit reduced activity in dorsolateral PFC and dorsal ACC during reinterpretation of social threat pictures (Goldin et al., 2009), structures implicated in cognitive regulation. Patients with SAD strive to avoid negative attention, and suppression aims at inhibiting the emotional outcome and outward display of feelings (J. J. Gross, 2002). Hence, the intent to suppress emotional reactions might even be increased under stress, where physiological reactions, such as blushing or trembling, are enhanced, overestimated (Mauss et al., 2004) and may be even more visible by others. Building on cognitive behavioral therapy, treatments specially aiming at these difficulties in emotion regulation have been developed (Barlow, Allen, & Choate, 2004; Linehan, 1993) and may be helpful in treatment of SAD as well.

The present findings further underline the significance of dysfunctional thought patterns in SAD. Although there was no difference to healthy controls apparent physiologically, participants with SAD evaluated the situation as much more stressful, as eliciting more tension, discomfort and anxiety and experienced themselves as being less in control. Thus, SAD patients processed the same situation as more stressful and threatening. This is indicative of a biased perception, as proposed by cognitive models of SAD (Clark & Wells, 1995; Rapee & Heimberg, 1997) and empirical evidence (for a review, see Bar-Haim et al., 2007). That is, participants with SAD might have been hypervigilant towards potential threats, resulting in an anxious emotional state. Additionally, one of the stress-inducing factors of the TSST-G is socio-evaluative threat (Dickerson & Kemeny, 2004), which might have triggered self-focused attention in SAD patients, resulting in a more conscious perception of bodily symptoms. This heightened awareness in turn might have let them sense bodily sensations more intensely and thus over-rate these feelings. This is in line with studies showing that patients with SAD (Gaebler, Daniels, Lamke, Fydrich, & Walter, 2013) and high socially anxious individuals (Mauss et al., 2004) are less accurate than healthy controls to estimate their bodily reactions to stress, e.g. heartbeat and respiratory rate. Moreover, while both participants with SAD and healthy controls reported increased stress and tension in response to the TSST-G, only SAD experienced increased *anxiety*. This underlines that the kind of stress induced by the TSST-G is at the core of fears of people with SAD: being exposed to the scrutiny by others. The same effect was apparent in the measure of in the desire to leave the situation. Again, there was an increase in response to stress only in the SAD group and not in HC, pointing to the characteristic avoidance behavior in this disorder (APA, 2013), which was increased by psychosocial stress. Thus, the present findings corroborate cognitive models of SAD (Clark & Wells, 1995; Rapee & Heimberg, 1997) that emphasize cognitive biases in SAD as crucial precipitating and maintaining factors. This may entail implications for treatment of this disorder.

A central aspect in the treatment of SAD is the conduction of behavioral experiments. Engaging in such experiments may become easier for patients once they know that their own bodily sensations are actually normal. Moreover, the awareness of supposedly exaggerated bodily symptoms may cause increased self-focused attention and safety-behaviors in order to hide the symptoms. Both self-focused attention and safety-behaviors contribute to maintenance of the disorder (Clark & Wells, 1995; McManus, Sacadura, & Clark, 2008; Spurr & Stopa, 2002). Psychoeducation regarding their physiological stress reaction may help patients to abstain from those behaviors.

In sum, in the present study, stress induction with a standardized laboratory protocol led to similar endocrine and cardiovascular responses in terms of increased salivary cortisol and heart rate in SAD and HC. Subjects with SAD, however, exhibited a markedly amplified subjective stress response compared to HC. The present findings suggest that patients with SAD exhibit a regular physiological stress response and a nevertheless elevated subjective response to stress. This discordance of physiological and psychological stress response builds on empirical evidence for cognitive models of SAD (Clark & Wells, 1995; Rapee & Heimberg, 1997) and their concept of a biased perception of social cues and bodily symptoms. The sample used here comprised of comorbidity-free patients. For a better understanding of the underlying psychophysiological mechanisms in SAD, it is important to investigate the stress response in a clear-cut sample. However, as comorbidity in SAD is high (B. F. Grant, Hasin, Blanco, et al., 2005; Ohayon & Schatzberg, 2010), future studies should directly compare HPA-axis and cardio-vascular responses in samples of patients with and without comorbidity such as depression or substance abuse, in order to disentangle the specifications of po-tentially aberrant stress reactivity in SAD with and without comorbid disorders. Further, the findings are of clinical relevance, as therapeutic approaches may have a wider scope for assessing the patient's self-concept, in view of the fact that the bodily sensations perceived by the patient as excessive are actually nor-mal.

8   Empirical Chapter II: Effects of Acute Stress on Social Interaction Behavior in Social Anxiety Disorder

8.1   Introduction

The way we act around others configures multiple aspects of our social life, such as being able to draw on help in difficult times, having a spouse or being integrated in social groups. We have a general need to affiliate with others and form stable relationships (Baumeister & Leary, 1995; Caporael, 1997). Belongingness and being in close relationships has a positive impact on health and well-being (Cacioppo et al., 2015; Holt-Lunstad et al., 2010). Accordingly, a vital source of coping is social support (Ditzen & Heinrichs, 2014).

The classical concept of the behavioral reaction to stress is the *fight-or-flight* response (W. B. Cannon, 1915), that is, showing aggressive behavior or escaping the situation, respectively. However, a growing body of research describes increased prosocial and affiliative behavior in healthy participants after stress (Berger et al., 2015; Buchanan & Preston, 2014; Takahashi et al., 2007; von Dawans et al., 2012). Those observations cannot be explained by the classical view of a *fight-or-flight* reaction but call for a broadening of the conceptualization of the human social behavioral reaction to stress. A concept that has provided a theoretical and empirical framework is the *tend-and-befriend* model, postulated by Taylor and colleagues (Taylor, 2006; Taylor et al., 2000). The model suggests that acute stress promotes affiliation to others, which in turn leads to stress reduction, resulting from positive social contacts. This very aspect may entail difficulties for people suffering from SAD, as key symptoms of this disorder are insecurity and worry about social contacts and avoidance of social situations (e.g. Rapee & Heimberg, 1997).

Social anxiety disorder (SAD) is characterized by a distinctive fear of behaving embarrassingly in interaction with others. Social encounters trigger distress and often bodily symptoms such as sweating, trembling or blushing. As a consequence, social situations are avoided or endured with intense distress (American Psychiatric Association, 2013). Thus, in SAD, fears of social interactions and subsequent avoidance function as an obstacle to social approach behavior, and stress reducing effects through affiliation may not be utilizable. The absence of this fundamental stress-protective resource would contribute to maintaining symptomatology and, in the long term, carry increased risk for additional, stress-related pathology (Chrousos, 2009).

Although SAD patients are stressed in social encounters by definition, little is known about the effects of stress on social interaction behavior in SAD. In a study by Mallott and colleagues (2009), healthy participants high in social anxiety acted less prosocially than participants low in social anxiety after social rejection. In accordance with this, highly socially anxious subjects have been shown to exhibit more aggressive and antisocial behavior after rejection than participants low in social anxiety (Maner, DeWall, Baumeister, & Schaller, 2007). Those observations indicate less prosocial behavior in socially anxious individuals after stressful situations. However, the studies did not investigate actual stress but paradigms of social rejection and social dominance. Although such situations can trigger a stress reaction, it is unclear if the participants were stressed, as stress-related parameters were not examined. Moreover, the samples consisted of healthy participants instead of patients who met criteria for SAD, thus not allowing clear-cut conclusions about the actual clinical picture. To the best of my knowledge, only one study (Roelofs et al., 2009) examined the influence of stress on socially relevant behavior in patients with SAD. There, participants had to engage in an approach-avoidance task after stress induction. Subjects with SAD were faster in avoiding angry faces after stress, indicating increased avoidance behavior. Most importantly, however, in none of the studies, the influence of stress on behavior in actual social interactions was examined, limiting possible conclusions about SAD patients' actual behavior in real social situations. In the current study, acute stress was induced with a well-established method, the TSST-G (von Dawans et al., 2011), and social behavior of patients with diagnosed SAD versus healthy controls was assessed in real interaction situations.

For the stress-reducing effect of *tend-and-befriend* behavior, positive social interactions are necessary, as they are thought to mediate the relation of affiliative behavior and decline of the stress responses (see chapter 3.1 for details). This may entail difficulties for patients with social anxiety disorder. Impairments in social contacts are at the core of suffering in social anxiety disorder (Alden & Taylor,

2004), and SAD patients exhibit actual deficits in social performance (Baker & Edelmann, 2002; Fydrich et al., 1998; Stopa & Clark, 1993; Voncken & Bögels, 2008), presumably impeding coping through social affiliation. In order to engage in social interactions smoothly, one needs to be able to infer another person's emotional and mental state, i.e. exhibit empathic abilities. Deficiencies in these abilities accordingly lead to miscommunication and impaired social functioning (Fett et al., 2011; Shanafelt et al., 2005). This is of special interest for disorders in which the core problem area concerns social interactions, as in SAD. As an underlying mechanism of social interaction behavior, empathic abilities might modulate the social response to stress.

Moreover, cognitive theories (e.g. Beck, 1979; Clark & Wells, 1995; Rapee & Heimberg, 1997) and empirical evidence (for a meta-analysis, see Bar-Haim et al., 2007; for a review on neuroimaging data, see Schulz et al., 2013) suggest an attentional bias for threat in SAD. That is, information processing in SAD seems to be biased to the effect that patients are hypervigilant to negative or threatening stimuli. This bias may be amplified in situations of stress. It is widely known that acute stress impairs the functioning of the prefrontal cortex (PFC). Thereby, stress affects socially important processes such as the working memory as well as the regulation of attention and emotion, limiting attention regulation in favor of a 'bottom up' control (for reviews, see Arnsten, 2009; McEwen & Morrison, 2013). That is, under stress, salient and threatening stimuli, such as signs of rejection in SAD, bind attention even more than under non-stressful conditions. In accordance, after cortisol administration, patients with SAD showed increased processing of threatening faces compared to placebo (van Peer, Spinhoven, Dijk, & Roelofs, 2009). Thus, in challenging or ambiguous situations, people suffering from SAD are expected to focus on possible snares instead of concentrating on positive possibilities that could arise from connecting with others. Additionally, with the impairment of prefrontal functioning, less attentional capacity is available. In SAD, it has been shown that attention under stress is rather self-focused and processing of external cues is reduced (Clark, 2005; Mansell, Clark, Ehlers, & Chen, 1999). This entails difficulties in social situations, as self-focused attention leaves less attention at the interaction partner and thus has been shown to compromise smooth social interactions (McManus et al., 2008). High empathic abilities might contain the adverse effects in SAD patients, as empathy has been shown to promote other-oriented motivation and prosocial behavior (Bateson, 2002; Eisenberg, 2007; Hoffmann, 2008).

The aim of the present study was to further elucidate the influences of acute stress on social behavior in people suffering from SAD under consideration of empathic abilities, thereby extending the knowledge of the psychopathology of this disorder. It was hypothesized that (I) SAD patients would show deficits in social performance compared to HC, irrespective of stress. Further, it was expected that (II) in healthy individuals, acute stress would lead to affiliative behavior in terms of increased social performance in the conversation and increased prosocial behavior in the social-decision task. Furthermore, it was hypothesized that (III) SAD patients would not exhibit affiliative behavior in reaction to stress but instead would be characterized by lower social performance ratings and reduced prosocial behavior and that (IV) empathic abilities would alleviate these effects of stress on social interaction behavior in SAD.

8.2   Methods

8.2.1   Study design and procedure

The study was a single-blind randomized controlled trial with a 2 x 2 between-subjects design with the factors group (SAD vs. HC) and stress (stress vs. no-stress). See chapter 6.3 for a detailed description of the experimental procedure.

8.2.2   Participants

For details on subject recruitment and sample description, see chapter 6.2. The sample consisted of N = 113 subjects, with n = 60 SAD, age 28.23 ± 8.98 years (mean ± SD) and n = 53 healthy controls, age 27.38 ± 6.51. Participants were randomly assigned to the stress and no-stress condition of the *Trier Social Stress Test for Groups* (TSST-G; von Dawans et al., 2011), resulting in n = 30 SAD stress; n = 30 SAD no-stress; n = 26 HC stress; n = 27 HC no-stress.

8.2.3 Stress paradigm

Stress was induced by the *Trier Social Stress Test for Groups* (TSST-G; von Dawans et al., 2011), an established standardized laboratory protocol for the induction of moderate psychosocial stress. See chapter 6.3.1 for details. At the end of the experiment, participants were asked to rate their performance in the TSST-G in terms of 1 = *average*, 2 = *below-average* or 3 = *above-average*.

8.2.4 Conversation paradigm

For the assessment of social performance under stress, a conversation paradigm was implemented. Paradigms like this allow for an experimentally controlled investigation of social interaction behavior while at the same time benefitting from high external validity. The conversation task used was based on Voncken and Bögels (2008) and consisted of a five-minute conversation with a confederate. The instructions for the participants, also adapted from the study by Voncken and Bögels, were as follows: "We would like you to have a conversation with another person. The purpose is to get to know each other. It is up to you to start the conversation and to keep it going." After the conversation, confederates rated the participants' social performance on a standardized questionnaire, also adapted from Voncken and Bögels (2008); see section 8.4.2.4. Concrete interactional elements such as gaze behavior, active listening and self-disclosure were measured. The conversation furthermore was videotaped and later rated by two independent video-raters. The main results of the paradigm were the external ratings (confederates' and video ratings), as they depict both the impression the participant makes and possible performance deficits. In addition, to assess possible biases in self-perception, participants rated their own social performance as well.

8.2.4.1 *Confederates*

Confederates were female undergraduate students. Across the sessions, a total of 16 confederates participated. All had received a three-hour training in rating social performance and remaining in a neutral but friendly posture during the conversation. Quality of behavior of the confederates was reviewed by M. Voncken through video-recordings. In addition, they were trained to answer with up to three pieces of information and only to ask a question after 7 seconds of silence. That way, the responsibility for keeping the conversation going remained with the participant. These instructions were also based on Voncken and Bögels (2008), which in turn were based on Boone et al. (1999) and Öst, Jerremalm, and Johansson (1981). In order to verify that confederates acted in the same way across groups, video-raters evaluated their behavior with respect to friendliness, attention towards the participant, and encouragement and discouragement (Voncken & Bögels, 2008).

8.2.4.2 Rating of social performance

Social performance in the conversation was assessed through ratings by the confederates, using a modified version of the *Social Behavior and Anxious Appearance rating scale* (SBA-rating scale; Voncken & Bögels, 2008). The original version was based on a rating scale by Bögels, Rijsemus, and De Jong (2002), which in turn was based on Rapee and Lim (1992). The SBA-rating-scale consists of 27 items and two scales: *anxious appearance* and *social behavior*. Anxious appearance comprises signs of nervousness such as trembling, blushing or stuttering. The second scale, social behavior, comprises items relating to formal aspects of interaction behavior, such as holding eye contact or formulating full sentences, as well as more complex aspects, such as the degree of self-disclosure or showing interest in the conversation partner. The two-factor structure has been confirmed by Bögels and colleagues (2002). As the SBA-rating scale was originally designed for a conversation with two confederates, the wording of five items had to be adapted to a version with one conversation partner (e.g. "Did the participant listen to what *you both* were saying?" into "Did the participant listen to what *you* were saying?") and one item had to be removed ("Could the participant divide attention between you both?"). The resulting questionnaire of 26 items was translated into German. Video-raters were also trained in rating social performance with the SBA-rating scale. The participants' social performance was additionally evaluated by two video-raters in order to determine inter-rater reliability between the video-raters and the confederates.

In order to assess self-focused attention, after the conversation, a translated German version of the *Self-focused Attention Scale* (SFA; Bögels, Alberts, & de Jong, 1996) was administered. The questionnaire comprises eleven items, which refer to the attention to one's own arousal and one's interpersonal behavior, e.g. *"In the presence of other people, I'm constantly focusing on whether I behave appropriately"*. The SFA has been demonstrated to have good internal consistency, Cronbach's alpha = 0.88 (Bögels et al., 1996).

8.2.5 Social decision paradigm

For the assessment of social interaction behavior under standardized controlled conditions, the paradigm from the study by von Dawans and colleagues (2012) was adapted: a behavioral economic experiment, based on game theory.

The main principle of these social-decision experiments is that different amounts of monetary units (MU) can be gained, depending on one's own decisions and the decisions of one's interaction partner. Participants decide if and how many points they want to transfer to their interaction partner via anonymous interactions. All decisions are based on real social interactions as the interaction partners are additional participants who are also invited into the lab on the day of the session. Anonymity allows for the measurement of baseline social preferences. This form of behavioral experiment is a well-established method for the investigation of social behavior under standardized controlled conditions (e.g. Fehr & Fischbacher, 2003; Sanfey, 2007). This way, prosocial behavior (trust, trustworthiness, sharing) as well as antisocial (punishment, envy) and non-social behavior (risk) can be examined.

Participants in the present study had to make binary decisions on paper right after stress induction (see section 6.3). More precisely, in the *trustworthiness* and *trust* games, player A could decide to trust player B or not. If he did not trust, both players received, for example, 18 MU and the session was over. If he did trust, the 18 MU were increased to 60 MU and player B had the option to keep all 60 MU (not trustworthy), while player A received nothing, or to keep only half of it and give the other half to player A (trustworthy). Participants played four rounds as player A *(trust game)* and player B *(trustworthiness game)* each. In the *sharing game*, participants had to decide whether to keep all MU or to divide them between themselves and the other player. In the *envy game,* the participant had to decide whether both players should get the same amount of MU (envy) or whether the other participant should receive a higher payoff, while the own payoff stayed the same (no envy). In the *punishment game,* player A could choose that both players should receive the same amount of MU or to "demand more." In case he chose the latter, player B could either condescend, which resulted in a high payoff for player A and a low payoff for himself (no punishment) or he could punish the other's greed, which resulted in zero outcome for both players. The nonsocial *risk game* did not include an interaction partner. Here, participants had to choose between two options regarding the payoff from a game of dice. One option was risky, as difference in payoff between winning and losing was high, while the other option was low-risk, with a lower profit opportunity. The whole experiment consisted of 28 rounds (each social game four times, risk game eight times), in each of which the participants had to choose between two options. All decisions were made before participants saw the decisions of the other players. The paradigm was programmed and conducted using the software *z-tree* (Fischbacher, 2007).

8.2.6   Assessment of empathic abilities

Empathic abilities were examined using the Multifaceted Empathy Test (MET; Dziobek et al., 2007). The MET allows for a separate assessment of cognitive and emotional empathy. It comprises of 30 pictures of people in different affective states (17 items with positive valence, 13 items with negative valence); see Fig. 8.1 for examples. For each picture, participants are asked to choose one of four possible labels describing the mental state of the person shown (cognitive

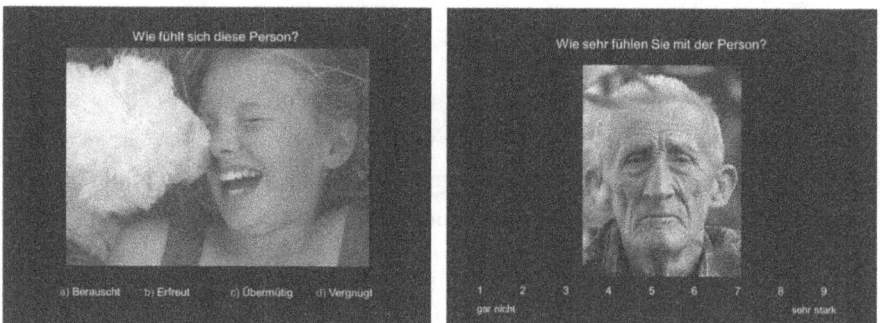

Figure 8.1. Example items from the *Multifaceted Empathy Test* (Dziobek et al., 2007) for cognitive (left) and emotional (right) empathy.

empathy). In a second step, they are asked to rate their concomitant degree of empathic concern on a 9-point Likert scale (emotional empathy). For cognitive empathy, scores represent the percentage of correct answers, and for emotional empathy, average rating scores are calculated.

8.2.7   Statistical analysis

Empathy scores of SAD and HC were compared using two-tailed t-tests. Within groups, empathy for negative and positive valence was compared, using paired t-tests. For the analyses of variance for repeated measures, Greenhouse-Geisser corrections were used in cases of violation of sphericity. Individual response curves, that is, areas under the curve with respect to increase (AUCi) were calculated for the endocrine stress response, using the trapezoid formula by Pruessner and colleagues (2003). This form of data handling allows us to obtain an individual aggregated parameter that includes repeated measurements over time for further analyses. The AUCi was then z-transformed and used as a dependent variable in multiple regression analyses. For the investigation of moderation effects, the *Process* macro for SPSS by Hayes (2013) was used (Model 1). This tool allows for mediation and moderation analyses. The macro computes the indirect effects by calculating the product of the coefficients. Unlike as described for classic regression analysis (Cleary & Kessler, 1982; Cohen, Cohen, & West, 1983), no manual computation of a product term of predictor and moderator variables is necessary, and conditional effects of predictor on the dependent variable at values of the moderator can be calculated. Prior to analysis, predictor variables were mean-centered and heteroscedasticity-consistent standard errors were employed to correct for heteroscedasticity (Long & Ervin, 2000). In order to further examine the conditional effects of the moderation, *regions of significance* were calculated, a statistical procedure, also called Johnson-Neyman technique (P. O. Johnson & Neyman, 1936). This was applied so as to go beyond the "pick-a-point" approach (Rogosa, 1980), which tests the conditional effect of X at designated values of the moderator, thereby reducing variance. Instead, the Johnson-Neyman technique identifies the point at which the significance level is exactly $p = .05$ and computes regions of significance. Effect sizes are reported in η_p^2 for analyses of variance and Cohen's d for t-tests. In cases of multiple testing, Bonferroni correction was applied. All tests were conducted two-sidedly, with level of significance at .05. Data analysis was run by SPSS Version 22.0.

8.3   Results

8.3.1   Manipulation check

The TSST-G increased cardiovascular, endocrine and subjective measures, indicating that the stress induction was successful. SAD and HC did not differ in their physiological stress responses but the SAD group had a significantly elevated subjective reaction to the stressor compared to the HC group (see chapter 7 for details). SAD participants rated themselves as performing worse in the stress condition (M = 1.72 ± 0.55) compared to the no-stress condition (M = 2.05 ± 0.40), U = -3.0, p < .01. Healthy controls did not differ with respect to condition (no-stress: M = 2.23 0.43; stress: M = 1.98 ± 0.55), U = -1.84, p = .066.

8.3.2   Interrater reliability and behavior of the confederates

The inter-rater reliability (Intraclass-Coefficient; ICC) of the *social behavior scale* was good for the confederates and video-raters together (ICC = .78, 95% CI = .69 -. 84) and even better for the video-raters only (ICC = .83, 95% CI = .75 - .88). These reliabilities are in concordance with those of previous studies (Alden & Wallace, 1995; Voncken & Bögels, 2008). Taken together, it can be concluded that the ratings for the *social behavior* scale were reliable. As both video-raters had evaluated all of the participants and standardization was high, an index (mean) of the two video ratings was calculated for further analyses.

Inter-rater reliability for the *anxious appearance scale* was poor for confederates and video-raters, (ICC = .64, 95% CI = .58 -. 78). This discrepancy might be due to the fact that many signs of anxiousness (blushing, trembling etc.) are not as reliably detectable via video recordings as they are face to face. Video recordings may have not displayed the precise color of the participant's face and enabled the view only from one angle, which may have led to less sensitive ratings of anxiety symptoms. This was confirmed by the poor internal consistency of the video-ratings for anxious appearance (Cronbach's α: .49 - .65) in contrast to the high internal consistency of the confederates ratings (Cronbach's α = .80). Thus, confederates' observations were considered to be more valid as they had been present in the situation. Therefore, for the anxious appearance scale, analyses were restricted to the confederates' ratings only.

In order to control for the confederates' behavior towards the two groups of participants, their friendliness was rated by the video-raters. Confederates acted in the same way towards healthy controls as they did towards patients, $t(106) = -.461$, $p = .646$. Thus, it can be inferred that their integrity was good.

8.3.3 Empathy

Cognitive and emotional empathy did not differ for groups, $t_{cog}(106) = 0.40$, $p = .690$; $t_{emo}(106) = 1.15$, $p = .216$. For **cognitive empathy**, there also was no group difference when taking the valence into consideration (see Table 4.1). Reaction times did not differ between groups, irrespective of valence. For **emotional empathy**, SAD showed lower scores regarding *positive* items than HC did, $t(116) = 2.37$, $p < .05$, $d = 0.45$, indicating less emotional empathy for positive emotions. This was not the case with *negative* items. Reaction times, again, did not differ between the groups, irrespective of valence (see Table 8.1).

Paired *t*-tests for **cognitive empathy** revealed that scores were higher for positive than for negative emotions in SAD, $t(56)= 5.54$, $p <.001$, as well as in HC, $t(50) = 5.91$, $p < .001$. Accordingly, reaction times for both SAD and HC were higher for negative than for positive emotions, $t_{SAD}(56) = -6.43$, $p < .001$; $t_{HC}(50)= -7.30$, $p < .001$, indicating that it took both groups longer to identify negative emotions (Table 8.1).

Paired *t*-tests for **emotional empathy** revealed that in SAD, valence had no influence on empathy score, $t(56) = 0.93$, $p =.355$ or reaction times, $t(56) = -0.73$, $p = .466$. In HC, scores were higher for positive than for negative items, $t(50)= -4.83$, $p < .001$ and RT lower, $t(50) = -2.58$, $p < .05$. This means that HC showed more emotional empathy and reacted faster for items with positive valence. Cognitive and emotional empathy were not associated with severity of social anxiety for SAD or HC, all $ps > .09$.

Regarding conditions of the TSST-G, there were no differences in cognitive or emotional empathy for SAD, $t_{cog}(55)= -0.32$, $p = .754$; $t_{emo}(55) = -0.21$, $p = .836$ or

HC, $t_{cog}(49)$= -0.48, p = .635; $t_{emo}(49)$ = 0.15, p = .882. For SAD patients who had been stressed, cognitive empathy was negatively correlated with self-focused attention during the conversation task, r = -.51, p < .01. This association was not apparent for SAD in the no-stress condition or for HC, all ps > .658.

Table 8.1. Results from the *Multifaceted Empathy Test* (MET) for SAD and HC.

	SAD M (SD)	HC M (SD)	t	p
Cognitive empathy	65.32 (9.16)	66.14 (12.12)	0.10	.971
Positive items	72.90 (13.01)	73.15 (14.71)	0.49	.629
Negative items	59.55 (12.73)	60.78 (13.80)	0.40	.690
Emotional empathy	5.57 (1.22)	5.87 (1.29)	0.12	.223
Positive items	5.66 (1.56)	6.33 (1.37)	**2.37**	**.021**
Negative items	5.50 (1.25)	5.51 (1.46)	0.05	.101
RT Cognitive empathy	8.78 (3.83)	7.81 (2.33)	-1.57	.124
Positive items	7.55 (3.22)	6.72 (2.12)	-1.56	.122
Negative items	9.51 (4.22)	8.64 (2.81)	-1.25	.212
RT Emotional empathy	4.11 (1.57)	3.90 (1.82)	-0.64	.522
Positive items	4.04 (1.63)	3.63 (1.64)	1.27	.213
Negative items	4.10 (1.82)	3.94 (2.22)	0.49	.702

Note: SAD = social anxiety disorder, HC = healthy control, RT = reaction time. Data are expressed as mean (SD). Effects in bold depict significance levels of p < .05.

8.3.4   Effects of stress on social interaction

8.3.4.1.1 Effects of stress on social performance

Social behavior

For the examination of the main research question of how stress influences social behavior in SAD compared to HC, a 2×2 (GROUP × CONDITION) ANOVA was conducted for video-raters and confederates, respectively. Both ANOVAs showed a main effect of GROUP, $F_{video}(1, 96)$ = 5.47, p < .05, η_p^2 = .05, $F_{confed}(1, 109)$ = 14.04, p < .001, η_p^2 = .144, but no effect of CONDITION, $F_{video}(1, 96)$ = 1.02, p = .31, $F_{confed}(1, 109)$ = 1.70, p = .196, and no interaction between the two factors, $F_{video}(1, 96)$ = 1.33, p = .25, $F_{confed}(1, 109)$ = 1.66, p = .20, indicating a better social performance of HC compared to SAD, irrespective of condition [**Fig. 8.2 (A)**].

Further, social behavior (as rated by video-raters) in the stress condition was negatively correlated with social anxiety symptomatology (SIAS), $r = -.41$, $p = .042$, but the effect did not withstand Bonferroni correction for multiple testing.

To further elucidate the influence of stress on social performance, the individual cortisol response (as depicted by the area under the curve with respect to increase, AUCi) was taken into account, as first, previous similar studies highlight the influence of HPA-axis reactivity on social behavior (Berger et al., 2015; Roelofs et al., 2009; Smeets et al., 2009) and second, small sample size might have covered a possible effect of stress on social performance.

Multiple regression analysis (backwards) with factors GROUP and z-transformed CORTISOL INCREASE (i.e. AUCi) were conducted. For the **video ratings**, the model explained 9.2% of variance, $R^2 = .092$, $F(3, 95) = 3.20$, $p < .05$. GROUP significantly contributed to predicting social behavior and there was a significant GROUP × CORTISOL INTERACTION, showing a differential effect for the endocrine stress response on social behavior as a function of GROUP (SAD vs. HC); see Table 8.1. Simple slopes analysis can be conducted to clarify whether the single slopes differ from zero or horizontal. The analysis revealed a trend for a positive relationship between cortisol increase and social behavior in HC, $b = .24$, $p = .080$, while in SAD there was no relationship and, on the descriptive level, a negative gradient, $b = -.14$, $p = .229$.

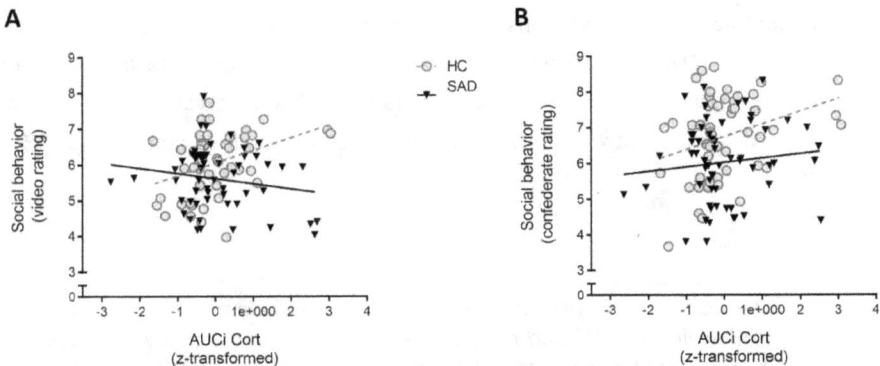

Figure 8.2. Regression of social behavior as a function of cortisol increase for subjects with SAD and for healthy controls. A: Rating of video-raters. B: Rating of confederates. SAD = social anxiety disorder, HC = healthy control, AUCi = area under the curve with respect to increase, Cort = cortisol.

For the **confederates ratings**, the model explained 15,2% of variance, R^2 = .152, $F(2, 109)$ = 9.73, p < .001. Here, both the factor GROUP and the CORTISOL IN-CREASE significantly contributed to the model, showing the general performance deficits of participants with SAD compared to healthy controls irrespective of stress, and a better social performance with higher CORTISOL INCREASE. The inter-action term did not reach significance (Table 4.2). As the slopes suggested that the effect for cortisol was mainly driven by HC, simple effects were conducted. There was a significant increase in the rating of social performance with higher CORTISOL INCREASE for HC, $F(1, 51)$= 5.15, β = .306, p < .05, R^2 = .093, while this was not the case for SAD, $F(1, 58)$= 1.40, β = .153, p =.243, R^2 = .023 [**Fig. 8.2 (B)**]. It should be noted that from a conservative point of view, simple effects analyses are not proper in absence of a significant interaction and presence of two main effects. Result therefore must be interpreted with caution (cf. Tybout et al., 2001).

Additionally, in order to explore the effect of cortisol increase on social behavior in HC, more detailed correlation analyses were conducted between the items of the *social behavior* scale of the SBA-rating scale and cortisol increase (AUC$_I$). On a descriptive level, a clear pattern emerged. Social behavior in HC was associated with cortisol increase (AUC$_I$) exclusively for items 23 - 26[3] of confederates' ratings (Pearson correlation, ranging from r = 0.30 to r = 0.34, all ps < .05), comprising more complex items and those indicating a connection to the conversation part-ner, in contrast to the other items, that focus more on formal aspects of the con-versation, i.e. *"Did the participant finish his sentences?"* or *"Was there silence many times?"* (all ps > .16). It should be noted that this observation is merely de-scriptive and would not withstand alpha correction for multiple testing (0.05/15 = 0.0033).

---

[3] Items 23 – 26 of the SBA-rating scale: *"Could the participant start the conversa-tion and keep it going?", "Did the participant listen to what you were saying?", "Did the participant show interest in what you were saying (understandingly nodding or using words like 'aha', 'hmm, hmm')?", "Did the participant discuss what you were saying (asking related questions, telling something that fits the subject of the discussion)?"*

Table 8.2. Multiple regressions: Effects of cortisol increase on social behavior, as rated by video-raters and confederates.

	b (SE)	ß	p
Video-ratings			
Step1			
Constant	6.04 (.13)		.000
Group (0 = HC, 1 = SAD)	-.38 (.17)	-.22	.030
Cortisol increase(standardized)	.240 (.13)	.27	.070
Group*Cortisol increase(standardized)	-.38 (.18)	-.32	.033
Confederates			
Step1			
Constant	6.747		.000
Group (0 = HC, 1 = SAD)	-.786	-.326	.000
Cortisol increase(standardized)	.358	.295	.025
Group*Cortisol increase(standardized)	-.185	-.112	.391
Step 2			
Constant	6.74 (.16)		.000
Group	-.79 (.21)	-.33	.000
Cortisol increase(standardized)	.26 (.11)	.27	.018

Note: B = Unstandardized coefficient. SE = Standard Deviation. R^2 = .108 for video ratings and R^2 = .162 for confederates ratings. Effects in bold depict significance levels of $p < .05$ or lower.

Anxious Appearance

For the examination of anxious appearance, 2×2 (GROUP × CONDITION) ANOVAs were conducted for confederates ratings. A significant effect of GROUP became apparent, $F(1, 109) = 8.87$, $p < .01$, $\eta_p^2 = .075$. That is, patients with SAD (M = 3.61 ± 1.27) showed more signs of anxiety than healthy controls did (M = 2.29 ± 1.27). There was no effect of CONDITION and no interaction between the two factors, all $ps < .11$, indicating that stress had no influence on the anxious appearance of HC or SAD.

For anxious appearance as well, a multiple regression analysis was conducted. A significant regression equation emerged, $F(1, 110) = 8.01$, $p < .01$, with an R^2 of .068 (Table 8.3), reflecting the results from the ANOVA. That is, participants with SAD were rated as more anxious than healthy controls. The individual cortisol response did not modulate anxious appearance.

Table 8.3. Multiple regressions: Effects of cortisol increase on anxious appearance (confederates rating).

		B (SE)	ß	p
Step1				
Constant		2.96 (0.18)		**.000**
Group		**0.62 (0.24)**	**.24**	**.012**
Cortisol increase(standardized)		0.12 (0.18)	.09	.510
Group* increase(standardized)	Cortisol	-0.18 (0.24)	-.10	.456
Step 2				
Constant		2.96 (0.18)		**.000**
Group		**0.62 (0.24)**	**.24**	**.011**
Group* increase(standardized)	Cortisol	0.06 (0.17)	-.04	.710
Step 3				
Group		**0.62 (0.24)**	**.24**	**.011**

Note: B = Unstandardized coefficient. SE = Standard Deviation. R^2 = .058 .Effects in bold depict significance levels of $p < .05$ or lower.

8.3.4.2 Effects of stress on social decision-making

In order to investigate effects of stress on decision-making, Mann-Whitney-U tests were conducted for SAD and HC, respectively. In SAD, there was a significant effect of CONDITION for trustworthiness, with participants in the stress condition being less trustworthy than participants in the no-stress condition, $U = -2.21$, $p < .05$, $r = .29$, see **Figure 8.3**. Additionally, there were trends for trust in the same direction, $U = -1.73$, $p = .084$ as well as for risk, $U = -1.76$, $p = .079$. Apart from that, CONDITION had no effect on the other variables tested (sharing, envy, punishment), all $ps > .634$. In HC, there was no effect for CONDITION in any of the parameters, all $ps > .140$. Ordinal regression analyses revealed that CORTISOL INCREASE (AUCi) did not modulate decision-behavior in either SAD or HC, all $ps > .202$.

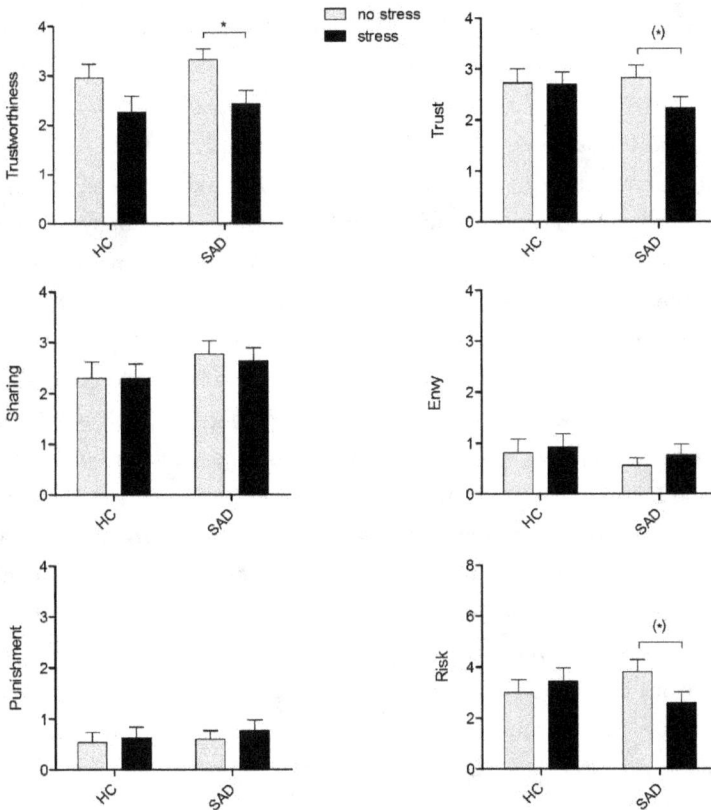

Figure 8.3. Mean scores in each game as a function of condition. Error bars represent SEM. SAD = social anxiety disorder, HC = healthy control. * $p < .05$. (*) $p = .084$ for *trust* and $p = .079$ for *risk*.

8.3.5   Influence of empathy on social interaction behavior under stress

8.3.5.1   *Social Performance and empathy*

Social Behavior

In order to examine a possible moderating effect of social cognition on the influence of stress on interaction behavior, the *Process* macro for SPSS by Hayes (2013) was used (Model 1). In order to take inter-individual differences in empathy into consideration, the cognitive and the emotional part of the MET were included into the model as moderators, respectively. Analyses were conducted separately for SAD and HC. For the confederates' ratings, the influence of stress on social behavior was moderated by the participants' **cognitive empathy**, $F(3, 56)$ = 10.23, $p < .001$, $R^2 = .29$, see Table 8.4. Further, *regions of significance* were calculated, using the Johnson-Neyman technique (see chapter 8.2.7 for description). It was revealed that at mean-centered scores lower than -4.82 in the MET-cog, stress/no-stress (condition) and social behavior were significantly related, $b = -0.92$, $t(53) = -2.00$, $p = .05$. With decreasing cognitive empathy, the relationship between stress/no-stress and social behavior became stronger, with the lowest cognitive empathy score of -6.60 (13 correct answers out of 30), $b = -1.28$, $t(53) =$ -2.16, $p < .05$. Further, at scores higher than 5.18, the interaction between condition and social behavior, again, became significant, $b = 1.05$, $t(53) = 2.01$, $p = .05$. With increasing cognitive empathy, the effect became stronger, with the highest score being 5.40 (25 correct answers), $b = 1.10$, $t(53) = 2.03$, $p < .05$. Only $n = 1$ participant of the SAD group yielded a score this high. **Figure 8.4** illustrates the conditional indirect effect at all values of the moderator with a 95% confidence band. These results cannot be explained by an association between empathy score and stress reactivity. Cognitive empathy was not correlated with the stress reaction (AUC$_I$ of cortisol, heart-rate, and subjective stress, respectively) in SAD or HC, all $ps > .179$. For the video ratings, there was no moderation effect of cognitive empathy in SAD, $F(3, 50) = 2.103$, $p = .112$, $R^2 = .112$.

Further, **emotional empathy** had no moderation effect on the relationship between stress and social behavior in SAD, for either confederates ratings, $F(3, 56)$ = .776, $p = .511$, $R^2 = .040$, or video ratings, $F(3, 47) = 1.82$, $p = .157$, $R^2 = .104$. In HC, neither cognitive nor emotional empathy modulated the influence of stress on social behavior (confederates and video ratings), all $ps > .157$. Consequently, no significant transition points could be calculated by the Johnson-Neyman technique.

Table 8.4 Moderation analysis for social anxiety disorder: Effects of condition on social behavior and anxious appearance (confederates rating) as mediated by cognitive empathy.

	b (SE)	t	p
Social behavior			
Constant	5.91 (0.13)	**32.32**	.000
Condition	0.03 (0.24)	0.12	.908
MET-cog	**0.32 (0.14)**	**2.34**	.023
Condition*MET-cog	**0.54 (0.23)**	**2.40**	.023
R^2 increase due to interaction: ΔR^2 = .058, $p < .05$			
Anxious appearance			
Constant	3.87 (0.24)	**16.32**	.000
Condition	-0.56 (0.33)	-1.69	.097
zMET-cog	0.29 (0.17)	0.18	.860
Condition*MET-cog	**-0.70 (0.33)**	**-2.12**	.039
R^2 increase due to interaction: ΔR^2 = .070, $p < .05$			

Note: B= unstandardized coefficient. SE = standard error. MET-cog = cognitive part of Multifaceted Empathy Test. Effects in bold depict significance levels of $p < .05$ or lower.

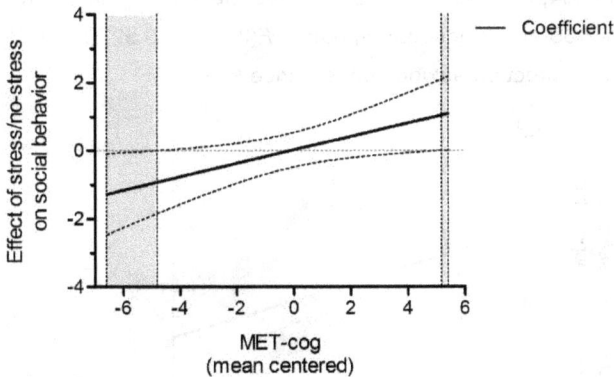

Figure 8.4. Results of the moderation analysis in social anxiety disorder. Conditional relation between stress/no-stress and social behavior (confederates rating), as a function of cognitive empathy. Solid line represents unstandardized coefficient (b). Dotted lines indicate 95%-confidence bands. Grey areas indicate region of significance (Johnson & Neyman, 1936). Predicted values are shown only for observed levels of the MET-cog. MET-cog = Multifaceted Empathy Test, cognitive part.

Anxious Appearance

In SAD, anxious appearance was moderated by **cognitive empathy**, $F(3, 53) =$ 3.26, $p < .05$, $R^2 = .16$ (Table 4.4). More precisely, higher cognitive empathy was associated with less anxious symptoms under stress in participants with SAD (**Fig. 8.5**). Johnson-Neyman technique revealed that at scores of a z-score in the MET-cog of at least 0.37 (20.0 out of 30 correct answers), condition (stress/no-stress) and anxious appearance were significantly related, $b = -0.65$, $t(53) = -2.01$, $p = .05$. As cognitive empathy increased, the relationship between stress/no-stress and anxious appearance became stronger, with the highest cognitive empathy score being 5.40, $b = -1.92$, $t(53) = -2.87$, $p < .01$. That is, SAD patients high in cognitive empathy could benefit from stress in terms of reduced anxious appearance, while this was not the case for patients low in cognitive empathy. The path model in **Figure 8.6** illustrates the effect of stress on social behavior and anxious appearance, moderated by cognitive empathy.

Again, there was no influence of **emotional empathy** on anxious appearance in SAD, $F(3, 53) = .94$, $p = . 430$, $R^2 = .061$. In HC, neither cognitive, $F(3, 47) = 1.83$, $p = .152$, $R^2 = .105$, nor emotional empathy, $F(3, 47) = 0.52$, $p = .671$, $R^2 = .035$, had a modulating effect on anxious appearance.

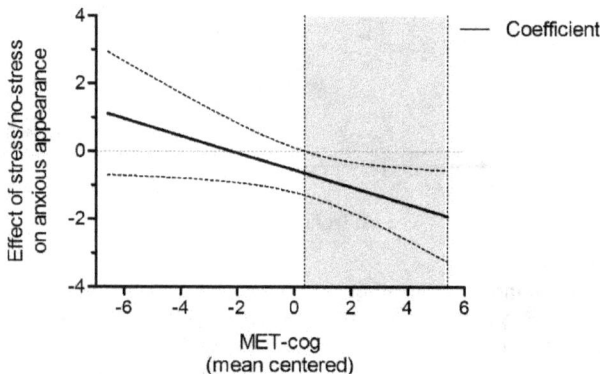

Figure 8.5. Results of the moderation analysis in social anxiety disorder. Conditional relation between stress/no-stress and anxious appearance (confederates rating), as a function of cognitive empathy. Solid line represents unstandardized coefficient (*b*). Dotted lines indicate 95%-confidence bands. Grey areas indicate region of significance (Johnson & Neyman, 1936). Predicted values are shown only for observed levels of the MET-cog. MET-cog = Multifaceted Empathy Test, cognitive part.

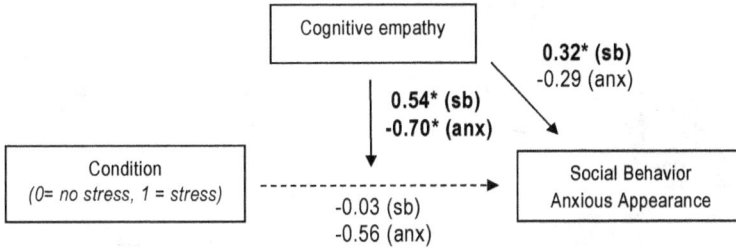

Figure 8.6. Path model of the effects of stress or no stress (condition) on social behavior and anxious appearance as mediated by cognitive empathy in the group of social anxiety disorder. Dotted lines represent nonsignificant paths. Values are unstandardized coefficients (*b*). sb = social behavior; anx = anxious appearance. *$p <$ .05.

8.3.5.2 Social decision making and empathy

In order to investigate if empathy had an impact on the relationship between stress and social decision-making in SAD, again, moderation analyses with the Process macro (Hayes, 2013) were conducted. For **cognitive empathy** overall, no moderation effect was found for trustworthiness, $F(3, 53) = 1.50$, $p = .224$, $R^2 = .09$, trust, $F(3, 53) = 2.08$, $p = .114$, $R^2 = .105$, or risk, $F(3, 53) = 2.14$, $p = .107$, $R^2 = .11$. However, cognitive empathy for *negative emotions* modulated the effect of stress on trustworthiness, $F(3, 53) = 3.85$, $p < .05$, $R^2 = .18$, and trust, $F(3, 51) = 2.81$, $p < .05$, $R^2 = .14$ (Table 4.5). Johnson-Neyman technique revealed that for mean-centered scores of the MET-cog of maximal 0.18 (10.3 correct answers out of 15), there was a significant effect of stress/no-stress on trustworthiness, $b = -0.69$, $t(53) = -2.01$, $p = .05$. With decreasing cognitive empathy, the effect became stronger, with the lowest score being -5.12, $b = -2.66$, $t(53) = -3.00$, $p < .01$ (**Fig. 8.7 (A)**). The same relationship emerged for trust, with a significant relationship between stress/no-stress and trust at scores of maximal -0.45 ($b = -0.68$, $t(53) = -2.01$, $p = .05$) and lower, with the lowest score being -5.12, $b = -2.45$, $t(53) = -2.81$, $p < .01$ (**Fig. 8.7 (B)**). That is, for SAD patients low in cognitive empathy for negative emotions, stress led to reduced trustworthiness and trust; however, it did not influence behavior in SAD patients high in cognitive empathy, reflecting the same pattern as for social behavior.

A

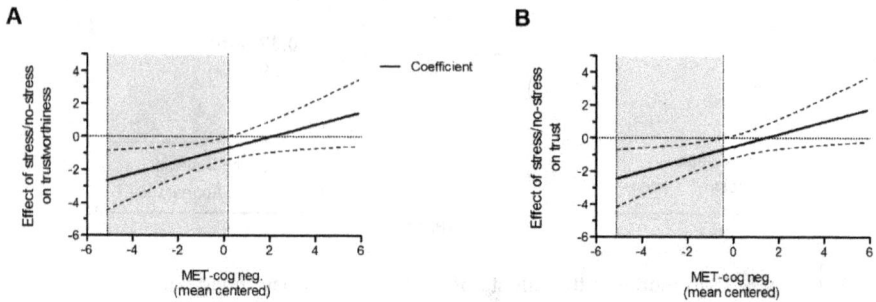

B

Figure 8.7. Results of the moderation analysis in social anxiety disorder. Conditional relation between stress/no-stress and trustworthiness (A) and trust (B), as a function of cognitive empathy for negative emotions. Solid lines represent unstandardized coefficients (*b*). Dotted lines indicate 95%-confidence bands. Grey areas indicate region of significance (Johnson & Neyman, 1936). Predicted values are shown only for observed levels of the MET. MET-cog neg. = Multifaceted Empathy Test, cognitive part for negative emotions.

There was no effect for risk in SAD, $F(3, 53) = 1.33$, $p = .273$, $R^2 = .07$. Moreover, there were no moderation effects apparent in SAD regarding cognitive empathy for *positive* emotions in the three parameters, all ps > .102. Further, as well as for social performance, **emotional empathy** did not modulate social decision-making in SAD, all ps < .201.

Table 8.5. Moderation analysis for participants with social anxiety disorder: Effects of condition on trustworthiness and trust as mediated by cognitive empathy (negative valence).

	b (SE)	t	p
Trustworthiness			
Constant	**3.16 (0.24)**	**13.23**	**.000**
Condition (0 = no-stress; 1 = stress)	**-0.75 (0.34)**	**-2.21**	**.032**
MET-cog_n	-0.08 (0.23)	-0.34	.735
Condition* MET-cog_n	**0.80 (0.35)**	**2.30**	**.025**
R^2 increase due to interaction: $\Delta R^2 = .085$, $p < .05$			
Trust			
Constant	**2.68 (0.23)**	**11.56**	**.000**
Condition (0 = no-stress; 1 = stress)	-0.51 (0.33)	-1.86	.128
MET-cog_n	-0.41 (0.22)	-1.55	.976
Condition* MET-cog_n	**0.82 (0.34)**	**2.42**	**.019**
R^2 increase due to interaction: $\Delta R^2 = .095$, $p < .05$			

Note: MET-cog_n = cognitive empathy (negative valence). *SE* = Standard Error. Effects in bold depict significance levels of $p < .05$ or lower.

In **Figure 8.8**, the observed pathways and strength of association for the modera-tion effect of stress on prosocial behavior (trustworthiness, trust) as moderated by cognitive empathy are shown.

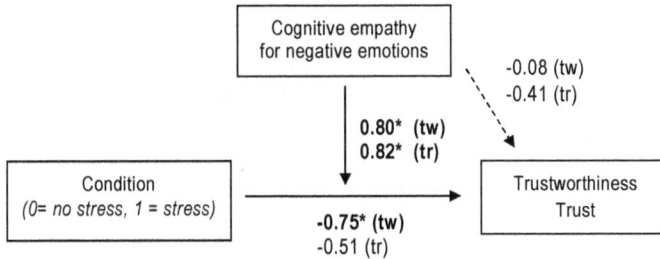

Figure 8.8. Path model of stress or no stress (condition) on trustworthiness and trust as mediated by cognitive empathy for negative emotions in the group of social anxiety disor-der. Dotted lines represent nonsignificant paths. Values are unstandardized coefficients (*b*). tw = trustworthiness; tr = trust. * *p* < .05.

8.3.6   Self-assessment of social performance and self-focused attention

Social behavior

For the additional assessment of the self-perception of participants' social behav-ior in the conversation, a 2×2 (GROUP × CONDITION) ANOVA was conducted. The ANOVA showed a strong effect of GROUP, $F(1, 109) = 29.37$, $p < .001$, $\eta_p^2 = .263$, indicating that SAD evaluated their social behavior as worse compared to HC (**Fig. 8.9**). Further, there was an effect of CONDITION, $F(1, 109) = 8.02$, $p < .01$, $\eta_p^2 = .069$. Post-hoc *t*-tests revealed that the effect of CONDITION was driven by the SAD-group, with higher self-ratings in the stress than in the no-stress condition $t(58) = -2.68$, $p < .05$, $d_{Cohen} = 0.69$, which was not apparent in the HC-group $t(51) = -1.34$, $p = .185$. That is, SAD rated their behavior as better under stress than under no-stress condition, while stress had no influence on self-ratings in healthy controls.

In order to examine the three ratings in comparison and test for potential biases in self-perception, two 3×2 RATERS (confederates/video/self) × CONDITION (no-stress/stress) repeated measures ANOVAs were conducted for the groups sepa-rately. In SAD, there was a significant effect of RATERS, $F(2, 104) = 5.02$, $p <.01$,

η_p^2 = .09 and RATERS × CONDITION, $F(2, 104)$ = 3.28, p <.05, η_p^2 = .06. Post hoc ANOVAs revealed, that the difference in raters was driven by the no-stress condition, $F(1, 50)$ = 6.89, p <.01, η_p^2 = .22 and dissolved in the stress condition, $F(1, 54)$ = 1.65, p = .202, due to an increase in participants' self-assessment (**Fig. 8.9**). In HC, repeated measures ANOVA yielded a significant effects for RATERS, $F(2, 88)$ = 8.18, p <.01, η_p^2 = .16. Post-hoc comparisons with Bonferroni correction revealed that video-ratings significantly differed from confederates- (p < .001) and self-ratings (p < .001).

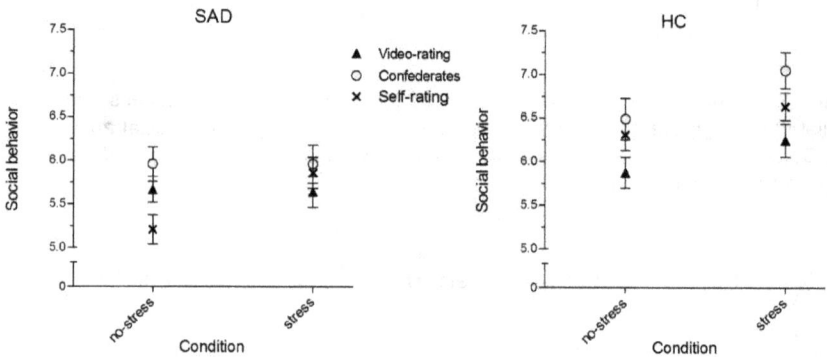

Figure 8.9. Mean ratings (confederates, video, self) of participants' social behavior (±SEM) for the two conditions of the Trier Social Stress Test (no stress/stress). SAD = social anxiety disorder; HC = healthy control.

Anxious appearance

For the assessment of the self-perception of participants' anxious appearance, a 2×2 (GROUP × CONDITION) ANOVA was conducted. A significant effect for CONDITION, $F(1, 109)$ = 10.03, p < .01, η_p^2 = 0.08, as well as for GROUP, $F(1, 109)$ = 30.64, p < .001, η_p^2 = 0.22 emerged, indicating that SAD rated themselves as appearing more anxious than as HC rated themselves (**Fig. 8.10**). Post hoc t-tests revealed that the effect of CONDITION was only apparent in the SAD group, $t(58)$ = 2.74, p < .01, d_{Cohen} = -0.71 , not in HC, $t(51)$ = 0.18, p = .087.

In order to examine the external- and self-rating in comparison, two 2×2 RATERS (confederates/self) × CONDITION (no-stress/stress) repeated measures ANOVAs were conducted for the groups separately. There was no significant effect for

RATERS or RATERS × CONDITION in both of the groups, all $ps > .453$. In SAD, there was a significant main effect of CONDITION, $F(1,58) = 8.68$, $p < .01$, $\eta_p^2 = 0.13$, indicating less anxious appearance in the stress compared to the no-stress condition, regardless of external or self-rating (**Fig. 8.10**).

Self-focused attention

For the examination of self-focused attention (SFA) during the conversation, a 2×2 (GROUP × CONDITION) ANOVA was conducted. Self-focused attention was higher for SAD ($M = 21.67$, ± 8.45) than for HC ($M = 13.23 ± 8.01$), a significant effect of GROUP, $F(1, 109) = 30.5$, $p < .001$, $\eta_p^2 = 0.22$. Further, there was an effect of CONDITION, $F(1, 109) = 6.29$, $p < .05$, $\eta_p^2 = 0.06$. Post-hoc ANOVAs revealed that this effect was driven by the SAD group, $F(1, 58) = 4.57$, $p < .05$, $\eta_p^2 = 0.07$, with higher SFA after no-stress ($M = 23.93 ± 8.08$) than after stress ($M = 19.40 ± 8.34$), and was not apparent in HC, $F(1, 51) = 2.03$, $p < .160$.

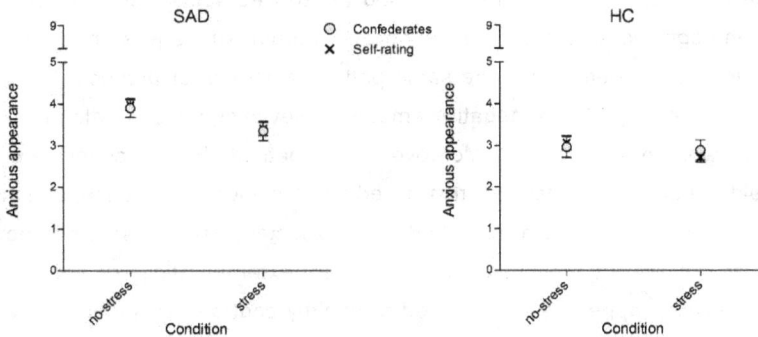

Figure 8.10. Mean ratings (confederates, self) of participants' anxious appearance (±SEM) for the two conditions of the TSST-G (no stress/stress). SAD = social anxiety disorder; HC = healthy control.

8.4 Discussion

The present study examined social affiliation behavior after stress in patients with social anxiety disorder and healthy controls under consideration of individual empathic abilities. As described previously (Chapter 7), stress induction via the

TSST-G (von Dawans et al., 2011) was successful. Participants in the stress condition exhibited higher increases in salivary cortisol, heart rate and subjective stress measures than in the control condition. While HC and SAD patients did not differ in their physiological stress reaction, patients showed significantly stronger increases in the psychological stress response compared to healthy controls.

Results regarding the effects of stress on social interaction behavior can be summarized as follows: Firstly, stress did not modulate social performance in the conversation in SAD or HC on a conditional level (stress/no-stress condition of the TSST-G). However, on the more sensitive stress measure of individual cortisol response, differential effects for SAD and HC became apparent. While HC showed increased social affiliative behavior in the conversation with increasing cortisol response, no such increase in social behavior was apparent in SAD. On the contrary, in line with the hypothesis, SAD showed reduced trustworthiness and (borderline significant) trust in the stress-condition compared to the no-stress condition. Secondly, cognitive empathy buffered these effects of stress on social interaction behavior in SAD. While stress led to reduced social behavior for patients low in cognitive empathy, no such decline through stress was apparent for SAD high in cognitive empathy. The same pattern emerged for prosocial behavior, with cognitive empathy for negative emotions alleviating stress-related reductions in trustworthiness and trust. Moreover, while patients high in cognitive empathy could benefit from stress in terms of reduced anxious appearance, patients low in cognitive empathy could not. Thirdly, as expected, patients showed social performance deficits in the conversation, i.e. poorer external ratings on social behavior and anxious appearance compared to healthy controls. This is in line with previous findings, reporting social performance deficits in SAD (Baker & Edelmann, 2002; Fydrich et al., 1998; Stopa & Clark, 1993; Voncken & Bögels, 2008) and corroborating the assumption that there is a core of truth in the patients' fear of negative evaluation.

This study for the first time showed that stress reduces prosocial behavior in patients with SAD in real social interactions and that high cognitive empathic abilities might buffer those effects. The study fits in nicely with previous findings of reduced approach behavior after stress in SAD (Roelofs et al., 2009) and less prosocial behavior in subclinical social anxiety (Mallott et al., 2009; Maner et al.,

2007). Our results furthermore suggest that the inherent coping mechanism of af-filiation under stress may be impaired in people suffering from SAD and, further-more, that interindividual differences in cognitive empathic abilities seem to be involved in the modulation of a withdrawing or affiliative response. In the follow-ing, the results are discussed in detail.

Acute stress led to reduced prosocial behavior in SAD. The prefrontal cortex is a target region for cortisol and increases of this hormone have been shown to im-pair prefrontal functioning (Oei et al., 2007; Wolf, Schommer, Hellhammer, McEwen, & Kirschbaum, 2001). Thus, under stress, attention regulation is limited by inhibition of prefrontal activity in favor of a 'bottom up' control of attention (Arn-sten, 2009). That is, under stress, salient stimuli bind attention even more than under non-stressful conditions; in SAD this applies especially to threatening social cues like signs of rejection (Bar-Haim et al., 2007; Cisler & Koster, 2010). An in-creased processing of such social threat cues may increase the likelihood of avoidant and withdrawing behavior. Aberrant attention processing in SAD might be a fruitful target for treatment of social anxiety. Accordingly, in a study by Amir and colleagues (2009), SAD patients received attention training with a variant of the dot-probe paradigm. The training directed attention away from threatening fa-cial cues and led to reduced symptomatology that maintained after a four-month follow-up. Trainings for modification of attentional bias have been applied in sev-eral anxiety disorders with an overall medium effect size regarding reduction of anxiety symptoms (for a meta-analysis, see Hakamata et al., 2010). Moreover, under stress, behavioral control is shifted from goal-directed to habitual and au-tomatic processing (Radenbach et al., 2015; Schwabe & Wolf, 2009). In SAD, stress may intensify negative cognitions about possible rejection by others through inhibition of otherwise corrective cognitions. The reaction of reduced pro-social behavior might evoke negative emotions in the interaction partner, who will more likely show rejection, confirming the patient's negative cognitions and ampli-fying his/her anxiety, resulting in a vicious circle.

Thinking from a resource-oriented perspective, it could be argued that in SAD a self-protection program applies, initiated to preserve the individual from the even more stressful experience of affiliation (e.g. Arkin, Lake, & Baumgardner, 1986; Rapee & Heimberg, 1997). As "blind faith" can have adverse consequences, such rather careful behavior may be functional in terms of stress reduction if one does not feel comfortable around others. However, though in the short term stress may be reduced, in the long term such behavior is not helpful, as it strengthens maintenance of the symptomatology and fosters isolation (Alden & Taylor, 2004); nonetheless, patients with SAD typically long for the company of others (Teo, Lerrigo, & Rogers, 2013).

In the present study, the individual capability for cognitive empathy in SAD moderated the influence of stress on social interaction behavior. Lower scores in cognitive empathy were associated with decreased social behavior under stress. Notably, this result was also reflected in social decision-making. Stress reduced trust and trustworthiness in SAD patients with low cognitive empathy for negative emotions, while no such decline was apparent for SAD high in cognitive empathy. Crucially, the modulation by empathy was not apparent in nonsocial risk-taking, underlining the social dimension of the effect. Thus, in line with our hypothesis, empathic abilities buffered the adverse effects of stress on social interaction behavior in SAD. That is, SAD patients low in cognitive empathy seem to cope differently with stress, i.e. by withdrawal instead of affiliation; conversely, SAD patients high in cognitive empathy seem to benefit from stress. These patients exhibited an improved impression on their conversation partner through reduced anxious appearance, and resistance against decreasing prosocial behavior under stress. With this pattern of behavior, SAD patients converged to the behavior of healthy controls under stress, reflecting a 'normalized' behavioral response and slight indications of *tend-and-befriend* behavior. There was no association between stress reaction and empathy score that could have driven these effects. Furthermore, the finding fits in nicely with literature that ties empathy to increased prosocial and reduced antisocial behavior (for a review, see Bateson, 2002; Lockwood et al., 2014).

The modulation of empathy was only apparent for cognitive empathy but not for emotional empathy. Having to participate in a getting-acquainted-task like the one in the present study constitutes a challenging and threatening experience for SAD patients. Under such threatening circumstances, a rather unemotional and sober projection of the other person's thoughts might be more feasible than generating and allowing compassionate feelings for the interaction partner. Thus, in the present study, cognitive empathic abilities might have had a stronger influence on patients' social behavior than their emotional empathic capacity did. Why did only those patients with high cognitive empathy exhibit unimpaired social interaction behavior under stress? One possible explanation could be a higher ability to distinguish between one's own and another person's emotional state. That is, a low ability in cognitive empathy could lead to an impairment in the differentiation between one's own and other people's emotions. In this regard, cognitive empathy is associated with self-reflection (e.g. Simone G. Shamay-Tsoory, 2011) and alexithymia impairments in self-other distinction and distinguishing emotions from bodily sensations (for a review, see Grynberg et al., 2012; Sifneos, 1973). The emotional state of the participants in the stress condition was more negative (uneasy, anxious, tensed) compared to that of the no-stress condition. Influenced by their own unpleasant status, the emotional state of the conversation partner might have been misconstrued as uneasy, hostile etc. and thus interpreted as rejecting rather than open and accepting. In other words, the participants' own discomfort may have been attributed on their conversation partner. This might have resulted in avoidant rather than affiliative and outgoing behavior.

On the neuronal level, patients low in empathic abilities may exhibit altered processing and/or connectivity of regions associated with self-state perception such as the precuneus (Cavanna & Trimble, 2006). Specifically, grey matter volume of the precuneus has been negatively associated with empathic abilities (Banissy, Kanai, Walsh, & Rees, 2012). Additionally, as part of the 'default brain network', activity in the precuneus typically decreases when switching from rest to tasks (Raichle & Snyder, 2007). Stress has been found to reduce this deactivation of precuneus activity (Soares et al., 2013). Thus, under stress, detachment from precuneus activity may be reduced in patients with low empathy, entailing heightened self-focused attention and leaving less attention for the interaction partner. In fact, the findings of the present study point towards this, as in SAD patients, cognitive empathy was negatively correlated with self-focused attention under stress.

Further, stress-related impairments in prefrontal functioning leads to heightened difficulties in verbalizing thoughts (Saslow et al., 2014). Thus, in the present study, the expression of sympathy for the interaction partner might have been restricted under stress. Such expressions of interest in one's interaction partner, however, are necessary in order to fluently interact. Another way to show interest is through mimicry, which functions as a marker of empathic concern for the other person (Preston et al., 2007). Accordingly, individuals high in empathy have been shown to exhibit more congruent facial electromyographic reactions (i.e. mimicry) in interactions than those low in empathy (Balconi & Canavesio, 2013; Sonnby-Borgström, 2002). Thus, in the present study, SAD patients high in empathy might have been compromised by stress to a lesser extent, as they might have been able to show interest through autonomic facial expressions of their own empathic response.

Further, the influence of stress on prosocial behavior was modulated by cognitive empathy for emotions with *negative* valence only. Why only for negative emotions? Firstly, methodological reasons may be possible. Reaction times for items with negative valence were longer and participants made more errors in identifying the emotion compared to items with positive valence, i.e. identification seemed to be harder for negative emotions. Thus, negative items might have distinguished more properly between subjects with high and low cognitive empathic abilities, which may have allowed us to detect the effect. Secondly, participants made the decisions of the paradigm while standing in front of the judges of the TSST-G, in contrast to the conversation, which took place in a separate room and not in front of the judges. The judges are trained to behave in a distant manner and abstain from positive emotions and encouragement (see chapter 6.3.1. for details). Moreover, the judges in the TSST have been shown to experience stress themselves (Buchanan et al., 2012). Thus, the ability to particularly infer this rather negative emotional state might have been triggered and thus influenced decision-making. Thirdly, contrary to difficulties in the identification of positive emotions, deficiencies in the understanding of negative emotions like anger, sadness, anxiety, despair etc. leaves the person with an ambiguous feeling about the other person's negative feelings and thus the degree of threat in that situation. Hence, feelings of insecurity and helplessness may be evoked, resulting in safety-seeking behavior such as withdrawal (e.g. Chen & Bargh, 1999; Herwig, Kaffenberger, Baumgartner, & Jäncke, 2007). Such engagement in safety behaviors might have led to poorer performance ratings in the conversation, as they have been shown to compromise smooth social interactions (McManus et al., 2008).

Regarding the influence of stress on patients' prosocial behavior in the social de-cision-paradigm, effects were apparent only for trustworthiness and trendwise for trust, while there was no effect for sharing, punishment and envy. This could be due to several reasons. Firstly, trustworthiness requires the trustee to live up to the other person's expectations, in as much as trust requires the person to ex-pose her-/himself to the reactions of others, which implies uncertainty and the possibility of harm. Both aspects entail difficulties for patients with SAD. Interper-sonal expectations, and beliefs about not meeting those expectations, as well as insecurity regarding acceptance from others and fear of social rejection, are at the core of SAD symptomatology. Those difficulties may be exacerbated under stress. Secondly, sharing depicts less of an interactional character as participants have to choose one of two allocation options, without having to integrate deci-sions from the other player. Thus, the decision may to a greater extent be driven by general motives of fairness and equity rather than being influenced by interac-tional preferences of seeking affiliation. As has been shown in economic games, a pure fairness motive can lead to prosocial behavior but also to the wish for re-taliation and revenge when the motive is violated (Fehr & Fischbacher, 2003; Fehr & Gächter, 2002). Thirdly, punishment and envy entail rather destructive in-teractional behavior. Participants in general showed low punishing and envying behavior. Considering motives of socially anxious individuals, the main goal in so-cial interactions is protection of the self, rather than harming the others. There-fore, it is not surprising that an effect of stress in SAD becomes evident more clearly in the prosocial than in the antisocial behaviors.

Furthermore, in the present study, SAD patients compared to HC exhibited social performance deficits in the conversation, irrespective of stress. This is in line with previous studies, showing similar deficiencies in SAD during social interactions (Baker & Edelmann, 2002; Fydrich et al., 1998; Stopa & Clark, 1993; Voncken & Bögels, 2008). The finding corroborates the assumption that there is a core of truth in the patients' fear of negative evaluation. While cognitive models stress the importance of problematic attentional processes and resulting negativity bias in SAD regarding their own performance (Clark & Wells, 1995; Rapee & Heimberg, 1997), this might not be the whole story. Patients with social anxiety disorder seem to display actual deficits in social interaction behavior. It is not yet clear what aspects drive the relationship between social anxiety and deficits in social performance. Clark and Wells (1995) have suggested performance deficits in SAD to being an epiphenomenon of safety behaviors and self-focused attention. That is, efforts to hide anxiety may result in a less outgoing, less friendly appearance. By engaging in behaviors that are intended to prevent possible negative evaluation (e.g. avoidance of eye-contact or grasping a glass very tightly in order not to drop it), people cannot gain the salutary learning experience that the feared negative evaluation does not necessarily occur. Moreover, by actually impairing social performance (e.g. avoiding eye-contact can be perceived as disinterest), safety behaviors can promote the eventuation of the feared outcome (Salkovskis, 1991; Wells et al., 1995). In line with this, exposure therapy that included reduction of safety-behaviors was superior to exposure alone (Wells et al., 1995). Others suggest that a lack of social skills is responsible (e.g. Segrin, 2001; Segrin & Flora, 2000). However, as a treatment, social skills training alone does not seem to be effective for symptom reduction (for a review, see Ponniah & Hollon, 2008). Moreover, socially anxious individuals can perform better when it is asked of them, indicating that social skills may be covert rather than non-existent (Thompson & Rapee, 2002). More research is needed to precisely understand what causes social performance deficits in SAD and under what circumstances this elicits social rejection.

Moreover, the observed association of social behavior and cortisol stress response in healthy controls is in accordance with previous studies, reporting an absence of a conditional effect but an influence of HPA-axis responsivity on social behavior (Berger et al., 2015; Smeets et al., 2009). Social behavior was associated specifically with the cortisol reaction and not with other stress measures, such as heart rate or subjective stress response. This, too, is in line with previous findings (Roelofs et al., 2009, 2005), strengthening the role of the HPA-axis in the modulation of social behavior under stress. In particular, healthy participants showed a positive relationship between increasing cortisol response and social behavior ratings, which builds on the accumulating evidence for a *tend-and-befriend* response in healthy individuals (for a review, see Buchanan & Preston, 2014). A closer look at the effect of the present study revealed that healthy controls under stress improved especially with those items that reflect a connection between the conversation partners (i.e. *"Did the participant show interest in what you were saying? (including non-verbal aspects like nodding)?"*), as opposed to items relating to more formal conversational aspects (i.e. *"Did the participant finish his sentences?"*). This is in line with previous findings, showing closeness and intimacy in dyadic interactions to rely on expression of concern for the disclosure made by the interaction partner (Berg & Archer, 1980; Jones & Archer, 1976) and on nonverbal behavior indicating interest, like smiling or nodding (Tickle-Degnen & Rosenthal, 1990; Tucker & Anders, 1998). Hence, the present finding indicates that increasing HPA-reactivity in healthy individuals may be associated with higher perceived closeness. It should, however, be noted that this effect was correlative and allows no causal conclusions. Nonetheless, this observation contributes to the accumulating evidence for the *tend-and-befriend* effect in healthy individuals (Buchanan & Preston, 2014), i.e., the tendency to affiliate with others under circumstances of stress (Taylor, 2006; Taylor et al., 2000). Cortisol increase had no influence on anxious appearance in HC. In fact, the results for social behavior in the conversation are particularly interesting, as goodness of interactions seem to be predicted by affiliating behavior rather than by visible symptoms of anxiety (Alden & Bieling, 1998; Taylor & Alden, 2011; Voncken & Dijk, 2013). Additionally, in contrast to anxious appearance, which is composed of physical reactions, social behavior is under voluntary control; thus, when it is impaired (as in SAD patients in the present study), it remains accessible for modification (namely via psychotherapy).

In contrast to our expectation and in contrast to the conversation task, there was no increase in prosocial behavior in healthy controls under stress, as measured by the social-decision paradigm. Whereas in the social-decision-paradigm interactions were realized via transfers on a computer, in the conversation task participants interacted with another person face-to-face. Being closer to real-life situations, the naturalistic setting might have triggered the perception of potential support from the interaction partner, leading to an impulse to affiliate with them. The absence of physical closeness in the decision paradigm might have promoted such feelings to a much lesser extent. However, stress effects in healthy controls in paradigms of social decision-making have been shown before. Von Dawans and colleagues (2012), for example, found increased trust, trustworthiness and sharing after acute stress induction in healthy men. The apparent inconsistency might be explained by several factors. First, under the no-stress condition, participants in the present study already behaved as prosocially as the stressed participants did in the previous study. That is, means for prosocial behavior under no-stress conditions were similar to those of the stressed participants in the study by von Dawans and colleagues. Thus, in the present study, a possible ceiling effect could have prevented a stress effect from showing. A sharper adjustment of parameters might have been necessary. Second, effects of stress on social decision-making may be variable and dependent on interindividual characteristics such as age. In fact, in the study by von Dawans and colleagues, the sample consisted of a homologous set of healthy students, while the present study comprised a broader profile of subjects with respect to education and age. Mean age in the study by von Dawans and colleagues was 21.31 years, $SD = 1.99$, while in the current study, the healthy sample was older ($M = 27.38$ years, $SD = 6.51$) and covered a broader age range (18-49 years). Age has been shown to modulate the extent to which trust is influenced by social information (Lee, Jolles, & Krabbendam, 2016). Moreover, activation (Güroğlu, van den Bos, van Dijk, Rombouts, & Crone, 2011) and cortical thickness (Steinbeis, Bernhardt, & Singer, 2012) of brain regions relevant for social decision-making, such as the temporoparietal junction and DLPFC, have been shown to be age-related, as those regions are late-developing (Gogtay et al., 2004; Johnson, 2001). In sum, sample characteristics and methodological aspects might partially account for the different findings. Future studies will need to elucidate the impact of those aspects in order to further disentangle the effects of stress on prosocial behavior.

The present findings give rise to the question of possible biological underpinnings of the observed effects of stress on social interaction behavior. The oxytocin system has been suggested as a crucial factor in the modulation of social behavior under stress (Heinrichs et al., 2013, 2009). Oxytocin produces anxiolytic effects by dampening the responsiveness of the HPA-axis (Cardoso, Kingdon, & Ellenbogen, 2014; Heinrichs et al., 2003) via downregulation of amygdala activity (Baumgartner et al., 2008; Domes, Heinrichs, Gläscher, et al., 2007; Kanat et al., 2015). Considering also that oxytocin is crucial for social behavior (Heinrichs & Domes, 2008) and facilitates social approach behavior (Donaldson & Young, 2008), the experience of stress may induce social affiliation behavior, modulated by an increase in central oxytocin. Accordingly, in nonhuman mammals, it has been shown that during stress, the oxytocin level in the extracellular fluid of the central nucleus of the amygdala is increased (Ebner, Bosch, Krömer, Singewald, & Neumann, 2005; Landgraf & Neumann, 2004). Evidence for such an approach-facilitating and stress-reducing mechanism in humans comes from studies on behavior (Radke, Roelofs, & de Bruijn, 2013; S. Taylor et al., 2006) and genetics (F. S. Chen et al., 2011). Accordingly, oxytocin has been suggested as a pivotal point in the regulation of approach/withdrawal behavior (Kemp & Guastella, 2010, 2011). Hence, the oxytocin system provides a neurobiological framework for the stress-buffering effects of social support and the modulation of affiliative behaviors in response to stress. Accordingly, it plays a central role in the conceptualization of the *tend-and-befriend* model (Taylor, 2006; Taylor et al., 2000), see Chapter 3.1. In SAD, administration of 24 IU oxytocin has been shown to reduce hyperactivation of the amygdala and medial prefrontal cortex in response to social threat (Labuschagne et al., 2010, 2011). Combining this observation with the findings from the present study, it could be assumed that alterations in underlying oxytocin system functioning in SAD might result in a reduced secretion of this hormone under stress, thus, impeding the motivation to affiliate with others. In support, a recent study found preliminary evidence for reduced plasma oxytocin levels after a trust game in SAD compared to healthy controls (Hoge et al., 2012). In another study, oxytocin administration combined with exposure therapy improved self-evaluation of appearance and speech performance in SAD patients; however, effects did not generalize to improve overall treatment outcome (Guastella, Howard, Dadds, Mitchell, & Carson, 2009). Regarding basal oxytocin levels, the only two studies that we are aware of either found no differences between SAD patients and healthy controls in plasma oxytocin (Hoge, Pollack, Kaufman, Zak, & Simon, 2008) or reduced baseline levels (Hoge et al., 2012). A recent study on the oxytocin receptor gene (OXTR) in SAD found reduced methylation of the OXTR under social threat. The authors interpreted this finding as upregulation of oxytocin receptor gene expression under threat due to presumably reduced basal levels in SAD (Ziegler et al., 2015). Although awaiting corroboration, those findings suggest that adaptability of oxytocin functioning in specific situations of social stress may be altered. Future studies are needed to further examine the role of the oxytocin system in SAD to reveal if secretion and/or functioning are altered and whether prolonged treatment of SAD with adjunct oxytocin improves social interaction behavior and facilitates seeking of social support (Heinrichs & Domes, 2008; Neumann & Slattery, 2016; van Honk, Bos, Terburg, Heany, & Stein, 2015).

Furthermore, SAD patients in the present study exhibited a negativity bias in self-ratings compared to external ratings regarding their social behavior in the conversation. This is in line with previous findings that report underestimation of oneself in patients with SAD (Alden & Wallace, 1995; Rapee & Lim, 1992; Stopa & Clark, 1993). The finding underlines the importance of dysfunctional cognitions in psychopathology of SAD. Although SAD patients actually appear less socially competent (Baker & Edelmann, 2002; Fydrich et al., 1998; Stopa & Clark, 1993; Voncken & Bögels, 2008), others do not see them as deficient to the extent that the patients view themselves as deficient. Further, the bias dissolved in the stress-condition, due to increased self-ratings. A possible explanation would be that stress may have positively influenced the patients' self-confidence. One would expect a higher degree of self-confidence to manifest itself in facilitated interaction behavior and thus improved external ratings. The improvement was, however, not reflected by increases in external ratings of social behavior. Alternatively, the increased self-assessment might reflect hints of positive effects of stress specifically on self-perception in SAD, possibly mediated by oxytocin. Stress is known to trigger oxytocin release (Ebner et al., 2005; Landgraf & Neumann, 2004) and in a study that administered oxytocin in conjunction with exposure therapy, SAD patients with oxytocin perceived their appearance as better than those receiving placebo (Guastella et al., 2009). The 'normalized' self-rating, i.e. dissolving of the negativity bias, in SAD patients was reflected by reduced self-focused attention during the conversation for stressed SAD patients. Notably, this reduction in self-focused attention, again, was associated with cognitive empathy. That is, stress reduced self-focused attention especially for those SAD patients with high cognitive empathic abilities, which may have resulted in perceiving and overrating fewer supposed flaws.

The present findings underline two crucial notions. The first one concerns the way SAD patients deal with stress and its interactional consequences. Lacking a vital function that normally promotes affiliation and belonging, SAD patients seem to be doubly burdened – they miss out on a powerful opportunity to reduce stress and, at the same time, create distance to others, thereby corroborating symptomatology. Secondly, more attention needs to be paid to the heterogeneity of disorders like SAD in research and clinical treatment. Taking fuller account of individual dispositions such as social cognitive abilities may allow for the development of individually adapted therapeutic approaches, thereby increasing the percentage of patients that benefit from therapy.

Healthy individuals may react by turning towards others, thereby having the chance of receiving social support, a powerful stress-reducing source (Ditzen & Heinrichs, 2014). For people suffering from social anxiety, however, this way of coping seems unusable, especially for those with low empathic abilities. As a consequence, an insufficient repertoire to deal with stress results in prolonged distress and eventually increases the risk for stress-related disorders such as hypertension or metabolic disorders (Chrousos, 2009; Repasky, Eng, & Hylander, 2015). Investigating the relation between stress and social behavior may also be of high relevance to other stress-related disorders, such as PTSD or depression (Sandi & Haller, 2015). People suffering from these disorders often suffer impairments in social functioning, such as social avoidance, anxiety, deficits in social cognition (Bora & Berk, 2016; Hames, Hagan, & Joiner, 2013), as well as hostile behavior (Freeman & Roca, 2001), especially when confronted with stress (Painuly, Sharan, & Mattoo, 2007).

In conclusion, the crucial result from the present study is that people suffering from social anxiety disorder, as opposed to healthy controls, seem not to display *tend-and-befriend* behavior in reaction to stress. While healthy controls could benefit from increasing HPA-reactivity under stress in terms of improved social behavior in a conversation, SAD patients did not deploy such coping mechanisms. Instead, they were characterized by an absence of increases in affiliative behavior and reduced prosocial behavior under stress. The capacity for cognitive empathy may be a pivotal point in the modulation of stress on social behavior. Maladaptive effects of stress may be attenuated by the capability for cognitive empathy. Essential questions for future research are what the neural underpinning of these effects might be and how they contribute to the development and maintenance of social anxiety disorder. Moreover, future studies should address whether these results are specific to social anxiety disorder or are more generally characteristic of anxiety disorders or psychiatric disorders with social impairments, such as autism or borderline personality disorder. And finally, future research needs to focus on how these findings may be utilized for improved diagnostics and therapy. Specifically, this may involve differentiated diagnostics that account for patients' individual capability of coping and their social cognitive abilities. Building on this, well-tailored treatments that include psychotherapy in conjunction with social cognition training and/or augmentation with oxytocin administration may improve today's therapeutic success.

IV GENERAL DISCUSSION

The present thesis has presented the effects of acute stress on social interaction behavior in social anxiety in two empirical chapters. The findings have been critically discussed regarding possible psychobiological mechanisms and have been embedded into the recent literature. This final chapter highlights and discusses the key findings of the investigation and addresses methodological considerations and limitations, before pointing out therapeutic implications as well as deriving open questions and possible leverage points for future research.

9 Summary of the Results and Conclusion

The first empirical chapter examined the stress reactivity in social anxiety disorder compared to healthy controls on an endocrine, cardiovascular and subjective level (Chapter 7). The second empirical chapter investigated the influence of stress on social interaction behavior in patients with SAD, under consideration of individual empathic abilities (Chapter 8).

9.1 Dissociated stress response in social anxiety disorder

To date, the stress reaction in patients with SAD is not well understood and the literature on the physiological stress reactivity is limited by inconsistent and partly unstandardized stress induction methods (see chapter 4.9). Hence, the objective of the first study was to examine the stress response in patients with social anxiety disorder (SAD) compared to matched healthy controls, using a standardized and well-established method for induction of moderate psychosocial stress, the *Trier Social Stress Test for Groups* (TSST-G; von Dawans et al., 2011).

A clear pattern of a dissociated reactivity between subjective and physiological stress response in patients with SAD compared to healthy controls emerged. That is, while SAD patients exhibited an increased reaction to stress in all of the subjective stress measures (stress, tension, discomfort, anxiety, avoidance, feeling of control), they did not differ to healthy controls regarding reaction in both physiological measures (salivary cortisol and heart rate). This is in line with previous studies that found no differences in the endocrine and/or autonomous stress reaction of SAD patients and healthy controls (Anderson & Hope, 2009; Beaton et al., 2006; Edelmann & Baker, 2002; Grossman, 2001; Klumbies et al., 2014; Martel et al., 1999). The results, however, contrast with studies that report an aberrant physiological stress reactivity for SAD (Condren et al., 2002; Furlan et al., 2001; Roelofs et al., 2009; van West et al., 2008). I have discussed several methodological aspects that may account for some of the differences, like method of stress induction or comorbidity status (see Chapter 7.4).

The findings are indicative of a biased perception, as proposed by cognitive models of SAD (Clark & Wells, 1995; Rapee & Heimberg, 1997). More precisely, dysfunctional appraisal and negative self-concept are associated with social anxiety (Beck et al., 1985; Clark & Wells, 1995; Hope, Gansler, & Heimberg, 1989). Hence, the present findings underline the role of cognitive processes in the generation of anxiety and subjective stress in SAD. This is underpinned by a recent study on CBT in SAD patients, where therapy-associated reductions in anxiety and avoidance were unrelated to physiological symptoms (Aderka, McLean, Huppert, Davidson, & Foa, 2013).

9.2 Cognitive empathy buffers adverse effects of stress on social behavior in social anxiety disorder

The second empirical chapter aimed at examining the effects of acute stress in SAD, with its influence on social interaction behavior and a possible modulating effect of social cognitive abilities (see Chapter 8). There is accumulating evidence for increased prosocial behavior in response to stress in healthy individuals (for a review, see Buchanan & Preston, 2014). Little is known, however, about whether this behavioral pattern can apply in patients with SAD, in whom social contacts are avoided or endured with intense distress (American Psychiatric Association, 2013). Moreover, empathy, i.e. the ability to infer other people's mental states, plays a fundamental role in social interactions and has been shown to promote prosocial behavior (Bateson, 2002; Eisenberg, 2007; Hoffmann, 2008).

The results from the present study suggest that people suffering from SAD exhibit a different social behavioral response pattern to acute stress than healthy individuals do. While healthy controls benefited from increasing HPA-reactivity under stress, in terms of improved social behavior in conversation, SAD patients did not show such improvements. On the contrary, they exhibited reduced prosocial be-havior, i.e. less trustworthiness (and, marginally significantly, less trust) under stress. Most notably, cognitive empathy buffered the effects of stress on social interaction behavior in SAD. Specifically, SAD patients low in cognitive empathy seem to cope differently with stress, i.e. by withdrawal instead of affiliation, while SAD patients high in cognitive empathy seem to benefit from stress in terms of an improved impression on their conversation partner through reduced anxious ap-pearance and resistance to decreasing prosocial behavior under stress. Exhibit-ing this pattern of behavior, SAD patients converged to the behavior of healthy controls under stress, reflecting a 'normalized' behavioral response and slight in-dications of *tend-and-befriend* behavior. There was no association between stress reaction and empathy score that could have driven these effects.

Turning to others in times of stress requires us to confide in the other person and feel safe around him/her. While this drive may be inherent in healthy controls, it may be deficient in people with SAD. The present findings suggest that high em-pathic abilities seem to accommodate this deficiency in SAD patients and play a crucial role in the modulation of social behavior. By inferring the other person's mind and comprehending his/her actions, we can perceive ourselves as an "ally" to the other person, feeling close to him/her in contrast to perceiving him/her as a potential threat and feeling distant. Moreover, empathy facilitates altruistic behav-ior (Bateson, 2002; Batson & Coke, 1981; Eisenberg, 2007), and several studies have found a negative association between empathy and aggressive and antiso-cial behavior (Kaukiainen et al., 1999; Robinson, Roberts, Strayer, & Koopman, 2007). It is likely that people who are willing to help others and who tend to be more other-oriented also show more affiliation under stress. Thereby, they have the chance to gain social support, which is tied to positive health outcomes (Ditzen & Heinrichs, 2014). In accordance, empathy has been associated with re-duced levels of burnout (Brazeau, Schroeder, Rovi, & Boyd, 2010; Gleichgerrcht & Decety, 2013; Lamothe, Boujut, Zenasni, & Sultan, 2014; Yuguero, Marsal, Es-querda, Vivanco, & Soler-González, 2017; Yuguero Torres, Esquerda Aresté, Marsal Mora, & Soler-González, 2015), suggesting a healthier processing of stress. Affiliation towards others could account for this association. This may be of specific relevance in people who usually exhibit aberrant social affiliation, in disorders such as SAD, autism or borderline personality disorder (Baron-Cohen, 2000; Dinsdale & Crespi, 2013; Jeung & Herpertz, 2014)

10   Methodological Considerations and Limitations

There are some limitations of the present study that need to be considered. First, the sample of patients with SAD was selective in terms of burden, as participants had no comorbidities, no use of drugs and no current medical or psychotherapeutic treatment. Social anxiety is often comorbid with other anxiety disorders and depression (Beesdo et al., 2007) and this is linked with more severe impairments (e.g. Erwin, Heimberg, Juster, & Mindlin, 2002; Kessler, Berglund, et al., 2005). For example, it has been shown that deviances in amygdala activity for emotion regulation are more pronounced in comorbid SAD patients than in SAD-only (Burklund, Craske, Taylor, & Lieberman, 2015). Thus, the sample of SAD patients may not represent the highly burdened comorbid SAD patients, and deficits in social behavior might be even more pronounced in the latter. However, symptom severity was still high, with mean LSAS scores of 65.8 (SD = 22.3), indicating a moderate to pronounced form of SAD. Additionally, it would be of interest to include a second control group next to healthy individuals, such as generalized anxiety disorder or specific phobia, in order to disentangle effects specific to social anxiety from general anxiety-related variance. Moreover, our sample consisted of male participants only, thus, findings cannot be generalized to female SAD patients. More precisely, sex differences have been reported for the neuroendocrine stress reaction (Kudielka & Kirschbaum, 2005; Zorn et al., 2016) and modulation of social behavior through stress may entail differences for women, as gonadal steroids play a crucial role in regulation of behavior (Lim & Young, 2006; Soma, Scotti, Newman, Charlier, & Demas, 2008). Accordingly, men and women have been suggested to differ in their ways of coping, with women seeking more social support than men (for a meta-analysis, see Tamres, Janicki, & Helgeson, 2002; S. Taylor et al., 2000). Considering these differences, studies examining the present topic in both males and females are needed. Further, patients in the stress-condition were older than patients in the no-stress-condition. Although not statistically significant (p = .062), it could have had an influence on the stress response, as age has been shown to influence heart rate as well as cortisol responses (Kudielka et al., 2004a, 2004b). However, in the study that directly compared the stress reaction in different age groups, reporting decreased heart rate reaction for older males (Kudielka et al., 2004b), the age difference between groups was at 40.90 years much higher than in the present study (2.77 years). Thus, it can be assumed that the marginal and non-significant age difference in the present sample did not bias results. Regarding HPA-axis reactivity, cortisol response in older men has been shown to be elevated compared to younger men (Kudielka et al., 2004a; Kudielka, Schmidt-Reinwald, Hellhammer, Schürmeyer, & Kirschbaum, 2000; Rohleder, Kudielka, Hellhammer, Wolf, & Kirschbaum, 2002). As the participants in the stress-condition were marginally older than those in the no-stress condition, an age effect would have, if anything, led to higher responses in the stress group, thereby underpinning our finding of a comparable cortisol reaction in SAD and HC. In addition, with the glucocorticoid cascade hypothesis (Robert M. Sapolsky, Krey, & McEwen, 1986), it has been stated that deficiencies in the termination of glucocorticoid secretion through hippocampal feedback would lead to increased HPA-axis reactivity in older organisms. This, however, has been called into question by De Kloet and colleagues (1998). Based on findings on changes in glucocorticoid and mineralocorticoid receptor binding in aging (De Kloet et al., 1991), they developed the corticosteroid receptor balance theory, claiming that aging would be accompanied by the creation of a balance between glucocorticoid and mineralocorticoid receptors, resulting in comparable endocrine responses in older and younger individuals.

Further, activity of the HPA axis and ANS was examined through the collection of salivary cortisol and recording of heart rate. Although both measures are well-established parameters in stress research, the stress response is a highly complex process with many substances and interactions involved. As such, stress also leads to changes in glucocorticoids, catecholamines, prolactin and growth hormone, so that the examination of heart rate and salivary cortisol as end-products are but two of many possible candidates (Foley & Kirschbaum, 2010). While heart rate depicts one aspect of SAM activity, assessment of epinephrine and norepinephrine levels in blood plasma would enable a direct derivation of adrenal medulla activity. Moreover, as regards HPA-axis activity, the additional examination of concentrations of ACTH, CRH or salivary alpha-amylase (sAA) could better depict the complete response and further elucidate whether possible deviations at another point in the physiological stress reaction in SAD occur. However, a recent study did not find differences in SAD compared to healthy controls in salivary and plasma cortisol, sAA, prolactin, heart rate and heart rate variability, corroborating the present findings (Klumbies et al., 2014). Moreover, assessment of other HPA-axis measures, such as ACTH, requires invasive sampling of blood plasma, which may act as an unwanted stressor and bias baseline measures.

The findings from previous studies on prosocial decision-making under stress in healthy participants were not replicated. Reasons for this might be differences in study design, sample characteristics and a possible ceiling effect. An investigation taking these aspects into consideration could help clarify under what circumstances tend-and-befriend behavior is shown in healthy controls, and what contributed to the difference in observations. Finally, the moderation of stress and social behavior by empathy during the conversation was apparent only in the rating by confederates but not in the video ratings. Although overall inter-rater reliability was good, differences in ratings due to different proximity to the participant might have accounted for this incongruity. As findings by Berg and Archer (1980) show, empathic concern for self-disclosure of one's interaction partner predicts likeability. Empathic concern is expressed via reactions such as mimic expressions or slight variations in posture (Niedenthal, 2007; Zahn-Waxler & Radke-Yarrow, 1990). Such subtle reactions might have been especially perceptible for confederates but not for video-raters, as video recordings of conversations are limited in comparison to being present in the actual situation. This may be due to several aspects, including: a restricted image section from outside; not being face-to-face with the participant; resolution and color rendering being dependent on technical quality; and inaccuracy in recording very low tones.

11   Implications for Psychopathology and Treatment

The findings of the present study entail implications for the understanding of the psychopathology of social anxiety disorder and for therapeutic approaches. Specifically, the findings underline the importance of dysfunctional cognitive processing in SAD in regards to threat intensity in social situations. The awareness that the patients' physiological reactions are within the normal range might soothe them and encourage them to make contact with others. With this, the therapist as well as the patient may have a broader groundwork to build on. Furthermore, the findings suggest that while stress can have a positive impact on social interactions in healthy controls, this association seems to be more complex for SAD patients. Especially those patients low in social cognitive abilities do not seem to engage in affiliation behavior in the sense of *tend-and-befriend*. If this observation is true, the consequences are wide ranging. With an absence of affiliative behavior in times of stress, they lack a powerful mechanism to reduce stress, thereby narrowing coping possibilities. This not only implies negative effects for general health (Ditzen & Heinrichs, 2014) but also most likely exacerbates symptomatology. If the tendency to avoid social contacts is amplified under stress, patients run the risk of forfeiting positive and corrective social experiences even more when daily stressors have to be endured. Therapists may pay specific attention to whether the patient is in possession of sufficient stress regulation strategies and consider integration of such in the treatment. Thereby, the risk of withdrawal due to high stress levels and resulting adverse effects on symptomatology and general health may be lowered.

Furthermore, high cognitive empathic abilities appear to buffer maladaptive social behavioral consequences of stress in SAD. DeWall and Baumeister (2006) showed that the mere prospect of loneliness decreases empathizing with others. Thus, SAD patients low in empathic abilities are confronted with an additional empathy reduction risk, as avoidance of social contacts and thoughts about exclusion and loneliness are everyday dangers, creating a vicious circle. An individually fitted treatment could include training of empathic abilities for those patients who exhibit deficiencies in that area. As empathy is a broad and complex construct, the concrete aspects to be targeted would need to be defined. The present study focused on basal aspects of empathy, i.e. recognizing the other person's mental state. More broadly, it would be interesting to investigate if differences in other aspects of the construct of empathy, such as mimicry as a form of communicative functioning (Bateson, 2011) or the motivation to help, would yield comparable results in modulating SAD patients' behavior under stress. And further, how can these and future findings be transferred into knowledge that actually becomes part of clinical practice? This opens a fruitful topic for future studies. Might those SAD patients low in empathic abilities benefit from training in basal emotional sharing, from exercises in mindfulness on compassion, or emotion regulation strategies for the reduction of personal distress (also see Singer & Lamm, 2009)? These questions await pursuit. An early training program on social cognition was proposed by Feshbach and Feshbach (1982), the *Empathy Training Program*. It included training of emotion identification and emotion discrimination, as well as lessons on perspective-taking. A 10-week training period on the program led to increased prosocial behavior in the intervention group compared to a control group (Feshbach, 1984). In patient groups, to date, several training programs have been developed regarding social cognitive remediation in schizophrenia (e.g. Horan et al., 2011; Kayser, Sarfati, Besche, & Hardy-Baylé, 2006; Penn, Roberts, Combs, & Sterne, 2007; Wölwer et al., 2005). A recent meta-analysis (Wykes, Huddy, Cellard, McGurk, & Czobor, 2011) revealed moderate effect sizes for social cognition, with durable improvements in the domain of emotion recognition and, in some of the studies, in attributional style. Notably, social cognition training only had positive effects on functioning when combined with psychiatric treatment.

In line with previous studies (Baker & Edelmann, 2002; Fydrich et al., 1998; Stopa & Clark, 1993; Voncken & Bögels, 2008), SAD patients exhibited social performance deficits compared to HC. The finding corroborates the assumption that there is a core of truth in the patients' fear of negative evaluation. The accumulating evidence for these deficiencies is of high therapeutic relevance. If patients with SAD appear less socially approachable and thus less likable, a therapy that mainly focuses on exposure therapy cannot necessarily be effective, as some of the cognitions might not be biased. In those cases, exposure might carry the risk of nurturing negative experiences and thus repeating the individual's learning history, maintaining fears. Accordingly, despite repeated exposures, patients with SAD mostly do not show habituation of their anxiety, in contrast to other anxiety disorders (Stangier, Heidenreich, & Peitz, 2003). In fact, a recent meta-analysis on therapy of anxiety disorders found no differences in the efficacy of CBT and exposure therapy for panic disorder and PTSD, but a clear superiority of CBT for SAD (Ougrin, 2011). From a classic behavior therapeutic view, the lack of habituation may seem paradoxical. Besides the assumption that SAD patients avoid full exposure by usage of safety behaviors (Clark, 2005), merely withstanding the feared situation may not account for what a person suffering from SAD actually needs. With awareness of individual performance deficits, their differentiation from actually biased cognitions, and the subsequent integration of that awareness in the therapy, we might get closer to a tailored therapy for SAD.

Previous work has reported a connection between social performance deficits, negative emotions in others and subsequent social rejection (Alden & Wallace, 1995; Creed & Funder, 1998; Meleshko & Alden, 1993; Voncken, Alden, Bögels, & Roelofs, 2008). The roles of stress and decreased prosocial behavior as a possible mediating factors, however, have not been considered so far. In social situations, stress is immanent for people with SAD. Social performance deficits may be a manifestation of reduced affiliative behavior, induced by the perceived stress. Cognitions that facilitate withdrawal and reductions in prosocial behavior (e.g. *"I don't need the others/care about them")* may be a form of dysfunctional coping by lowering the patient's own high standards and expectations for the interaction (Alden, Ryder, & B, 2002; Clark & Wells, 1995; Juster et al., 1996). Lowered expectations may lead to short-term reduction of anxiety, while symptomatology and social impairment are fueled in the long-term. Dysfunctional coping strategies like this have been described as disengagement (Carver, Scheier, & Weintraub, 1989) and have been associated with social anxiety (Thomasson & Psouni, 2010). Such strategies basically aim at avoiding the experience of threatening situations or emotional distress. Further, another way to cope is substance abuse (Blumenthal, Ham, Cloutier, Bacon, & Douglas, 2016; Thomasson & Psouni, 2010; for a review, see Carrigan & Randall, 2003). Those SAD patients with higher social cognitive abilities may engage less in such disengagement coping. More studies are needed to confirm the present findings. When stress proves to reduce prosocial and affiliative behavior in SAD, this may open a valuable leverage point in the treatment of this disorder. Patients may train to engage in functional stress regulation strategies in order to prevent the need for withdrawing and reduced prosocial behavior. For example, mindfulness-based stress reduction in SAD may contribute to improving symptomatology and flexibility in emotion regulation (Goldin & Gross, 2010).

More fine-tuned diagnostics are needed that consider the patient's individual capacity for emotional regulation and social cognitive abilities. Building on this, well-tailored treatments that include psychotherapy in conjunction with social cognition training and/or augmentation with oxytocin administration may help improve today's insufficient efficacy in the treatment of disorders like social anxiety disorder.

12   Integrational Model of Stress-Related Behavior and Social Impairment

In this thesis, the oxytocin system has been discussed as a possible underlying biological mechanism involved in the modulation of social behavior after acute stress (see Chapter 3.1). Oxytocin produces anxiolytic effects by dampening responsiveness of the HPA-axis (Cardoso et al., 2014; Heinrichs et al., 2003) via downregulation of amygdala activity (Baumgartner et al., 2008; Domes, Heinrichs, Gläscher, et al., 2007; Kanat et al., 2015). Moreover, oxytocin improves cognitive empathy (Domes, Heinrichs, Michel, et al., 2007; Lischke et al., 2012; Schulze et al., 2011) and is crucial for social behavior (Heinrichs & Domes, 2008). Plasma oxytocin levels on the one hand have been shown to be relatively stable over time (Feldman, Weller, Zagoory-Sharon, & Levine, 2007) and on the other hand to exhibit situation-specific modulation depending on the social contacts (Feldman, Gordon, Schneiderman, Weisman, & Zagoory-Sharon, 2010). There is preliminary evidence of reduced plasma oxytocin levels in SAD compared to healthy controls (Hoge et al., 2012). Moreover, oxytocin administration in SAD has been shown to reduce hyperactivation of the amygdala and medial prefrontal cortex in response to social threat (Labuschagne et al., 2010, 2011). Alterations in underlying oxytocin system functioning in SAD might result in a reduced secretion of this hormone under stress, thereby impeding the motivation to affiliate with others. In SAD patients with high social cognitive abilities, central oxytocin levels may be higher, facilitating approach under stress.

The behavioral response to stress is complex and dependent on various situational and individual aspects (see Buchanan & Preston, 2014; Preston & De Waal, 2002). Being able to flexibly adapt to contextual demands is supposed to be crucial for physical and mental health (Aldao, Sheppes, & Gross, 2015; Kashdan & Rottenberg, 2010). Patients with SAD have been shown to exhibit more rigid, inflexible reactions to social stress (Farmer & Kashdan, 2015; Werner, Goldin, Ball, Heimberg, & Gross, 2011).

The model in **Figure 12.1** integrates this observation into the findings from the present study, building on the models by Heinrichs & Domes (2008) and von Dawans (2008). Healthy individuals are able to adaptively modulate their social behavior in response to stress, according to situational and individual demands (see Buchanan & Preston, 2014; Preston & De Waal, 2002). That is, depending on contextual aspects and personal goals, one may engage in either amenable or aggressive behavior. For example, affiliation behavior in reaction to receiving bad news enables social support. These positive social contacts stimulate oxytocin release, which in turn alleviates HPA-axis and amygdala reactivity. However, a more aggressive or defensive behavior may be functional in situations such as in a contest, in order to prevail against the competition, or in an actual threat situation, such as being mugged. In psychopathology associated with impairments in social functioning, such as social anxiety disorder or borderline personality disorder, only limited adaptation might be possible. Moreover, behavioral outcomes seem to be dependent on social cognitive abilities, with high social cognitive abilities facilitating affiliative behavior, modulated by the oxytocin system. Notably, affiliation behavior is shown to be less likely, although context and individual goals might promote affiliative social interaction behavior. Showing withdrawal or anti-social behavior in such situations, on the other hand, elicits negative emotions in others and leads to social rejection. Thereby, patients miss out on the anxiolytic, stress reducing effects of positive social contacts, forfeiting a vital coping mechanism.

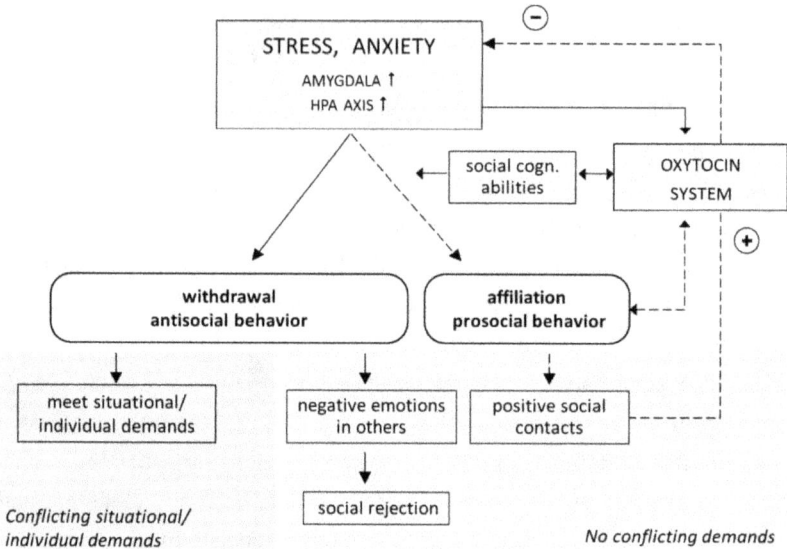

Figure 12.1. Model of the effects of stress on social behavior and interactional consequences in health and psychopathology. Adapted from Heinrichs & Domes (2008) and von
Dawans (2008). Healthy individuals adaptively modulate social behavior in response to
stress, according to situational and individual requirements. When there are no conflicting
situational or individual demands, stress leads to affiliation behavior. Resulting positive
social contacts stimulate oxytocin release, which in turn alleviates HPA axis and amygdala reactivity. In psychopathology, adaption, especially affiliation behavior, is only limitedly
possible (indicated by dotted lines) and is dependent on social cognitive abilities, modulated by the oxytocin system.   Showing withdrawal/antisocial behavior elicits negative
emotions in others and leads to social rejection. HPA axis = hypothalamus pituitary adrenal axis; cogn. = cognitive.

13   Remaining Questions and Future Goals

Over one-hundred years after Cannon (1915) described the *fight-or-flight* response to acute stress, our understanding of the manifold consequences of stress
has expanded but there are no fewer open questions.

The findings of the present study suggest the physiological stress response of
SAD patients is similar to that of HC. Nonetheless, ambiguity in the data situation
calls for further investigation of the stress systems in social anxiety. Despite
growing research on endocrine and autonomous stress reactivity in social anxiety
disorder, as well as on the stress-related neuronal correlates in this disorder, par-

adoxes regarding the physiological stress reaction in SAD remain. Studies are needed that implement a combined investigation of endocrine stress markers and brain imaging in response to acute stress processing in social anxiety. The implemented stress induction should exhibit characteristics of a general stressor instead of cues that depict a 'social threat' to SAD patients but not to non-socially anxious individuals, in order to detect a possibly divergent activity pattern in SAD compared to healthy controls. Such approaches would contribute to extending our understanding of underlying mechanisms and to disentangling neuronal correlates associated with a potentially elevated stress reactivity that is also reflected on the endocrine level and in an exaggerated response to social cues. Moreover, it would be of interest to explore whether changes on the epigenetic level may account for some of these differences. For example, adverse developmental experience has been associated with hypermethylation of the promoter region of the glucocorticoid receptor gene, which in turn facilitates heightened stress sensitivity and dysregulation of the HPA axis (for reviews, see Heim & Nemeroff, 2001; Meyer-Lindenberg & Tost, 2012). For social anxiety, indications in this regard come from a study on childhood abuse. Therein, SAD patients with childhood abuse exhibited increased cortisol reactivity to a stressor compared to patients without childhood abuse (Elzinga, Spinhoven, Berretty, de Jong, & Roelofs, 2010)[4]. Similar results have been found for depression (Heim et al., 2000). The increasing consideration of epigenetic influences like DNA methylation and gene expression in the research on stress reactivity (e.g. Cole, 2014; Turecki & Meaney, 2016) may help us gain more insight into fundamental physiological characteristics of disorders such as SAD and may contribute to clarifying the divergent results of the stress reaction in SAD, for example by identification of different subtypes.

From neuroimaging studies, there is considerable evidence that SAD patients exhibit elevated amygdala reactivity in response to social threat cues (for meta-analyses, see Brühl et al., 2014; Etkin & Wager, 2007). However, the amygdala is a highly heterogeneous structure. A popular approach in fMRI studies on the neural correlates of mental disorders is the definition of regions of interest (ROI),

---

[4] Study is not additionally included in the overview in chapter 4.9, as the sample was part of the larger study by Roeloefs and colleagues (2009).

whereby most studies define the amygdala as a single ROI. Ventral areas like the amygdala and adjacent regions are especially prone to artefacts due to their proximity to the pharynx. A more differentiated picture of the involvement of the individual nuclei and the extended amygdala in SAD specific stress processing is needed, in order to differentiate which subregions of the amygdala and their pathways are overactive under stress and whether they are directly involved in HPA-axis functioning. This view of a more complex relation between amygdalar activation and stress processing is in line with a recent study on socio-emotional threat processing in SAD (Ziv, Goldin, Jazaieri, Hahn, & Gross, 2013). The study found similar reactivity in amygdala and insula in SAD compared to healthy individuals in three different tasks, despite highly increased subjective stress measures. The same pattern of comparable activity has been reported by other studies (Doehrmann et al., 2013; Nakao et al., 2011; Quadflieg, Mohr, Mentzel, Miltner, & Straube, 2008). Regarding future studies, the combined investigation of endocrine stress markers and brain imaging in response to stress induction could contribute to elucidating the physiological processes of the stress reaction in SAD. To date, there are few studies engaging in such multilevel approaches. Accordingly, Åhs and colleagues (Ahs, Sollers, Furmark, Fredrikson, & Thayer, 2009) found positive correlations of salivary cortisol with activity in the hypothalamus but not with the amygdala in SAD. Moreover, improved spatial resolution of very high-resolution fMRI and connectivity-based approaches, like diffusion tensor imaging, might enable more fine-tuned detection of activity in SAD-related structures (Sladky et al., 2015; Solano-Castiella et al., 2010; Ugurbil, 2016), thereby disentangling subregions relevant for the subjective and physiological stress reactions.

Furthermore, future studies are needed to further examine the role of the oxytocin system in SAD to reveal if secretion and/or functioning are altered and whether prolonged treatment of SAD with adjunct oxytocin improves social interaction behavior and facilitates seeking of social support (Heinrichs & Domes, 2008; Neumann & Slattery, 2016; van Honk et al., 2015).

Orienting towards others in times of stress constitutes a potent coping mechanism to reduce stress via closeness to other human beings. This kind of stress reduction is available and achievable in many situations. If this mechanism does not work, a crucial option to reduce adverse repercussions of stress in everyday life is missing, thereby increasing risk for stress-related diseases such as hypertension, type-2 diabetes mellitus or psychiatric disorders like anxiety and depression (Chrousos, 2009; McEwen & Stellar, 1993). Moreover, how we deal with stress does not affect us solely on the individual level. Rather, due to its social dimensions there are multiple consequences for social interactions and, eventually, for society as a whole. Whether individuals show withdrawing, aggressive and violent behavior or act prosocial in response to stress makes an enormous difference for communal life. With a better understanding of what environmental and personal conditions facilitate an affiliative, prosocial attitude in response to stress, corresponding innovations in the structure of society (for instance, in educational systems or with regards to socioeconomic status) become possible. The study presented in this thesis makes a first contribution to this understanding by suggesting facilitated affiliative behavior through the promotion of empathic abilities as a form of treatment.

The scope of the present thesis goes beyond social anxiety disorder. In particular, the finding that cognitive empathy can function as a buffer against social withdrawal under stress, here shown on the basis of SAD, might not be restricted solely to this disorder; indeed, it may be of relevance to other disorders associated with social impairments, including autism (e.g. Baron-Cohen, 2000; Bons et al., 2013; Dziobek et al., 2007), borderline personality disorder (e.g. Dinsdale & Crespi, 2013; Domes, Schulze, & Herpertz, 2009; Jeung & Herpertz, 2014) or even little noticed disorders like body dysmorphic disorder (Buhlmann, Gleiss, Rupf, Zschenderlein, & Kathmann, 2011). Accordingly, the research on transdiagnostic factors has gained much attention in recent years, specifically with development of the Research Domain Criteria (RDoC) project (Insel et al., 2010). This approach abandons a nosology that views diagnostic conceptualizations as actual disorder entities and induces researchers to find the underlying neural, genetic etc. correlates (Kozak & Cuthbert, 2016). Rather, the new approach focuses on dimensional constructs, integrating findings from psychological and biological research, leading towards an empirically based understanding of fundamental mechanisms and their anomalies and associated symptoms. Major aspects of the current RDoC matrix relevant to social anxiety are the construct *Potential Threat*

("Anxiety") and the domain *Social Processes* ("NIMH » Research Domain Criteria (RDoC)," n.d.). In this regard, the present investigation of individual empathic abilities fits in nicely in the RDoC sub-construct *Understanding Mental States* of the domain *Social Processes*. Therefore, large sample based studies are warranted that encompass a multimodal investigation of the stress reaction and an assessment of social cognitive abilities and social interaction, using behavioral, hormonal, as well as neural and genetic approaches. With such a translational focus on our behavior, its underlying biological processes and how behavior adapts to stress, research may portray associated psychopathology more accurately and eventually enable the development of individually tailored and thus more efficient treatment approaches.

REFERENCES

Acarturk, C., Cuijpers, P., van Straten, A., & de Graaf, R. (2009). Psychological treatment of social anxiety disorder: a meta-analysis. *Psychological Medicine, 39*(2), 241–254.

Ackerman, J. M., Huang, J. Y., & Bargh, J. A. (2012). Evolutionary perspectives on social cognition. *The Handbook of Social Cognition*, 451–473.

Aderka, I. M., Hofmann, S. G., Nickerson, A., Hermesh, H., Gilboa-Schechtman, E., & Marom, S. (2012). Functional impairment in social anxiety disorder. *Journal of Anxiety Disorders, 26*(3), 393–400.

Aderka, I. M., McLean, C. P., Huppert, J. D., Davidson, J. R. T., & Foa, E. B. (2013). Fear, avoidance and physiological symptoms during cognitive-behavioral therapy for social anxiety disorder. *Behaviour Research and Therapy, 51*(7), 352–358.

Ahs, F., Sollers, J. J., Furmark, T., Fredrikson, M., & Thayer, J. F. (2009). High-frequency heart rate variability and cortico-striatal activity in men and women with social phobia. *NeuroImage, 47*(3), 815–820.

Aktar, E., Majdandžić, M., de Vente, W., & Bögels, S. M. (2014). Parental social anxiety disorder prospectively predicts toddlers' fear/avoidance in a social referencing paradigm. *Journal of Child Psychology and Psychiatry, and Allied Disciplines, 55*(1), 77–87.

Aldao, A., Sheppes, G., & Gross, J. J. (2015). Emotion Regulation Flexibility. *Cognitive Therapy and Research, 39*(3), 263–278.

Alden, L. E., & Bieling, P. (1998). Interpersonal consequences of the pursuit of safety. *Behaviour Research and Therapy, 36*(1), 53–64.

Alden, L. E., Ryder, A. G., & B, M. (2002). Perfectionism in the context of social fears: Toward a two-component model. In G. L. Flett & P. L. Hewitt (Eds.), *Perfectionism: Theory, research, and treatment* (pp. 373–391). Washington, DC, US: American Psychological Association.

Alden, L. E., & Taylor, C. T. (2004). Interpersonal processes in social phobia. *Clinical Psychology Review, 24*(7), 857–882.

Alden, L. E., & Wallace, S. T. (1995). Social phobia and social appraisal in successful and unsuccessful social interactions. *Behaviour Research and Therapy, 33*(5), 497–505.

American Psychiatric Association. (2013). *Diagnostic and Statistical Manual of Mental Disorders (DSM)* (5th ed.). Washington, DC.

Amin, N., Foa, E. B., & Coles, M. E. (1998). Negative interpretation bias in social phobia. *Behaviour Research and Therapy, 36*(10), 945–957.

Amir, N., Beard, C., Taylor, C. T., Klumpp, H., Elias, J., Burns, M., & Chen, X. (2009). Attention Training in Individuals with Generalized Social Phobia: A Randomized Controlled Trial. *Journal of Consulting and Clinical Psychology, 77*(5), 961–973.

Anderson, E. R., & Hope, D. A. (2009). The relationship among social phobia, objective and perceived physiological reactivity, and anxiety sensitivity in an adolescent population. *Journal of Anxiety Disorders, 23*(1), 18–26.

Arbelle, S., Benjamin, J., Golin, M., Kremer, I., Belmaker, R. H., & Ebstein, R. P. (2003). Relation of Shyness in Grade School Children to the Genotype for the Long Form of the Serotonin Transporter Promoter Region Polymorphism. *American Journal of Psychiatry, 160*(4), 671–676.

Argyle, M., & Kendon, A. (1967). The Experimental Analysis of Social Performance. In L. Berkowitz (Ed.), *Advances in Experimental Social Psychology* (Vol. 3, pp. 55–98). Elsevier.

Arkin, R. M., Lake, E. A., & Baumgardner, A. H. (1986). Shyness and Self-Presentation. In W. H. Jones, J. M. Cheek, & S. R. Briggs (Eds.), *Shyness* (pp. 189–203). Springer US.

Arkowitz, H., Lichtenstein, E., McGovern, K., & Hines, P. (1975). The behavioral assessment of social competence in males. *Behavior Therapy, 6*(1), 3–13.

Arnsten, A. F. T. (2009). Stress signalling pathways that impair prefrontal cortex structure

Aron, A., Melinat, E., Aron, E. N., Vallone, R. D., & Bator, R. J. (1997). The Experimental Generation of Interpersonal Closeness: A Procedure and Some Preliminary Findings. *Personality and Social Psychology Bulletin, 23*(4), 363–377.

Aureli, F., Van Schaik, C. P., & Van Hooff, J. A. R. A. M. (1989). Functional aspects of reconciliation among captive long-tailed macaques (Macaca fascicularis). *American Journal of Primatology, 19*(1), 39–51.

Auyeung, B., Lombardo, M. V., Heinrichs, M., Chakrabarti, B., Sule, A., Deakin, J. B., ... Baron-Cohen, S. (2015). Oxytocin increases eye contact during a real-time, naturalistic social interaction in males with and without autism. *Translational Psychiatry, 5*, e507.

Auyeung, K. W., & Alden, L. E. (2016). Social Anxiety and Empathy for Social Pain. *Cognitive Therapy and Research, 40*(1), 38–45.

Baker, S. R., & Edelmann, R. J. (2002). Is social phobia related to lack of social skills? Duration of skill-related behaviours and ratings of behavioural adequacy. *The British Journal of Clinical Psychology / the British Psychological Society, 41* (3), 243–257.

Balconi, M., & Canavesio, Y. (2013). Emotional contagion and trait empathy in prosocial behavior in young people: the contribution of autonomic (facial feedback) and balanced emotional empathy scale (BEES) measures. *Journal of Clinical and Experimental Neuropsychology, 35*(1), 41–48.

Ball, T. M., Sullivan, S., Flagan, T., Hitchcock, C. A., Simmons, A., Paulus, M. P., & Stein, M. B. (2012). Selective effects of social anxiety, anxiety sensitivity, and negative affectivity on the neural bases of emotional face processing. *NeuroImage, 59*(2), 1879–1887.

Bandelow, B., Sher, L., Bunevicius, R., Hollander, E., Kasper, S., Zohar, J., ... WFSBP Task Force on Anxiety Disorders, OCD and PTSD. (2012). Guidelines for the pharmacological treatment of anxiety disorders, obsessive-compulsive disorder and posttraumatic stress disorder in primary care. *International Journal of Psychiatry in Clinical Practice, 16*(2), 77–84.

Banissy, M. J., Kanai, R., Walsh, V., & Rees, G. (2012). Inter-individual differences in empathy are reflected in human brain structure. *Neuroimage, 62*(3), 2034–2039.

Barden, N., Reul, J. M., & Holsboer, F. (1995). Do antidepressants stabilize mood through actions on the hypothalamic-pituitary-adrenocortical system? *Trends in Neurosciences, 18*(1), 6–11.

Bar-Haim, Y., Lamy, D., Pergamin, L., Bakermans-Kranenburg, M. J., & van IJzendoorn, M. H. (2007). Threat-related attentional bias in anxious and nonanxious individuals: A meta-analytic study. *Psychological Bulletin, 133*(1), 1–24.

Barlow, D. H., Allen, L. B., & Choate, M. L. (2004). Toward a unified treatment for emotional disorders. *Behavior Therapy, 35*(2), 205–230.

Barnes, L. L. B., Harp, D., & Jung, W. S. (2002). Reliability Generalization of Scores on the Spielberger State-Trait Anxiety Inventory. *Educational and Psychological Measurement, 62*(4), 603–618.

Baron-Cohen, S. (2000). Theory of mind and autism: A fifteen year review. In S. Baron-Cohen, H. Tager-Flusberg, & D. J. Cohen (Eds.), *Understanding other minds: Perspectives from developmental cognitive neuroscience (2nd ed.)* (pp. 3–20). New York, NY, US: Oxford University Press.

Barraza, J. A., & Zak, P. J. (2009). Empathy toward strangers triggers oxytocin release and subsequent generosity. *Annals of the New York Academy of Sciences, 1167*, 182–189.

Bateson, C. D. (1998). Altruism and prosocial behavior. In D. T. Gilbert, S. T. Fiske, & G. Lindzey (Eds.), *Handbook of Social Psychology* (4., Vol. 2, pp. 282–316). New York: McGraw- Hill.

Bateson, C. D. (2002). Adressing the Altruism Question Experimentally. In *Altruism and Altruistic Love: Science, Philosophy, and Religion in Dialogue* (pp. 89–105). Oxford University Press.

Bateson, C. D. (2011). These Things called Empathy: Eight Related but Distinct Phenomena. *The Social Neuroscience of Empathy*, 3–15.

Batson, C. D., & Coke, J. S. (1981). Empathy: A source of altruistic motivation for helping? In J. P. Rushton & R. M. Sorrentino (Eds.), *Altruism and helping behavior: Social, personality, and developmental perspectives.* (pp. 167–187). Hillsdale, NJ: Erlbaum.

Bauman, M. D., & Amaral, D. G. (2005). The distribution of serotonergic fibers in the macaque monkey amygdala: an immunohistochemical study using antisera to 5-hydroxytryptamine. *Neuroscience, 136*(1), 193–203.

Baumeister, R. F., & Leary, M. R. (1995). The need to belong: desire for interpersonal attachments as a fundamental human motivation. *Psychological Bulletin, 117*(3), 497–529.

Baumgartner, T., Heinrichs, M., Vonlanthen, A., Fischbacher, U., & Fehr, E. (2008). Oxytocin shapes the neural circuitry of trust and trust adaptation in humans. *Neuron, 58*(4), 639–650.

Baur, V., Hänggi, J., Rufer, M., Delsignore, A., Jäncke, L., Herwig, U., & Beatrix Brühl, A. (2011). White matter alterations in social anxiety disorder. *Journal of Psychiatric Research, 45*(10), 1366–1372.

Beard, C., Moitra, E., Weisberg, R. B., & Keller, M. B. (2010). Characteristics and predictors of social phobia course in a longitudinal study of primary-care patients. *Depression and Anxiety, 27*(9), 839–845.

Beaton, E. A., Schmidt, L. A., Ashbaugh, A. R., Santesso, D. L., Antony, M. M., McCabe, R. E., ... Schulkin, J. (2006). Low salivary cortisol levels among socially anxious young adults: Preliminary evidence from a selected and a non-selected sample. *Personality and Individual Differences, 41*(7), 1217–1228.

Beck, A. T. (1979). *Cognitive Therapy and the Emotional Disorders.* Penguin.

Beck, A. T., Emery, G., & Greenberg, R. L. (1985). *Anxiety Disorders and Phobias: A Cognitive Perspective.* New York: Basic Books.

Beck, A. T., Steer, R. A., & Brown, G. K. (1996). *Manual for the Beck Depression Inventory-II.* San Antonio, TX: Psychological Corporation.

Beesdo, K., Bittner, A., Pine, D. S., Stein, M. B. M., Hofler, M. D.-S., Lieb, R., & Wittchen, H.-U. (2007). Incidence of Social Anxiety Disorder and the Consistent Risk for Secondary Depression in the First Three Decades of Life. *Archives of General Psychiatry, 64*(8), 903–912.

Beesdo-Baum, K., Knappe, S., Fehm, L., Höfler, M., Lieb, R., Hofmann, S. G., & Wittchen, H.-U. (2012). The natural course of social anxiety disorder among adolescents and young adults. *Acta Psychiatrica Scandinavica, 126*(6), 411–425.

Beidel, D. C., Turner, S. M., & Dancu, C. V. (1985). Physiological, cognitive and behavioral aspects of social anxiety. *Behaviour Research and Therapy, 23*(2), 109–117.

Beidel, D. C., Turner, S. M., & Morris, T. L. (1999). Psychopathology of childhood social phobia. *Journal of the American Academy of Child and Adolescent Psychiatry, 38*(6), 643–650.

Berg, J. H., & Archer, R. L. (1980). Disclosure or concern: A second look at liking for the norm breaker1. *Journal of Personality, 48*(2), 245–257.

Berger, J., Heinrichs, M., von Dawans, B., Way, B. M., & Chen, F. S. (2015). Cortisol modulates men's affiliative responses to acute social stress. *Psychoneuroendocrinology, 63*, 1–9.

Bernard, C. (1878). *Les Phénomènes de la Vie*. Paris: two vols.

Birbaumer, N., & Schmidt, R. F. (2002). *Biologische Psychologie* (5th ed.). Berlin u.a.: Springer.

Blakemore, S.-J. (2008). The social brain in adolescence. *Nature Reviews Neuroscience, 9*(4), 267–277.

Blakemore, S.-J., Bristow, D., Bird, G., Frith, C., & Ward, J. (2005). Somatosensory activations during the observation of touch and a case of vision-touch synaesthesia. *Brain: A Journal of Neurology, 128*(Pt 7), 1571–1583.

Blanco, C., Xu, Y., Schneier, F. R., Okuda, M., Liu, S.-M., & Heimberg, R. G. (2011). Predictors of persistence of social anxiety disorder: a national study. *Journal of Psychiatric Research, 45*(12), 1557–1563.

Blom, R. M., Samuels, J. F., Riddle, M. A., Joseph Bienvenu, O., Grados, M. A., Reti, I. M., ... Nestadt, G. (2011). Association between a serotonin transporter promoter polymorphism (5HTTLPR) and personality disorder traits in a community sample. *Journal of Psychiatric Research, 45*(9), 1153–1159.

Blumenthal, H., Ham, L. S., Cloutier, R. M., Bacon, A. K., & Douglas, M. E. (2016). Social anxiety, disengagement coping, and alcohol-use behaviors among adolescents. *Anxiety, Stress, and Coping, 29*(4), 432–446.

Boesch, M., Sefidan, S., Ehlert, U., Annen, H., Wyss, T., Steptoe, A., & La Marca, R. (2014). Mood and autonomic responses to repeated exposure to the Trier Social Stress Test for Groups (TSST-G). *Psychoneuroendocrinology, 43*, 41–51.

Bögels, S. M., Alberts, M., & de Jong, P. J. (1996). Self-consciousness, self-focused attention, blushing propensity and fear of blushing. *Personality and Individual Differences, 21*(4), 573–581.

Bögels, S. M., Alden, L. E., Beidel, D. C., Clark, L. A., Pine, D. S., Stein, M. B., & Voncken, M. (2010). Social anxiety disorder: questions and answers for the DSM-V. *Depression and Anxiety, 27*(2), 168–189.

Bögels, S. M., Rijsemus, W., & Jong, P. J. D. (2002). Self-Focused Attention and Social Anxiety: The Effects of Experimentally Heightened Self-Awareness on Fear, Blushing, Cognitions, and Social Skills. *Cognitive Therapy and Research, 26*(4), 461–472.

Bögels, S. M., van Oosten, A., Muris, P., & Smulders, D. (2001). Familial correlates of social anxiety in children and adolescents. *Behaviour Research and Therapy, 39*(3), 273–287.

Bögels, S. M., Wijts, P., Oort, F. J., & Sallaerts, S. J. M. (2014). Psychodynamic psychotherapy versus cognitive behavior therapy for social anxiety disorder: an efficacy and partial effectiveness trial. *Depression and Anxiety, 31*(5), 363–373.

Bons, D., van den Broek, E., Scheepers, F., Herpers, P., Rommelse, N., Buitelaar, J. K., & Buitelaaar, J. K. (2013). Motor, emotional, and cognitive empathy in children and adolescents with autism spectrum disorder and conduct disorder. *Journal of Abnormal Child Psychology, 41*(3), 425–443.

Boone, M. L., McNeil, D. W., Masia, C. L., Turk, C. L., Carter, L. E., Ries, B. J., & Lewin, M. R. (1999). Multimodal comparisons of social phobia subtypes and avoidant personality disorder. *Journal of Anxiety Disorders, 13*(3), 271–292.

Bora, E., & Berk, M. (2016). Theory of mind in major depressive disorder: A meta-analysis. *Journal of Affective Disorders, 191*, 49–55.

Brazeau, C. M. L. R., Schroeder, R., Rovi, S., & Boyd, L. (2010). Relationships between medical student burnout, empathy, and professionalism climate. *Academic Medicine: Journal of the Association of American Medical Colleges, 85*(10 Suppl), S33-36.

Brook, C. A., & Schmidt, L. A. (2008). Social anxiety disorder: A review of environmental risk factors. *Neuropsychiatric Disease and Treatment, 4*(1), 123–143.

Brothers, L. (1990). The social brain: A project for integrating primate behavior and neurophysiology in a new domain. *Concepts in Neuroscience, 1,* 27–51.

Brownstein, M. J., Russell, J. T., & Gainer, H. (1980). Synthesis, transport, and release of posterior pituitary hormones. *Science (New York, N.Y.), 207*(4429), 373–378.

Bruce, S. E., Yonkers, K. A., Otto, M. W., Eisen, J. L., Weisberg, R. B., Pagano, M., ... Keller, M. B. (2005). Influence of psychiatric comorbidity on recovery and recurrence in generalized anxiety disorder, social phobia, and panic disorder: a 12-year prospective study. *The American Journal of Psychiatry, 162*(6), 1179–1187.

Brühl, A. B., Delsignore, A., Komossa, K., & Weidt, S. (2014). Neuroimaging in social anxiety disorder—a meta-analytic review resulting in a new neurofunctional model. *Neuroscience and Biobehavioral Reviews, 47,* 260–280.

Buchanan, T. W., Bagley, S. L., Stansfield, R. B., & Preston, S. D. (2012). The empathic, physiological resonance of stress. *Social Neuroscience, 7*(2), 191–201.

Buchanan, T. W., & Preston, S. D. (2014). Stress leads to prosocial action in immediate need situations. *Frontiers in Behavioral Neuroscience, 8.*

Buckert, M., Kudielka, B. M., Reuter, M., & Fiebach, C. J. (2012). The COMT Val158Met polymorphism modulates working memory performance under acute stress. *Psychoneuroendocrinology, 37*(11), 1810–1821.

Buhlmann, U., Gleiss, M. J. L., Rupf, L., Zschenderlein, K., & Kathmann, N. (2011). Modifying emotion recognition deficits in body dysmorphic disorder: an experimental investigation. *Depression and Anxiety, 28*(10), 924–931.

Buhlmann, U., Wacker, R., & Dziobek, I. (2015). Inferring other people's states of mind: Comparison across social anxiety, body dysmorphic, and obsessive-compulsive disorders. *Journal of Anxiety Disorders, 34,* 107–113.

Burke, H. M., Davis, M. C., Otte, C., & Mohr, D. C. (2005). Depression and cortisol responses to psychological stress: A meta-analysis. *Psychoneuroendocrinology, 30*(9), 846–856.

Burklund, L. J., Craske, M. G., Taylor, S., & Lieberman, M. D. (2015). Altered emotion regulation capacity in social phobia as a function of comorbidity. *Social Cognitive and Affective Neuroscience, 10*(2), 199–208.

Button, K. S., Ioannidis, J. P. A., Mokrysz, C., Nosek, B. A., Flint, J., Robinson, E. S. J., & Munafò, M. R. (2013). Power failure: why small sample size undermines the reliability of neuroscience. *Nature Reviews Neuroscience, 14*(5), 365–376.

Cacioppo, J. T., Cacioppo, S., Capitanio, J. P., & Cole, S. W. (2015). The neuroendocrinology of social isolation. *Annual Review of Psychology, 66,* 733–767.

Calder, A. J., Lawrence, A. D., & Young, A. W. (2001). Neuropsychology of fear and loathing. *Nature Reviews Neuroscience, 2*(5), 352–363.

Cannon, W. B. (1915). *Bodily changes in pain, hunger, fear and rage, an account of recent researches into the function of emotional excitement.* New York and London,: D. Appleton and Co.

Cannon, W. B. (1929). Organization for Physiological Homeostasis. *Physiological Reviews, 9*(3), 399–431.

Cannon, W. B. (1932). *The wisdom of the body.* New York, NY, US: W W Norton & Co.

Canton, J., Scott, K. M., & Glue, P. (2012). Optimal treatment of social phobia: systematic review and meta-analysis. *Neuropsychiatric Disease and Treatment, 8*, 203–215.

Caporael, L. R. (1997). The evolution of truly social cognition: the core configurations model. *Personality and Social Psychology Review: An Official Journal of the Society for Personality and Social Psychology, Inc, 1*(4), 276–298.

Cardoso, C., Kingdon, D., & Ellenbogen, M. A. (2014). A meta-analytic review of the impact of intranasal oxytocin administration on cortisol concentrations during laboratory tasks: moderation by method and mental health. *Psychoneuroendocrinology, 49*, 161–170.

Carré, A., Gierski, F., Lemogne, C., Tran, E., Raucher-Chéné, D., Béra-Potelle, C., ... Limosin, F. (2014). Linear association between social anxiety symptoms and neural activations to angry faces: from subclinical to clinical levels. *Social Cognitive and Affective Neuroscience, 9*(6), 880–886.

Carrigan, M. H., & Randall, C. L. (2003). Self-medication in social phobia: a review of the alcohol literature. *Addictive Behaviors, 28*(2), 269–284.

Carroll, D., Phillips, A. C., & Der, G. (2008). Body mass index, abdominal adiposity, obesity, and cardiovascular reactions to psychological stress in a large community sample. *Psychosomatic Medicine, 70*(6), 653–660.

Carter, S. A., & Wu, K. D. (2010). Relations among symptoms of social phobia subtypes, avoidant personality disorder, panic, and depression. *Behavior Therapy, 41*(1), 2–13.

Carver, C. S., Scheier, M. F., & Weintraub, J. K. (1989). Assessing coping strategies: a theoretically based approach. *Journal of Personality and Social Psychology, 56*(2), 267–283.

Cavanna, A. E., & Trimble, M. R. (2006). The precuneus: a review of its functional anatomy and behavioural correlates. *Brain, 129*(3), 564–583.

Cervenka, S., Hedman, E., Ikoma, Y., Djurfeldt, D. R., Rück, C., Halldin, C., & Lindefors, N. (2012). Changes in dopamine D2-receptor binding are associated to symptom reduction after psychotherapy in social anxiety disorder. *Translational Psychiatry, 2*, e120.

Chambless, D. L., Fydrich, T., & Rodebaugh, T. L. (2008). Generalized social phobia and avoidant personality disorder: meaningful distinction or useless duplication? *Depression and Anxiety, 25*(1), 8–19.

Charmandari, E., Tsigos, C., & Chrousos, G. P. (2005). Endocrinology of the stress response. *Annual Review of Physiology, 67*, 259–284.

Charney, D. S., Woods, S. W., Krystal, J. H., & Heninger, G. R. (1990). Serotonin function and human anxiety disorders. *Annals of the New York Academy of Sciences, 600*, 558-572-573.

Chartier, M. J., Walker, J. R., & Stein, M. B. (2001). Social phobia and potential childhood risk factors in a community sample. *Psychological Medicine, 31*(2), 307–315.

Chavira, D. A., & Stein, M. B. (2005). Childhood social anxiety disorder: from understanding to treatment. *Child and Adolescent Psychiatric Clinics of North America, 14*(4), 797–818, ix.

Chen, F. S., Kumsta, R., von Dawans, B., Monakhov, M., Ebstein, R. P., & Heinrichs, M. (2011). Common oxytocin receptor gene (OXTR) polymorphism and social support interact to reduce stress in humans. *Proceedings of the National Academy of Sciences of the United States of America, 108*(50), 19937–19942.

Chen, M., & Bargh, J. A. (1999). Consequences of Automatic Evaluation: Immediate Behavioral Predispositions to Approach or Avoid the Stimulus. *Personality and Social Psychology Bulletin, 25*(2), 215–224.

131

131

Chrousos, G. P. (1992). Regulation and dysregulation of the hypothalamic-pituitary-adrenal axis. The corticotropin-releasing hormone perspective. *Endocrinology and Metabolism Clinics of North America, 21*(4), 833–858.

Chrousos, G. P. (1995). The Hypothalamic–Pituitary–Adrenal Axis and Immune-Mediated Inflammation. *New England Journal of Medicine, 332*(20), 1351–1363.

Chrousos, G. P. (2009). Stress and disorders of the stress system. *Nature Reviews Endocrinology, 5*(7), 374–381.

Chrousos, G. P., & Gold, P. (1992). The concepts of stress and stress system disorders: Overview of physical and behavioral homeostasis. *JAMA, 267*(9), 1244–1252.

Cisler, J. M., & Koster, E. H. W. (2010). Mechanisms of attentional biases towards threat in anxiety disorders: An integrative review. *Clinical Psychology Review, 30*(2), 203–216.

Clark, D. A., & Beck, A. T. (2011). *Cognitive Therapy of Anxiety Disorders: Science and Practice*. Guilford Press.

Clark, D. M. (2005). A cognitive perspective on social phobia. *The Essential Handbook of Social Anxiety for Clinicians*, 193–218.

Clark, D. M., Ehlers, A., Hackmann, A., McManus, F., Fennell, M., Grey, N., ... Wild, J. (2006). Cognitive therapy versus exposure and applied relaxation in social phobia: A randomized controlled trial. *Journal of Consulting and Clinical Psychology, 74*(3), 568–578.

Clark, D. M., Ehlers, A., McManus, F., Hackmann, A., Fennell, M., Campbell, H., ... Louis, B. (2003). Cognitive therapy versus fluoxetine in generalized social phobia: a randomized placebo-controlled trial. *Journal of Consulting and Clinical Psychology, 71*(6), 1058–1067.

Clark, D. M., & Wells, A. (1995). A cognitive model of social phobia. In R. G. Heimberg (Ed.), *Social Phobia: Diagnosis, Assessment, and Treatment* (pp. 69–93). Guilford Press.

Clark, J. V., & Arkowitz, H. (1975). Social anxiety and self-evaluation of interpersonal performance. *Psychological Reports, 36*(1), 211–221.

Clauss, J. A., Avery, S. N., VanDerKlok, R. M., Rogers, B. P., Cowan, R. L., Benningfield, M. M., & Blackford, J. U. (2014). Neurocircuitry underlying risk and resilience to social anxiety disorder. *Depression and Anxiety, 31*(10), 822–833.

Cleary, P. D., & Kessler, R. C. (1982). The Estimation and Interpretation of Modifier Effects. *Journal of Health and Social Behavior, 23*(2), 159–169.

Cohen, J., Cohen, P., & West, S. G. (1983). *Applied Multiple Regression/Correlation Analysis for the Behavioral Sciences* (2nd ed.). Mahwah, N.J: Taylor & Francis Ltd.

Cole, S. W. (2014). Human social genomics. *PLoS Genetics, 10*(8), e1004601.

Coll, C. G., Kagan, J., & Reznick, J. S. (1984). Behavioral Inhibition in Young Children. *Child Development, 55*(3), 1005–1019.

Condren, R. M., O'Neill, A., Ryan, M. C. M., Barrett, P., & Thakore, J. H. (2002). HPA axis response to a psychological stressor in generalised social phobia. *Psychoneuroendocrinology, 27*(6), 693–703.

Coplan, R. J., Rubin, K. H., Fox, N. A., Calkins, S. D., & Stewart, S. L. (1994). Being alone, playing alone, and acting alone: distinguishing among reticence and passive and active solitude in young children. *Child Development, 65*(1), 129–137.

Cougle, J. R., Keough, M. E., Riccardi, C. J., & Sachs-Ericsson, N. (2009). Anxiety disorders and suicidality in the National Comorbidity Survey-Replication. *Journal of Psychiatric Research, 43*(9), 825–829.

Couture, S. M., Penn, D. L., & Roberts, D. L. (2006). The Functional Significance of Social Cognition in Schizophrenia: A Review. *Schizophrenia Bulletin, 32*(suppl_1), S44–S63.

Craig, A. D. B. (2009). How do you feel--now? The anterior insula and human awareness. *Nature Reviews. Neuroscience, 10*(1), 59–70.

Craig, I. W. (2007). The importance of stress and genetic variation in human aggression. *BioEssays: News and Reviews in Molecular, Cellular and Developmental Biology, 29*(3), 227–236.

Creed, A. T., & Funder, D. C. (1998). Social anxiety: from the inside and outside. *Personality and Individual Differences, 25*(1), 19–33.

Damasio, A. R., Grabowski, T. J., Bechara, A., Damasio, H., Ponto, L. L., Parvizi, J., & Hichwa, R. D. (2000). Subcortical and cortical brain activity during the feeling of self-generated emotions. *Nature Neuroscience, 3*(10), 1049–1056.

Danti, S., Ricciardi, E., Gentili, C., Gobbini, M. I., Pietrini, P., & Guazzelli, M. (2010). Is Social Phobia a "Mis-Communication" Disorder? Brain Functional Connectivity during Face Perception Differs between Patients with Social Phobia and Healthy Control Subjects. *Frontiers in Systems Neuroscience, 4*, 152.

Davidson, J. R. T., Foa, E. B., Huppert, J. D., Keefe, F. J., Franklin, M. E., Compton, J. S., ... Gadde, K. M. (2004). Fluoxetine, comprehensive cognitive behavioral therapy, and placebo in generalized social phobia. *Archives of General Psychiatry, 61*(10), 1005–1013.

Davis, M. H. (1983). Measuring individual differences in empathy: Evidence for a multidimensional approach. *Journal of Personality and Social Psychology, 44*(1), 113–126.

Davis, M., & Whalen, P. J. (2001). The amygdala: vigilance and emotion. *Molecular Psychiatry, 6*(1), 13–34.

Dawans, B. von. (2008). *Neuropeptidergic Modulation of Social Behavior in Health and Social Phobia*. Cuvillier Verlag.

de Kloet, E. R., Oitzl, M. S., & Joëls, M. (1999). Stress and cognition: are corticosteroids good or bad guys? *Trends in Neurosciences, 22*(10), 422–426.

de Kloet, E. R., Rots, N. Y., & Cools, A. R. (1996). Brain-corticosteroid hormone dialogue: slow and persistent. *Cellular and Molecular Neurobiology, 16*(3), 345–356.

De Kloet, E. R., Sutanto, W., Rots, N., van Haarst, A., van den Berg, D., Oitzl, M., ... Voorhuis, D. (1991). Plasticity and function of brain corticosteroid receptors during aging. *Acta Endocrinologica, 125 Suppl 1*, 65–72.

De Kloet, E. R., Vreugdenhil, E., Oitzl, M. S., & Joëls, M. (1998). Brain corticosteroid receptor balance in health and disease. *Endocrine Reviews, 19*(3), 269–301.

de Rosnay, M., Cooper, P. J., Tsigaras, N., & Murray, L. (2006). Transmission of social anxiety from mother to infant: an experimental study using a social referencing paradigm. *Behaviour Research and Therapy, 44*(8), 1165–1175.

de Vignemont, F., & Singer, T. (2006). The empathic brain: how, when and why? *Trends in Cognitive Sciences, 10*(10), 435–441.

Decety, J. (2011). The neuroevolution of empathy. *Annals of the New York Academy of Sciences, 1231*, 35–45.

Decety, J., & Lamm, C. (2009). The biological basis of empathy. *Handbook of Neuroscience for the Behavioral Sciences. New York: John Wiley and Sons*, 940–957.

Derogatis, L. R., & Melisaratos, N. (1983). The Brief Symptom Inventory: an introductory report. *Psychological Medicine, 13*(3), 595–605.

DeVries, A. C., Guptaa, T., Cardillo, S., Cho, M., & Carter, C. S. (2002). Corticotropin-releasing factor induces social preferences in male prairie voles. *Psychoneuroendocrinology, 27*(6), 705–714.

DeWall, C. N., & Baumeister, R. F. (2006). Alone but feeling no pain: Effects of social exclusion on physical pain tolerance and pain threshold, affective forecasting, and interpersonal empathy. *Journal of Personality and Social Psychology, 91*(1), 1–15.

DeWit, D. J., Ogborne, A., Offord, D. R., & MacDonald, K. (1999). Antecedents of the risk of recovery from DSM-III-R social phobia. *Psychological Medicine, 29*(3), 569–582.

Di Simplicio, M., Massey-Chase, R., Cowen, P. J., & Harmer, C. J. (2009). Oxytocin enhances processing of positive versus negative emotional information in healthy male volunteers. *Journal of Psychopharmacology (Oxford, England), 23*(3), 241–248.

Dickerson, S. S., & Kemeny, M. E. (2004). Acute Stressors and Cortisol Responses: A Theoretical Integration and Synthesis of Laboratory Research. *Psychological Bulletin, 130*(3), 355–391.

Dieleman, G. C., Huizink, A. C., Tulen, J. H. M., Utens, E. M. W. J., Creemers, H. E., van der Ende, J., & Verhulst, F. C. (2015). Alterations in HPA-axis and autonomic nervous system functioning in childhood anxiety disorders point to a chronic stress hypothesis. *Psychoneuroendocrinology, 51*, 135–150.

Ding, J., Chen, H., Qiu, C., Liao, W., Warwick, J. M., Duan, X., ... Gong, Q. (2011). Disrupted functional connectivity in social anxiety disorder: a resting-state fMRI study. *Magnetic Resonance Imaging, 29*(5), 701–711.

Dinsdale, N., & Crespi, B. J. (2013). The borderline empathy paradox: evidence and conceptual models for empathic enhancements in borderline personality disorder. *Journal of Personality Disorders, 27*(2), 172–195.

Ditzen, B., & Heinrichs, M. (2014). Psychobiology of social support: The social dimension of stress buffering. *Restorative Neurology and Neuroscience, 32*(1), 149-62.

Ditzen, B., Schaer, M., Gabriel, B., Bodenmann, G., Ehlert, U., & Heinrichs, M. (2009). Intranasal oxytocin increases positive communication and reduces cortisol levels during couple conflict. *Biological Psychiatry, 65*(9), 728–731.

Doehrmann, O., Ghosh, S. S., Polli, F. E., Reynolds, G. O., Horn, F., Keshavan, A., ... Gabrieli, J. D. (2013). Predicting Treatment Response in Social Anxiety Disorder From Functional Magnetic Resonance Imaging. *JAMA Psychiatry (Chicago, Ill.), 70*(1).

Domes, G., Heinrichs, M., Gläscher, J., Büchel, C., Braus, D. F., & Herpertz, S. C. (2007). Oxytocin attenuates amygdala responses to emotional faces regardless of valence. *Biological Psychiatry, 62*(10), 1187–1190.

Domes, G., Heinrichs, M., Michel, A., Berger, C., & Herpertz, S. C. (2007). Oxytocin improves "mind-reading" in humans. *Biological Psychiatry, 61*(6), 731–733.

Domes, G., Schulze, L., & Herpertz, S. C. (2009). Emotion recognition in borderline personality disorder-a review of the literature. *Journal of Personality Disorders, 23*(1), 6–19.

Domes, G., Sibold, M., Schulze, L., Lischke, A., Herpertz, S. C., & Heinrichs, M. (2013). Intranasal oxytocin increases covert attention to positive social cues. *Psychological Medicine, 43*(8), 1747–1753.

Domschke, K., Stevens, S., Beck, B., Baffa, A., Hohoff, C., Deckert, J., & Gerlach, A. L. (2008). Blushing propensity in social anxiety disorder: influence of serotonin transporter gene variation. *Journal of Neural Transmission, 116*(6), 663–666.

Donaldson, Z. R., & Young, L. J. (2008). Oxytocin, vasopressin, and the neurogenetics of sociality. *Science (New York, N.Y.), 322*(5903), 900–904.

Dvash, J., & Shamay-Tsoory, S. G. (2014). Theory of Mind and Empathy as Multidimensional Constructs: Neurological Foundations. *Topics in Language Disorders, 34*(4), 282–295.

Dziobek, I., Rogers, K., Fleck, S., Bahnemann, M., Heekeren, H. R., Wolf, O. T., & Convit, A. (2007). Dissociation of Cognitive and Emotional Empathy in Adults with Asperger Syndrome Using the Multifaceted Empathy Test (MET). *Journal of Autism and Developmental Disorders, 38*(3), 464–473.

Earle, T. L., Linden, W., & Weinberg, J. (1999). Differential effects of harassment on cardiovascular and salivary cortisol stress reactivity and recovery in women and men. *Journal of Psychosomatic Research*, *46*(2), 125–141.

Ebner, K., Bosch, O. J., Krömer, S. A., Singewald, N., & Neumann, I. D. (2005). Release of oxytocin in the rat central amygdala modulates stress-coping behavior and the release of excitatory amino acids. *Neuropsychopharmacology: Official Publication of the American College of Neuropsychopharmacology*, *30*(2), 223–230.

Edelmann, R. J., & Baker, S. R. (2002). Self-reported and actual physiological responses in social phobia. *British Journal of Clinical Psychology*, *41*(1), 1–14.

Eikenaes, I., Hummelen, B., Abrahamsen, G., Andrea, H., & Wilberg, T. (2013). Personality functioning in patients with avoidant personality disorder and social phobia. *Journal of Personality Disorders*, *27*(6), 746.

Eisenberg, N. (2000). Emotion, regulation, and moral development. *Annual Review of Psychology*, *51*, 665–697.

Eisenberg, N. (2007). Empathy-related responding and prosocial behaviour. *Novartis Foundation Symposium*, *278*, 71-80-96, 216–221.

Eisenberg, N., & Miller, P. A. (1987). The relation of empathy to prosocial and related behaviors. *Psychological Bulletin*, *101*(1), 91–119.

Elenkov, null, & Chrousos, G. P. (1999). Stress Hormones, Th1/Th2 patterns, Pro/Anti-inflammatory Cytokines and Susceptibility to Disease. *Trends in Endocrinology and Metabolism: TEM*, *10*(9), 359–368.

Elzinga, B. M., Spinhoven, P., Berretty, E., de Jong, P., & Roelofs, K. (2010). The role of childhood abuse in HPA-axis reactivity in Social Anxiety Disorder: a pilot study. *Biological Psychology*, *83*(1), 1–6.

Erwin, B. A., Heimberg, R. G., Juster, H., & Mindlin, M. (2002). Comorbid anxiety and mood disorders among persons with social anxiety disorder. *Behaviour Research and Therapy*, *40*(1), 19–35.

Erwin, B. A., Heimberg, R. G., Schneier, F. R., & Liebowitz, M. R. (2003). Anger experience and expression in social anxiety disorder: Pretreatment profile and predictors of attrition and response to cognitive-behavioral treatment. *Behavior Therapy*, *34*(3), 331–350.

Eslinger, P. J. (1998). Neurological and neuropsychological bases of empathy. *European Neurology*, *39*(4), 193–199.

Etkin, A. (2012). Neurobiology of Anxiety: From Neural Circuits to Novel Solutions? *Depression and Anxiety*, *29*(5), 355–358.

Etkin, A., & Wager, T. D. (2007). Functional Neuroimaging of Anxiety: A Meta-Analysis of Emotional Processing in PTSD, Social Anxiety Disorder, and Specific Phobia. *American Journal of Psychiatry*, *164*(10), 1476–1488.

Evans, K. C., Wright, C. I., Wedig, M. M., Gold, A. L., Pollack, M. H., & Rauch, S. L. (2008). A functional MRI study of amygdala responses to angry schematic faces in social anxiety disorder. *Depression and Anxiety*, *25*(6), 496–505.

Farmer, A., & Kashdan, T. B. (2012). Social anxiety and emotion regulation in daily life: Spillover effects on positive and negative social events. *Cognitive Behaviour Therapy*, *41*(2), 152–162.

Farmer, A., & Kashdan, T. B. (2015). Stress sensitivity and stress generation in social anxiety disorder: A temporal process approach. *Journal of Abnormal Psychology*, *124*(1), 102–114.

Fedoroff, I. C., & Taylor, S. (2001). Psychological and Pharmacological Treatments of Social Phobia: A Meta-Analysis. *Journal of Clinical Psychopharmacology*, *21*(3), 311–324.

Fehm, L., Pelissolo, A., Furmark, T., & Wittchen, H.-U. (2005). Size and burden of social phobia in Europe. *European Neuropsychopharmacology: The Journal of the European College of Neuropsychopharmacology, 15*(4), 453–462.

Fehr, E., & Fischbacher, U. (2003). The nature of human altruism. *Nature, 425*(6960), 785–791.

Fehr, E., & Gächter, S. (2002). Altruistic punishment in humans. *Nature, 415*(6868), 137–140.

Feldman, R., Gordon, I., Schneiderman, I., Weisman, O., & Zagoory-Sharon, O. (2010). Natural variations in maternal and paternal care are associated with systematic changes in oxytocin following parent-infant contact. *Psychoneuroendocrinology, 35*(8), 1133–1141.

Feldman, R., Weller, A., Zagoory-Sharon, O., & Levine, A. (2007). Evidence for a neuroendocrinological foundation of human affiliation: plasma oxytocin levels across pregnancy and the postpartum period predict mother-infant bonding. *Psychological Science, 18*(11), 965–970.

Feshbach, N. D. (1984). Empathy, Empathy Training and the Regulation of Aggression in Elementary School Children. In D. R. M. Kaplan, D. V. J. Konečni, & D. R. W. Novaco (Eds.), *Aggression in Children and Youth* (pp. 192–208). Springer Netherlands.

Feshbach, N. D., & Feshbach, S. (1982). Empathy training and the regulation of aggression: Potentialities and limitations. *Academic Psychology Bulletin, 4*(3), 399–413.

Feske, U., & Chambless, D. L. (1995). Cognitive behavioral versus exposure only treatment for social phobia: A meta-analysis. *Behavior Therapy, 26*(4), 695–720.

Fett, A.-K. J., Shergill, S. S., & Krabbendam, L. (2015). Social neuroscience in psychiatry: unravelling the neural mechanisms of social dysfunction. *Psychological Medicine, 45*(06), 1145–1165.

Fett, A.-K. J., Viechtbauer, W., Dominguez, M.-G., Penn, D. L., van Os, J., & Krabbendam, L. (2011). The relationship between neurocognition and social cognition with functional outcomes in schizophrenia: a meta-analysis. *Neuroscience and Biobehavioral Reviews, 35*(3), 573–588.

Fisak, B., & Grills-Taquechel, A. E. (2007). Parental Modeling, Reinforcement, and Information Transfer: Risk Factors in the Development of Child Anxiety? *Clinical Child and Family Psychology Review, 10*(3), 213–231.

Fischbacher, U. (2007). z-Tree: Zurich toolbox for ready-made economic experiments. *Experimental Economics, 10*(2), 171–178.

Foa, E. B., Franklin, M. E., Perry, K. J., & Herbert, J. D. (1996). Cognitive biases in generalized social phobia. *Journal of Abnormal Psychology, 105*(3), 433–439.

Foley, P., & Kirschbaum, C. (2010). Human hypothalamus–pituitary–adrenal axis responses to acute psychosocial stress in laboratory settings. *Neuroscience & Biobehavioral Reviews, 35*(1), 91–96.

Folkman, S. (1997). Positive psychological states and coping with severe stress. *Social Science & Medicine (1982), 45*(8), 1207–1221.

Folkman, S. (2008). The case for positive emotions in the stress process. *Anxiety, Stress, and Coping, 21*(1), 3–14.

Forray, M. I., & Gysling, K. (2004). Role of noradrenergic projections to the bed nucleus of the stria terminalis in the regulation of the hypothalamic-pituitary-adrenal axis. *Brain Research. Brain Research Reviews, 47*(1–3), 145–160.

Fox, N. A., Henderson, H. A., Marshall, P. J., Nichols, K. E., & Ghera, M. M. (2005). Behavioral inhibition: linking biology and behavior within a developmental framework. *Annual Review of Psychology, 56*, 235–262.

Franke, G. H. (2000). *BSI -Brief Symptom Inventory - Deutsche Version*. Göttingen: Beltz.

Fraser, O. N., Stahl, D., & Aureli, F. (2008). Stress reduction through consolation in chimpanzees. *Proceedings of the National Academy of Sciences, 105*(25), 8557–8562.

Freeman, R. (2006). Assessment of cardiovascular autonomic function. *Clinical Neurophysiology: Official Journal of the International Federation of Clinical Neurophysiology, 117*(4), 716–730.

Freeman, T. W., & Roca, V. (2001). Gun use, attitudes toward violence, and aggression among combat veterans with chronic posttraumatic stress disorder. *Journal of Nervous and Mental Diseases, 189*(5), 317–320.

Frick, A., Howner, K., Fischer, H., Kristiansson, M., & Furmark, T. (2013). Altered fusiform connectivity during processing of fearful faces in social anxiety disorder. *Translational Psychiatry, 3*(10), e312.

Frith, C. D. (2007). The social brain? *Philosophical Transactions of the Royal Society of London. Series B, Biological Sciences, 362*(1480), 671–678.

Frith, C. D., & Frith, U. (2006). The neural basis of mentalizing. *Neuron, 50*(4), 531–534.

Frith, C. D., & Frith, U. (2007). Social cognition in humans. *Current Biology: CB, 17*(16), R724-732.

Furlan, P. M., DeMartinis, N., Schweizer, E., Rickels, K., & Lucki, I. (2001). Abnormal salivary cortisol levels in social phobic patients in response to acute psychological but not physical stress. *Biological Psychiatry, 50*(4), 254–259.

Furmark, T., Henningsson, S., Appel, L., Åhs, F., Linnman, C., Pissiota, A., ... Fredrikson, M. (2009). Genotype over-diagnosis in amygdala responsiveness: affective processing in social anxiety disorder. *Journal of Psychiatry & Neuroscience: JPN, 34*(1), 30–40.

Furmark, T., Tillfors, M., Garpenstrand, H., Marteinsdottir, I., Långström, B., Oreland, L., & Fredrikson, M. (2004). Serotonin transporter polymorphism related to amygdala excitability and symptom severity in patients with social phobia. *Neuroscience Letters, 362*(3), 189–192.

Fydrich, T., Chambless, D. L., Perry, K. J., Buergener, F., & Beazley, M. B. (1998). Behavioral assessment of social performance: a rating system for social phobia. *Behaviour Research and Therapy, 36*(10), 995–1010.

Fyer, A. J., Mannuzza, S., Chapman, T. F., Liebowitz, M. R., & Klein, D. F. (1993). A direct interview family study of social phobia. *Archives of General Psychiatry, 50*(4), 286–293.

Fyer, A. J., Mannuzza, S., Chapman, T. F., Martin, L. Y., & Klein, D. F. (1995). Specificity in familial aggregation of phobic disorders. *Archives of General Psychiatry, 52*(7), 564–573.

Gaebler, M., Daniels, J. K., Lamke, J.-P., Fydrich, T., & Walter, H. (2013). Heart rate variability and its neural correlates during emotional face processing in social anxiety disorder. *Biological Psychology, 94*(2), 319–330.

Gallagher, H. L., & Frith, C. D. (2003). Functional imaging of "theory of mind." *Trends in Cognitive Sciences, 7*(2), 77–83.

Ganasen, K. A., Ipser, J. C., & Stein, D. J. (2010). Augmentation of cognitive behavioral therapy with pharmacotherapy. *The Psychiatric Clinics of North America, 33*(3), 687–699.

Geary, D. C., & Flinn, M. V. (2002). Sex differences in behavioral and hormonal response to social threat: Commentary on Taylor et al. (2000). *Psychological Review, 109*(4), 745–750.

Gelernter, J., Page, G. P., Stein, M. B., & Woods, S. W. (2004). Genome-wide linkage scan for loci predisposing to social phobia: evidence for a chromosome 16 risk locus. *The American Journal of Psychiatry, 161*(1), 59–66.

Gentili, C., Cristea, I. A., Angstadt, M., Klumpp, H., Tozzi, L., Phan, K. L., & Pietrini, P. (2016). Beyond emotions: A meta-analysis of neural response within face processing system in social anxiety. *Experimental Biology and Medicine (Maywood, N.J.)*, *241*(3), 225–237.

Gerlach, A. L., Wilhelm, F. H., Gruber, K., & Roth, W. T. (2001). Blushing and physiological arousability in social phobia. *Journal of Abnormal Psychology*, *110*(2), 247–258.

Giménez, M., Pujol, J., Ortiz, H., Soriano-Mas, C., López-Solà, M., Farré, M., ... Martín-Santos, R. (2012). Altered brain functional connectivity in relation to perception of scrutiny in social anxiety disorder. *Psychiatry Research*, *202*(3), 214–223.

Gleichgerrcht, E., & Decety, J. (2013). Empathy in Clinical Practice: How Individual Dispositions, Gender, and Experience Moderate Empathic Concern, Burnout, and Emotional Distress in Physicians. *PLOS ONE*, *8*(4), e61526.

Gogtay, N., Giedd, J. N., Lusk, L., Hayashi, K. M., Greenstein, D., Vaituzis, A. C., ... Thompson, P. M. (2004). Dynamic mapping of human cortical development during childhood through early adulthood. *Proceedings of the National Academy of Sciences of the United States of America*, *101*(21), 8174–8179.

Goldin, P. R., & Gross, J. J. (2010). Effects of mindfulness-based stress reduction (MBSR) on emotion regulation in social anxiety disorder. *Emotion (Washington, D.C.)*, *10*(1), 83–91.

Goldin, P. R., Manber, T., Hakimi, S., Canli, T., & Gross, J. J. (2009). Neural bases of social anxiety disorder: emotional reactivity and cognitive regulation during social and physical threat. *Archives of General Psychiatry*, *66*(2), 170–180.

Gorman, J. M., & Kent, J. M. (1999). SSRIs and SNRIs: broad spectrum of efficacy beyond major depression. *The Journal of Clinical Psychiatry*, *60 Suppl 4*, 33–38; discussion 39.

Gould, R. A., Buckminster, S., Pollack, M. H., Otto, M. W., & Massachusetts, L. Y. (1997). Cognitive-Behavioral and Pharmacological Treatment for Social Phobia: A Meta-Analysis. *Clinical Psychology: Science and Practice*, *4*(4), 291–306.

Grant, B. F., Hasin, D. S., Blanco, C., Stinson, F. S., Chou, S. P., Goldstein, R. B., ... Huang, B. (2005). The Epidemiology of Social Anxiety Disorder in the United States: Results From the National Epidemiologic Survey on Alcohol and Related Conditions. *The Journal of Clinical Psychiatry*, *66*(11), 1351–1361.

Grant, B. F., Hasin, D. S., Stinson, F. S., Dawson, D. A., Patricia Chou, S., June Ruan, W., & Huang, B. (2005). Co-occurrence of 12-month mood and anxiety disorders and personality disorders in the US: results from the national epidemiologic survey on alcohol and related conditions. *Journal of Psychiatric Research*, *39*(1), 1–9.

Grant, S., Aitchison, T., Henderson, E., Christie, J., Zare, S., McMurray, J., & Dargie, H. (1999). A comparison of the reproducibility and the sensitivity to change of visual analogue scales, Borg scales, and Likert scales in normal subjects during submaximal exercise. *Chest*, *116*(5), 1208–1217.

Gray, T. S. (1993). Amygdaloid CRF pathways. Role in autonomic, neuroendocrine, and behavioral responses to stress. *Annals of the New York Academy of Sciences*, *697*, 53–60.

Green, M. F., Horan, W. P., & Lee, J. (2015). Social cognition in schizophrenia. *Nature Reviews. Neuroscience*, *16*(10), 620–631.

Green, M. F., Penn, D. L., Bentall, R., Carpenter, W. T., Gaebel, W., Gur, R. C., ... Heinssen, R. (2008). Social Cognition in Schizophrenia: An NIMH Workshop on Definitions, Assessment, and Research Opportunities. *Schizophrenia Bulletin*, *34*(6), 1211–1220.

Grosbras, M.-H., & Paus, T. (2006). Brain networks involved in viewing angry hands or faces. *Cerebral Cortex (New York, N.Y.: 1991)*, *16*(8), 1087–1096.

Gross, J. J. (2002). Emotion regulation: affective, cognitive, and social consequences. *Psychophysiology*, *39*(3), 281–291.

Gross, R., Olfson, M., Gameroff, M. J., Shea, S., Feder, A., Lantigua, R., ... Weissman, M. M. (2005). Social anxiety disorder in primary care. *General Hospital Psychiatry*, *27*(3), 161–168.

Grossman, F. H. W. (2001). Gender Differences in Psychophysiological Responses to Speech Stress Among Older Social Phobics. *Psychosomatic Medicine*, *63*(5), 765–77.

Grynberg, D., Chang, B., Corneille, O., Maurage, P., Vermeulen, N., Berthoz, S., & Luminet, O. (2012). Alexithymia and the processing of emotional facial expressions (EFEs): systematic review, unanswered questions and further perspectives. *PloS One*, *7*(8), e42429.

Guastella, A. J., Howard, A. L., Dadds, M. R., Mitchell, P., & Carson, D. S. (2009). A randomized controlled trial of intranasal oxytocin as an adjunct to exposure therapy for social anxiety disorder. *Psychoneuroendocrinology*, *34*(6), 917–923.

Guastella, A. J., Mitchell, P. B., & Dadds, M. R. (2008). Oxytocin increases gaze to the eye region of human faces. *Biological Psychiatry*, *63*(1), 3–5.

Gunnar, M., & Quevedo, K. (2007). The neurobiology of stress and development. *Annual Review of Psychology*, *58*, 145–173.

Güroğlu, B., van den Bos, W., van Dijk, E., Rombouts, S. A. R. B., & Crone, E. A. (2011). Dissociable brain networks involved in development of fairness considerations: understanding intentionality behind unfairness. *NeuroImage*, *57*(2), 634–641.

Hahn, A., Stein, P., Windischberger, C., Weissenbacher, A., Spindelegger, C., Moser, E., ... Lanzenberger, R. (2011). Reduced resting-state functional connectivity between amygdala and orbitofrontal cortex in social anxiety disorder. *NeuroImage*, *56*(3), 881–889.

Hakamata, Y., Lissek, S., Bar-Haim, Y., Britton, J. C., Fox, N., Leibenluft, E., ... Pine, D. S. (2010). Attention Bias Modification Treatment: A meta-analysis towards the establishment of novel treatment for anxiety. *Biological Psychiatry*, *68*(11), 982–990.

Hallett, V., Ronald, A., Rijsdijk, F., & Happé, F. (2012). Disentangling the Associations Between Autistic-Like and Internalizing Traits: A Community Based Twin Study. *Journal of Abnormal Child Psychology*, *40*(5), 815–827.

Hames, J. L., Hagan, C. R., & Joiner, T. E. (2013). Interpersonal processes in depression. *Annual Review of Clinical Psychology*, *9*, 355–377.

Hankin, B. L., & Abela, D. J. R. Z. (2005). *Development of Psychopathology: A Vulnerability-Stress Perspective* (New.). Manchester; New York: New York: Sage Publications, Inc.

Hariri, A. R., Mattay, V. S., Tessitore, A., Kolachana, B., Fera, F., Goldman, D., ... Weinberger, D. R. (2002). Serotonin transporter genetic variation and the response of the human amygdala. *Science (New York, N.Y.)*, *297*(5580), 400–403.

Haug, T. T., Blomhoff, S., Hellström, K., Holme, I., Humble, M., Madsbu, H. P., & Wold, J. E. (2003). Exposure therapy and sertraline in social phobia: I-year follow-up of a randomised controlled trial. *The British Journal of Psychiatry*, *182*(4), 312–318.

Hautzinger, M., Keller, F., & Kühner, C. (2006). *BDI-II-Beck Depressions- Inventar*. Frankfurt am Main: Harcourt Test Services.

Hayes, A. F. (2013). *Introduction to Mediation, Moderation, and Conditional Process Analysis: A Regression-Based Approach*. Guilford Press.

Heils, A., Teufel, A., Petri, S., Stöber, G., Riederer, P., Bengel, D., & Lesch, K. P. (1996). Allelic variation of human serotonin transporter gene expression. *Journal of Neurochemistry*, *66*(6), 2621–2624.

Heim, C., Ehlert, U., & Hellhammer, D. H. (2000). The potential role of hypocortisolism in the pathophysiology of stress-related bodily disorders. *Psychoneuroendocrinology*, *25*(1), 1–35.

Heim, C., & Nemeroff, C. B. (2001). The role of childhood trauma in the neurobiology of mood and anxiety disorders: preclinical and clinical studies. *Biological Psychiatry*, *49*(12), 1023–1039.

Heimberg, R. G., Hofmann, S. G., Liebowitz, M. R., Schneier, F. R., Smits, J. A. J., Stein, M. B., ... Craske, M. G. (2014). Social anxiety disorder in DSM-5. *Depression and Anxiety*, *31*(6), 472–479.

Heimberg, R. G., Hope, D. A., Dodge, C. S., & Becker, R. E. (1990). DSM-III-R subtypes of social phobia. Comparison of generalized social phobics and public speaking phobics. *The Journal of Nervous and Mental Disease*, *178*(3), 172–179.

Heimberg, R. G., Horner, K. J., Juster, H. R., Safren, S. A., Brown, E. J., Schneier, F. R., & Liebowitz, M. R. (1999). Psychometric properties of the Liebowitz social anxiety scale. *Psychological Medicine*, *29*(01), 199–212.

Heinrichs, M., Baumgartner, T., Kirschbaum, C., & Ehlert, U. (2003). Social support and oxytocin interact to suppress cortisol and subjective responses to psychosocial stress. *Biological Psychiatry*, *54*(12), 1389–1398.

Heinrichs, M., Chen, F., & Domes, G. (2013). Social neuropeptides in the human brain. In S. Baron-Cohen, H. Tager-Flusberg, & M. Lombardo (Eds.), *Understanding other minds* (3rd ed.). Oxford: Oxyford University Press.

Heinrichs, M., & Domes, G. (2008). Neuropeptides and social behaviour: effects of oxytocin and vasopressin in humans. *Progress in Brain Research*, *170*, 337–350.

Heinrichs, M., von Dawans, B., & Domes, G. (2009). Oxytocin, vasopressin, and human social behavior. *Frontiers in Neuroendocrinology*, *30*(4), 548–557.

Helfinstein, S. M., Fox, N. A., & Pine, D. S. (2012). Approach–withdrawal and the role of the striatum in the temperament of behavioral inhibition. *Developmental Psychology*, *48*(3), 815–826.

Herman, J. P., Figueiredo, H., Mueller, N. K., Ulrich-Lai, Y., Ostrander, M. M., Choi, D. C., & Cullinan, W. E. (2003). Central mechanisms of stress integration: hierarchical circuitry controlling hypothalamo-pituitary-adrenocortical responsiveness. *Frontiers in Neuroendocrinology*, *24*(3), 151–180.

Herwig, U., Kaffenberger, T., Baumgartner, T., & Jäncke, L. (2007). Neural correlates of a "pessimistic" attitude when anticipating events of unknown emotional valence. *NeuroImage*, *34*(2), 848–858.

Hettema, J. M., Neale, M. C., & Kendler, K. S. (2001). A review and meta-analysis of the genetic epidemiology of anxiety disorders. *The American Journal of Psychiatry*, *158*(10), 1568–1578.

Hettema, J. M., Neale, M. C., Myers, J. M., Prescott, C. A., & Kendler, K. S. (2006). A Population-Based Twin Study of the Relationship Between Neuroticism and Internalizing Disorders. *American Journal of Psychiatry*, *163*(5), 857–864.

Hezel, D. M., & McNally, R. J. (2014). Theory of Mind Impairments in Social Anxiety Disorder. *Behavior Therapy*, *45*(4), 530–540.

Hirsch, C. R., & Mathews, A. (2000). Impaired positive inferential bias in social phobia. *Journal of Abnormal Psychology*, *109*(4), 705–712.

Hoffmann, M. L. (2008). Empthy and Prosocial Behavior. In M. Lewis, J. Haviland-Jones, & L. F. Barrett (Eds.), *Handbook of Emotions* (3rd ed.). New York: Guilford Press.

140

Hofmann, S. G. (2004). Cognitive Mediation of Treatment Change in Social Phobia. Journal of Consulting and Clinical Psychology, 72(3), 392–399.

Hofmann, S. G., & Barlow, D. H. (2002). Social Phobia (Social Anxety Disorder). In Anxiety and its disorders: the nature and treatment of anxiety and panic (2nd ed, pp. 454–476). New York: Guilford Press.

Hofmann, S. G., Gerlach, A. L., Wender, A., & Roth, W. T. (1997). Speech disturbances and gaze behavior during public speaking in subtypes of social phobia. Journal of Anxiety Disorders, 11(6), 573–585.

Hofmann, S. G., & Hinton, D. E. (2014). Cross-cultural aspects of anxiety disorders. Current Psychiatry Reports, 16(6), 450.

Hoge, E. A., Lawson, E. A., Metcalf, C. A., Keshaviah, A., Zak, P. J., Pollack, M. H., & Simon, N. M. (2012). Plasma oxytocin immunoreactive products and response to trust in patients with social anxiety disorder: Research Article: Oxytocin and Trust in Social Anxiety Disorder. Depression and Anxiety, 29(11), 924–930.

Hoge, E. A., Pollack, M. H., Kaufman, R. E., Zak, P. J., & Simon, N. M. (2008). Oxytocin levels in social anxiety disorder. CNS Neuroscience & Therapeutics, 14(3), 165–170.

Holt-Lunstad, J., Smith, T. B., & Layton, J. B. (2010). Social relationships and mortality risk: a meta-analytic review. PLoS Medicine, 7(7), e1000316.

Honess, P. E., & Marin, C. M. (2006). Behavioural and physiological aspects of stress and aggression in nonhuman primates. Neuroscience and Biobehavioral Reviews, 30(3), 390–412.

Hope, D. A., Gansler, D. A., & Heimberg, R. G. (1989). Attentional focus and causal attributions in social phobia: Implications from social psychology. Clinical Psychology Review, 9(1), 49–60.

Hopko, D. R., McNeil, D. W., Zvolensky, M. J., & Eifert, G. H. (2001). The relation between anxiety and skill in performance-based anxiety disorders: A behavioral formulation of social phobia. Behavior Therapy, 32(1), 185–207.

Horan, W. P., Kern, R. S., Tripp, C., Hellemann, G., Wynn, J. K., Bell, M., ... Green, M. F. (2011). Efficacy and specificity of Social Cognitive Skills Training for outpatients with psychotic disorders. Journal of Psychiatric Research, 45(8), 1113–1122.

Hostinar, C. E., McQuillan, M. T., Mirous, H. J., Grant, K. E., & Adam, E. K. (2014). Cortisol responses to a group public speaking task for adolescents: Variations by age, gender, and race. Psychoneuroendocrinology, 50, 155–166.

Hudson, J. L., & Rapee, R. M. (2000). The Origins of Social Phobia. Behavior Modification, 24(1), 102–129.

Ibañez, A., Gleichgerrcht, E., & Manes, F. (2010). Clinical effects of insular damage in humans. Brain Structure & Function, 214(5–6), 397–410.

Insel, T., Cuthbert, B., Garvey, M., Heinssen, R., Pine, D. S., Quinn, K., ... Wang, P. (2010). Research domain criteria (RDoC): toward a new classification framework for research on mental disorders. The American Journal of Psychiatry, 167(7), 748–751.

Ioannidis, J. P. A. (2005). Why Most Published Research Findings Are False. PLOS Medicine, 2(8), e124.

Irle, E., Ruhleder, M., Lange, C., Seidler-Brandler, U., Salzer, S., Dechent, P., ... Leichsenring, F. (2010). Reduced amygdalar and hippocampal size in adults with generalized social phobia. Journal of Psychiatry & Neuroscience : JPN, 35(2), 126–131.

Jackson, P. L., Brunet, E., Meltzoff, A. N., & Decety, J. (2006). Empathy examined through the neural mechanisms involved in imagining how I feel versus how you feel pain. Neuropsychologia, 44(5), 752–761.

Jacobs, M., Snow, J., Geraci, M., Vythilingam, M., Blair, R. J. R., Charney, D. S., ... Blair, K. S. (2008). Association between Level of Emotional Intelligence and Severity of Anxiety in Generalized Social Phobia. *Journal of Anxiety Disorders, 22*(8), 1487–1495.

Jankord, R., & Herman, J. P. (2008). Limbic regulation of hypothalamo-pituitary-adrenocortical function during acute and chronic stress. *Annals of the New York Academy of Sciences, 1148*, 64–73.

Jeung, H., & Herpertz, S. C. (2014). Impairments of interpersonal functioning: empathy and intimacy in borderline personality disorder. *Psychopathology, 47*(4), 220–234.

Johnson, E. O., Kamilaris, T. C., Chrousos, G. P., & Gold, P. W. (1992). Mechanisms of stress: a dynamic overview of hormonal and behavioral homeostasis. *Neuroscience and Biobehavioral Reviews, 16*(2), 115–130.

Johnson, M. H. (2001). Functional brain development in humans. *Nature Reviews. Neuroscience, 2*(7), 475–483.

Johnson, P. O., & Neyman, J. (1936). Tests of certain linear hypotheses and their application to some educational problems. *Statistical Research Memoirs, 1*, 57–93.

Jones, E. E., & Archer, R. L. (1976). Are there special effects of personalistic self-disclosure? *Journal of Experimental Social Psychology, 12*(2), 180–193.

Joormann, J., & Gotlib, I. H. (2006). Is this happiness I see? Biases in the identification of emotional facial expressions in depression and social phobia. *Journal of Abnormal Psychology, 115*(4), 705–714.

Juster, H. R., Heimberg, R. G., Frost, R. O., Holt, C. S., Mattia, J. I., & Faccenda, K. (1996). Social phobia and perfectionism. *Personality and Individual Differences, 21*(3), 403–410.

Kagan, J., Reznick, J. S., & Gibbons, J. (1989). Inhibited and uninhibited types of children. *Child Development, 60*(4), 838–845.

Kagan, J., Reznick, J. S., & Snidman, N. (1987). The physiology and psychology of behavioral inhibition in children. *Child Development, 58*(6), 1459–1473.

Kalia, M. (2002). Assessing the economic impact of stress--the modern day hidden epidemic. *Metabolism: Clinical and Experimental, 51*(6 Suppl 1), 49–53.

Kalin, N. H., Shelton, S. E., Rickman, M., & Davidson, R. J. (1998). Individual differences in freezing and cortisol in infant and mother rhesus monkeys. *Behavioral Neuroscience, 112*(1), 251–254.

Kanat, M., Heinrichs, M., Mader, I., van Elst, L. T., & Domes, G. (2015). Oxytocin Modulates Amygdala Reactivity to Masked Fearful Eyes. *Neuropsychopharmacology: Official Publication of the American College of Neuropsychopharmacology, 40*(11), 2632–2638.

Karlsson, B., Sigström, R., Waern, M., Ostling, S., Gustafson, D., & Skoog, I. (2010). The prognosis and incidence of social phobia in an elderly population. A 5-year follow-up. *Acta Psychiatrica Scandinavica, 122*(1), 4–10.

Kashdan, T. B., & Rottenberg, J. (2010). Psychological flexibility as a fundamental aspect of health. *Clinical Psychology Review, 30*(7), 865–878.

Katzelnick, D. J., Kobak, K. A., DeLeire, T., Henk, H. J., Greist, J. H., Davidson, J. R., ... Helstad, C. P. (2001). Impact of generalized social anxiety disorder in managed care. *The American Journal of Psychiatry, 158*(12), 1999–2007.

Kaukiainen, A., Björkqvist, K., Lagerspetz, K, Österman, K., Salmivalli, C., Rothberg, S., & Ahlbom, A. (1999). The relationships between social intelligence, empathy, and three types of aggression. *Aggressive Behavior, 25*(2), 81–89.

Kawachi, I., Sparrow, D., Vokonas, P. S., & Weiss, S. T. (1994). Symptoms of anxiety and risk of coronary heart disease. The Normative Aging Study. *Circulation, 90*(5), 2225–2229.

Kawaguchi, A., Nemoto, K., Nakaaki, S., Kawaguchi, T., Kan, H., Arai, N., ... Akechi, T. (2016). Insular Volume Reduction in Patients with Social Anxiety Disorder. *Frontiers in Psychiatry, 7*, 3.

Kayser, N., Sarfati, Y., Besche, C., & Hardy-Baylé, M.-C. (2006). Elaboration of a rehabilitation method based on a pathogenetic hypothesis of "theory of mind" impairment in schizophrenia. *Neuropsychological Rehabilitation, 16*(1), 83–95.

Kemp, A. H., & Guastella, A. J. (2010). Oxytocin: prosocial behavior, social salience, or approach-related behavior? *Biological Psychiatry, 67*(6), e33–34; author reply e35.

Kemp, A. H., & Guastella, A. J. (2011). The Role of Oxytocin in Human Affect: A Novel Hypothesis. *Current Directions in Psychological Science, 20*(4), 222–231.

Kendler, K. S., Neale, M. C., Kessler, R. C., Heath, A. C., & Eaves, L. J. (1992). The Genetic Epidemiology of Phobias in Women: The Interrelationship of Agoraphobia, Social Phobia, Situational Phobia, and Simple Phobia. *Archives of General Psychiatry, 49*(4), 273–281.

Kennedy, B., Dillon, E., Mills, P. J., & Ziegler, M. G. (2001). Catecholamines in human saliva. *Life Sciences, 69*(1), 87–99.

Kennedy, D. P., & Adolphs, R. (2012). The social brain in psychiatric and neurological disorders. *Trends in Cognitive Sciences, 16*(11), 559–572.

Kent, J. M., & Rauch, S. L. (2003). Neurocircuitry of anxiety disorders. *Current Psychiatry Reports, 5*(4), 266–273.

Kessler, R. C., Berglund, P., Demler, O., Jin, R., Merikangas, K. R., & Walters, E. E. (2005). Lifetime prevalence and age-of-onset distributions of DSM-IV disorders in the National Comorbidity Survey Replication. *Archives of General Psychiatry, 62*(6), 593–602.

Kessler, R. C., Chiu, W. T., Demler, O., Merikangas, K. R., & Walters, E. E. (2005). Prevalence, severity, and comorbidity of 12-month DSM-IV disorders in the National Comorbidity Survey Replication. *Archives of General Psychiatry, 62*(6), 617–627.

Kirschbaum, C., & Hellhammer, D. H. (1989). Salivary cortisol in psychobiological research: an overview. *Neuropsychobiology, 22*(3), 150–169.

Kirschbaum, C., Kudielka, B. M., Gaab, J., Schommer, N. C., & Hellhammer, D. H. (1999). Impact of gender, menstrual cycle phase, and oral contraceptives on the activity of the hypothalamus-pituitary-adrenal axis. *Psychosomatic Medicine, 61*(2), 154–162.

Kirschbaum, C., Pirke, K.-M., & Hellhammer, D. H. (1993). The "Trier Social Stress Test" - A Tool for Investigating Psychobiological Stress Response in a Laboratory Setting. *Neuropsychobiology*, (28), 76–81.

Klumbies, E., Braeuer, D., Hoyer, J., & Kirschbaum, C. (2014). The reaction to social stress in social phobia: discordance between physiological and subjective parameters. *PloS One, 9*(8), e105670.

Klumpp, H., Angstadt, M., Nathan, P. J., & Phan, K. L. (2010). Amygdala reactivity to faces at varying intensities of threat in generalized social phobia: An event-related functional MRI study. *Psychiatry Research: Neuroimaging, 183*(2), 167–169.

Koch, S. B., van Zuiden, M., Nawijn, L., Frijling, J. L., Veltman, D. J., & Olff, M. (2016). Intranasal Oxytocin Administration Dampens Amygdala Reactivity towards Emotional Faces in Male and Female PTSD Patients. *Neuropsychopharmacology: Official Publication of the American College of Neuropsychopharmacology, 41*(6), 1495–1504.

Koen, N., & Stein, D. J. (2011). Pharmacotherapy of anxiety disorders: a critical review. *Dialogues in Clinical Neuroscience, 13*(4), 423–437.

Kosfeld, M., Heinrichs, M., Zak, P. J., Fischbacher, U., & Fehr, E. (2005). Oxytocin increases trust in humans. *Nature, 435*(7042), 673–676.

Koski, S. E., Koops, K., & Sterck, E. H. M. (2007). Reconciliation, relationship quality, and postconflict anxiety: testing the integrated hypothesis in captive chimpanzees. *American Journal of Primatology, 69*(2), 158–172.

Koszycki, D., Benger, M., Shlik, J., & Bradwejn, J. (2007). Randomized trial of a meditation-based stress reduction program and cognitive behavior therapy in generalized social anxiety disorder. *Behaviour Research and Therapy, 45*(10), 2518–2526.

Kozak, M. J., & Cuthbert, B. N. (2016). The NIMH Research Domain Criteria Initiative: Background, Issues, and Pragmatics. *Psychophysiology, 53*(3), 286–297.

Krämer, M., Seefeldt, W. L., Heinrichs, N., Tuschen-Caffier, B., Schmitz, J., Wolf, O. T., & Blechert, J. (2012). Subjective, autonomic, and endocrine reactivity during social stress in children with social phobia. *Journal of Abnormal Child Psychology, 40*(1), 95–104.

Krebs, D. (1975). Empathy and altruism. *Journal of Personality and Social Psychology, 32*(6), 1134–1146.

Kudielka, B. M., Buske-Kirschbaum, A., Hellhammer, D. ., & Kirschbaum, C. (2004a). HPA axis responses to laboratory psychosocial stress in healthy elderly adults, younger adults, and children: impact of age and gender. *Psychoneuroendocrinology, 29*(1), 83–98.

Kudielka, B. M., Buske-Kirschbaum, A., Hellhammer, D. H., & Kirschbaum, C. (2004b). Differential heart rate reactivity and recovery after psychosocial stress (TSST) in healthy children, younger adults, and elderly adults: the impact of age and gender. *International Journal of Behavioral Medicine, 11*(2), 116–121.

Kudielka, B. M., Hellhammer, D. H., & Wüst, S. (2009). Why do we respond so differently? Reviewing determinants of human salivary cortisol responses to challenge. *Psychoneuroendocrinology, 34*(1), 2–18.

Kudielka, B. M., & Kirschbaum, C. (2005). Sex differences in HPA axis responses to stress: a review. *Biological Psychology, 69*(1), 113–132.

Kudielka, B. M., Schmidt-Reinwald, A. K., Hellhammer, D. H., Schürmeyer, T., & Kirschbaum, C. (2000). Psychosocial stress and HPA functioning: no evidence for a reduced resilience in healthy elderly men. *Stress (Amsterdam, Netherlands), 3*(3), 229–240.

Kudielka, B. M., & Wüst, S. (2010). Human models in acute and chronic stress: assessing determinants of individual hypothalamus-pituitary-adrenal axis activity and reactivity. *Stress (Amsterdam, Netherlands), 13*(1), 1–14.

Kuhnert, R.-L., Begeer, S., Fink, E., & de Rosnay, M. (2016). Gender-differentiated effects of theory of mind, emotion understanding, and social preference on prosocial behavior development: A longitudinal study. *Journal of Experimental Child Psychology, 154*, 13–27.

Kumsta, R., Chen, F. S., Pape, H.-C., & Heinrichs, M. (2013). Neuropeptide S receptor gene is associated with cortisol responses to social stress in humans. *Biological Psychology, 93*(2), 304–307.

Kuzma, J. M., & Black, D. W. (2004). Integrating pharmacotherapy and psychotherapy in the management of anxiety disorders. *Current Psychiatry Reports, 6*(4), 268–273.

La Greca, A. M., & Harrison, H. M. (2005). Adolescent peer relations, friendships, and romantic relationships: do they predict social anxiety and depression? *Journal of Clinical Child and Adolescent Psychology: The Official Journal for the Society of Clinical Child and Adolescent Psychology, American Psychological Association, Division 53, 34*(1), 49–61.

Labuschagne, I., Phan, K. L., Wood, A., Angstadt, M., Chua, P., Heinrichs, M., ... Nathan, P. J. (2010). Oxytocin attenuates amygdala reactivity to fear in generalized social anxiety disorder. *Neuropsychopharmacology, 35*(12), 2403–2413.

Labuschagne, I., Phan, K. L., Wood, A., Angstadt, M., Chua, P., Heinrichs, M., ... Nathan, P. J. (2011). Medial frontal hyperactivity to sad faces in generalized social anxiety disorder and modulation by oxytocin. *The International Journal of Neuropsychopharmacology*, 1–14.

Lamm, C., Batson, C. D., & Decety, J. (2007). The neural substrate of human empathy: effects of perspective-taking and cognitive appraisal. *Journal of Cognitive Neuroscience*, *19*(1), 42–58.

Lamm, C., Decety, J., & Singer, T. (2011). Meta-analytic evidence for common and distinct neural networks associated with directly experienced pain and empathy for pain. *NeuroImage*, *54*(3), 2492–2502.

Lamothe, M., Boujut, E., Zenasni, F., & Sultan, S. (2014). To be or not to be empathic: the combined role of empathic concern and perspective taking in understanding burnout in general practice. *BMC Family Practice*, *15*, 15.

Landgraf, R., & Neumann, I. D. (2004). Vasopressin and oxytocin release within the brain: a dynamic concept of multiple and variable modes of neuropeptide communication. *Frontiers in Neuroendocrinology*, *25*(3–4), 150–176.

Lanzenberger, R. R., Mitterhauser, M., Spindelegger, C., Wadsak, W., Klein, N., Mien, L.-K., ... Tauscher, J. (2007). Reduced Serotonin-1A Receptor Binding in Social Anxiety Disorder. *Biological Psychiatry*, *61*(9), 1081–1089.

Laux, L., Glanzmann, P., Schaffner, P., & Spielberger, C. D. (1981). *STAI. Das State-Trait-Angstinventar*. Weinheim: Beltz.

Lazarus, R. S. (1966). *Psychological stress and the coping process*. New York: McGraw-Hill.

Lazarus, R. S., & Folkman, S. (1984). *Stress, appraisal, and coping*. New York: Springer Pub. Co.

LeDoux, J. E. (2000). Emotion circuits in the brain. *Annual Review of Neuroscience*, *23*, 155–184.

Lee, N. C., Jolles, J., & Krabbendam, L. (2016). Social information influences trust behaviour in adolescents. *Journal of Adolescence*, *46*, 66–75.

Leichsenring, F., Salzer, S., Beutel, M. E., Herpertz, S., Hiller, W., Hoyer, J., ... Leibing, E. (2013). Psychodynamic therapy and cognitive-behavioral therapy in social anxiety disorder: a multicenter randomized controlled trial. *The American Journal of Psychiatry*, *170*(7), 759–767.

Lesch, K. P., Bengel, D., Heils, A., Sabol, S. Z., Greenberg, B. D., Petri, S., ... Murphy, D. L. (1996). Association of anxiety-related traits with a polymorphism in the serotonin transporter gene regulatory region. *Science (New York, N.Y.)*, *274*(5292), 1527–1531.

Levin, A. P., Saoud, J. B., Strauman, T., Gorman, J. M., Fyer, A. J., Crawford, R., & Liebowitz, M. R. (1993). Responses of "generalized" and "discrete" social phobics during public speaking. *Journal of Anxiety Disorders*, *7*(3), 207–221.

Liao, W., Qiu, C., Gentili, C., Walter, M., Pan, Z., Ding, J., ... Chen, H. (2010). Altered Effective Connectivity Network of the Amygdala in Social Anxiety Disorder: A Resting-State fMRI Study. *PLOS ONE*, *5*(12), e15238.

Lieb, R., Wittchen, H.-U., Höfler, M., Fuetsch, M., Stein, M. B., & Merikangas, K. R. (2000). Parental psychopathology, parenting styles, and the risk of social phobia in offspring: a prospective-longitudinal community study. *Archives of General Psychiatry*, *57*(9), 859–866.

Liebowitz, M. R. (1987). Social phobia. *Modern Problems of Pharmacopsychiatry*, *22*, 141–173.

Liebowitz, M. R., Gorman, J. M., Fyer, A. J., & Klein, D. F. (1985). Social phobia. Review of a neglected anxiety disorder. *Archives of General Psychiatry*, *42*(7), 729–736.

Liebowitz, M. R., Heimberg, R. G., Schneier, F. R., Hope, D. A., Davies, S., Holt, C. S., ... Klein, D. F. (1999). Cognitive-behavioral group therapy versus phenelzine in social phobia: long-term outcome. *Depression and Anxiety, 10*(3), 89–98.

Lim, M. M., & Young, L. J. (2006). Neuropeptidergic regulation of affiliative behavior and social bonding in animals. *Hormones and Behavior, 50*(4), 506–517.

Linehan, M. M. (1993). *Skills training manual for treating borderline personality disorder* (Vol. xii). New York, NY, US: Guilford Press.

Lischke, A., Berger, C., Prehn, K., Heinrichs, M., Herpertz, S. C., & Domes, G. (2012). Intranasal oxytocin enhances emotion recognition from dynamic facial expressions and leaves eye-gaze unaffected. *Psychoneuroendocrinology, 37*(4), 475–481.

Lockwood, P. L., Seara-Cardoso, A., & Viding, E. (2014). Emotion Regulation Moderates the Association between Empathy and Prosocial Behavior. *PLoS ONE, 9*(5).

Long, J. S., & Ervin, L. H. (2000). Using Heteroscedasticity Consistent Standard Errors in the Linear Regression Model. *The American Statistician, 54*(3), 217–224.

Loo, C. K., & Mitchell, P. B. (2005). A review of the efficacy of transcranial magnetic stimulation (TMS) treatment for depression, and current and future strategies to optimize efficacy. *Journal of Affective Disorders, 88*(3), 255–267.

Lorberbaum, J. P., Kose, S., Johnson, M. R., Arana, G. W., Sullivan, L. K., Hamner, M. B., ... George, M. S. (2004). Neural correlates of speech anticipatory anxiety in generalized social phobia. *Neuroreport, 15*(18), 2701–2705.

Losiak, W., Blaut, A., Klosowska, J., & Slowik, N. (2016). Social Anxiety, Affect, Cortisol Response and Performance on a Speech Task. *Psychopathology*.

Lovallo, W. R., Farag, N. H., Vincent, A. S., Thomas, T. L., & Wilson, M. F. (2006). Cortisol responses to mental stress, exercise, and meals following caffeine intake in men and women. *Pharmacology, Biochemistry, and Behavior, 83*(3), 441–447.

Luria, R. E. (1975). The validity and reliability of the visual analogue mood scale. *Journal of Psychiatric Research, 12*(1), 51–57.

Machado-de-Sousa, J. P., Osório, F. de L., Jackowski, A. P., Bressan, R. A., Chagas, M. H. N., Torro-Alves, N., ... Hallak, J. E. C. (2014). Increased amygdalar and hippocampal volumes in young adults with social anxiety. *PloS One, 9*(2), e88523.

Mallott, M. A., Maner, J. K., DeWall, N., & Schmidt, N. B. (2009). Compensatory deficits following rejection: the role of social anxiety in disrupting affiliative behavior. *Depression and Anxiety, 26*(5), 438–446.

Malnick, S. D. H., & Knobler, H. (2006). The medical complications of obesity. *QJM: Monthly Journal of the Association of Physicians, 99*(9), 565–579.

Maner, J. K., DeWall, C. N., Baumeister, R. F., & Schaller, M. (2007). Does social exclusion motivate interpersonal reconnection? Resolving the "porcupine problem." *Journal of Personality and Social Psychology, 92*(1), 42–55.

Mannuzza, S., Schneier, F. R., Chapman, T. F., Liebowitz, M. R., Klein, D. F., & Fyer, A. J. (1995). Generalized social phobia. Reliability and validity. *Archives of General Psychiatry, 52*(3), 230–237.

Mansell, W., Clark, D. M., Ehlers, A., & Chen, Y.-P. (1999). Social Anxiety and Attention away from Emotional Faces. *Cognition and Emotion, 13*(6), 673–690.

Margittai, Z., Strombach, T., van Wingerden, M., Joëls, M., Schwabe, L., & Kalenscher, T. (2015). A friend in need: Time-dependent effects of stress on social discounting in men. *Hormones and Behavior, 73*, 75–82.

Marsh, A. A., Yu, H. H., Pine, D. S., & Blair, R. J. R. (2010). Oxytocin improves specific recognition of positive facial expressions. *Psychopharmacology, 209*(3), 225–232.

Martel, F. L., Hayward, C., Lyons, D. M., Sanborn, K., Varady, S., & Schatzberg, A. F. (1999). Salivary cortisol levels in socially phobic adolescent girls. *Depression and Anxiety, 10*(1), 25–27.

Mason, J. W. (1971). A re-evaluation of the concept of "non-specificity" in stress theory. *Journal of Psychiatric Research, 8*(3), 323–333.

Mathew, S. J., Coplan, J. D., & Gorman, J. M. (2001). Neurobiological mechanisms of social anxiety disorder. *The American Journal of Psychiatry, 158*(10), 1558–1567.

Mattick, R. P., & Clarke, J. C. (1998). Development and validation of measures of social phobia scrutiny fear and social interaction anxiety. *Behaviour Research and Therapy, 36*(4), 455–470.

Mauss, I., Wilhelm, F., & Gross, J. (2004). Is there less to social anxiety than meets the eye? Emotion experience, expression, and bodily responding. *Cognition and Emotion, 18*(5), 631–642.

McDonald, A. J. (1998). Cortical pathways to the mammalian amygdala. *Progress in Neurobiology, 55*(3), 257–332.

McEwen, B. S. (1998). Stress, adaptation, and disease. Allostasis and allostatic load. *Annals of the New York Academy of Sciences, 840*, 33–44.

McEwen, B. S., & Morrison, J. H. (2013). The brain on stress: vulnerability and plasticity of the prefrontal cortex over the life course. *Neuron, 79*(1), 16–29.

McEwen, B. S., & Stellar, E. (1993). Stress and the individual. Mechanisms leading to disease. *Archives of Internal Medicine, 153*(18), 2093–2101.

McManus, F., Sacadura, C., & Clark, D. M. (2008). Why social anxiety persists: an experimental investigation of the role of safety behaviours as a maintaining factor. *Journal of Behavior Therapy and Experimental Psychiatry, 39*(2), 147–161.

Meleshko, K. G., & Alden, L. E. (1993). Anxiety and self-disclosure: toward a motivational model. *Journal of Personality and Social Psychology, 64*(6), 1000–1009.

Mendlowicz, M. V., & Stein, M. B. (2000). Quality of life in individuals with anxiety disorders. *American Journal of Psychiatry, 157*(5), 669–682.

Meng, Y., Lui, S., Qiu, C., Qiu, L., Lama, S., Huang, X., ... Zhang, W. (2013). Neuroanatomical deficits in drug-naïve adult patients with generalized social anxiety disorder: a voxel-based morphometry study. *Psychiatry Research, 214*(1), 9–15.

Merikangas, K. R., Lieb, R., Wittchen, H.-U., & Avenevoli, S. (2003). Family and high-risk studies of social anxiety disorder. *Acta Psychiatrica Scandinavica. Supplementum,* (417), 28–37.

Meyer-Lindenberg, A., & Tost, H. (2012). Neural mechanisms of social risk for psychiatric disorders. *Nature Neuroscience, 15*(5), 663–668.

Miller, A. H., Spencer, R. L., Pulera, M., Kang, S., McEwen, B. S., & Stein, M. (1992). Adrenal steroid receptor activation in rat brain and pituitary following dexamethasone: implications for the dexamethasone suppression test. *Biological Psychiatry, 32*(10), 850–869.

Miller, G. A., & Chapman, J. P. (2001). Misunderstanding analysis of covariance. *Journal of Abnormal Psychology, 110*(1), 40–48.

Miller, R., Plessow, F., Kirschbaum, C., & Stalder, T. (2013). Classification criteria for distinguishing cortisol responders from nonresponders to psychosocial stress: evaluation of salivary cortisol pulse detection in panel designs. *Psychosomatic Medicine, 75*(9), 832–840.

Miskovic, V., & Schmidt, L. A. (2012). Early information processing biases in social anxiety. *Cognition & Emotion, 26*(1), 176–185.

Mogg, K., Philippot, P., & Bradley, B. P. (2004). Selective attention to angry faces in clinical social phobia. *Journal of Abnormal Psychology, 113*(1), 160–165.

Molenberghs, P., Johnson, H., Henry, J. D., & Mattingley, J. B. (2016). Understanding the minds of others: A neuroimaging meta-analysis. *Neuroscience & Biobehavioral Reviews*, *65*, 276–291.

Morrison, A. S., Mateen, M. A., Brozovich, F. A., Zaki, J., Goldin, P. R., Heimberg, R. G., & Gross, J. J. (2016). Empathy for positive and negative emotions in social anxiety disorder. *Behaviour Research and Therapy*, *87*, 232–242.

Moser, J. S., Hajcak, G., Huppert, J. D., Foa, E. B., & Simons, R. F. (2008). Interpretation bias in social anxiety as detected by event-related brain potentials. *Emotion*, *8*(5), 693–700.

Moskowitz, G. B. (2005). *Social Cognition: Understanding Self and Others*. Guilford Press.

Murray, L., Cooper, P., Creswell, C., Schofield, E., & Sack, C. (2007). The effects of maternal social phobia on mother-infant interactions and infant social responsiveness. *Journal of Child Psychology and Psychiatry, and Allied Disciplines*, *48*(1), 45–52.

Nakao, T., Sanematsu, H., Yoshiura, T., Togao, O., Murayama, K., Tomita, M., ... Kanba, S. (2011). fMRI of patients with social anxiety disorder during a social situation task. *Neuroscience Research*, *69*(1), 67–72.

Nel, P. (2003). *Dr. Seuss: American Icon*. New York: Bloomsbury Academic.

Neumann, I. D., Krömer, S. A., Toschi, N., & Ebner, K. (2000). Brain oxytocin inhibits the (re)activity of the hypothalamo-pituitary-adrenal axis in male rats: involvement of hypothalamic and limbic brain regions. *Regulatory Peptides*, *96*(1–2), 31–38.

Neumann, I. D., & Slattery, D. A. (2016). Oxytocin in General Anxiety and Social Fear: A Translational Approach. *Biological Psychiatry*, *79*(3), 213–221.

Niedenthal, P. M. (2007). Embodying Emotion. *Science*, *316*(5827), 1002–1005.

NIMH » Research Domain Criteria (RDoC). (n.d.). Retrieved February 8, 2017, from https://www.nimh.nih.gov/research-priorities/rdoc/index.shtml

Ochsner, K. N., & Gross, J. J. (2005). The cognitive control of emotion. *Trends in Cognitive Sciences*, *9*(5), 242–249. h

Oei, N. Y. L., Elzinga, B. M., Wolf, O. T., de Ruiter, M. B., Damoiseaux, J. S., Kuijer, J. P. A., ... Rombouts, S. A. R. B. (2007). Glucocorticoids Decrease Hippocampal and Prefrontal Activation during Declarative Memory Retrieval in Young Men. *Brain Imaging and Behavior*, *1*(1–2), 31–41.

Ohayon, M. M., & Schatzberg, A. F. (2010). Social phobia and depression: Prevalence and comorbidity. *Journal of Psychosomatic Research*, *68*(3), 235–243.

Okumura, T., Nakajima, Y., Matsuoka, M., & Takamatsu, T. (1997). Study of salivary catecholamines using fully automated column-switching high-performance liquid chromatography. *Journal of Chromatography. B, Biomedical Sciences and Applications*, *694*(2), 305–316.

Olthuis, J. V., Watt, M. C., Bailey, K., Hayden, J. A., & Stewart, S. H. (2015). Therapist-supported Internet cognitive behavioural therapy for anxiety disorders in adults. *The Cochrane Database of Systematic Reviews*, (3), CD011565.

Öst, L.-G., Jerremalm, A., & Johansson, J. (1981). Individual response patterns and the effects of different behavioral methods in the treatment of social phobia. *Behaviour Research and Therapy*, *19*(1), 1–16.

O'Toole, M. S., Hougaard, E., & Mennin, D. S. (2013). Social anxiety and emotion knowledge: A meta-analysis. *Journal of Anxiety Disorders*, *27*(1), 98–108.

Otte, C., Hart, S., Neylan, T. C., Marmar, C. R., Yaffe, K., & Mohr, D. C. (2005). A meta-analysis of cortisol response to challenge in human aging: importance of gender. *Psychoneuroendocrinology*, *30*(1), 80–91.

Ougrin, D. (2011). Efficacy of exposure versus cognitive therapy in anxiety disorders: systematic review and meta-analysis. *BMC Psychiatry, 11*, 200.

Paes, F., Baczynski, T., Novaes, F., Marinho, T., Arias-Carrión, O., Budde, H., ... Machado, S. (2013). Repetitive Transcranial Magnetic Stimulation (rTMS) to Treat Social Anxiety Disorder: Case Reports and a Review of the Literature. *Clinical Practice and Epidemiology in Mental Health: CP & EMH, 9*, 180–188.

Paes, F., Machado, S., Arias-Carrión, O., Silva, A. C., & Nardi, A. E. (2013). rTMS to treat social anxiety disorder: a case report. *Revista Brasileira De Psiquiatria (Sao Paulo, Brazil: 1999), 35*(1), 99–100.

Painuly, N., Sharan, P., & Mattoo, S. K. (2007). Antecedents, concomitants and consequences of anger attacks in depression. *Psychiatry Research, 153*(1), 39–45.

Papez, J. W. (1937). A Proposed Mechanism of Emotion. *Archives of Neurology & Psychiatry, 38*(4), 725–743.

Pariante, C. M., Papadopoulos, A. S., Poon, L., Cleare, A. J., Checkley, S. A., English, J., ... Lightman, S. (2004). Four days of citalopram increase suppression of cortisol secretion by prednisolone in healthy volunteers. *Psychopharmacology, 177*(1–2), 200–206.

Penn, D. L., Roberts, D. L., Combs, D., & Sterne, A. (2007). Best practices: The development of the Social Cognition and Interaction Training program for schizophrenia spectrum disorders. *Psychiatric Services (Washington, D.C.), 58*(4), 449–451.

Petrovic, P., Kalisch, R., Singer, T., & Dolan, R. J. (2008). Oxytocin attenuates affective evaluations of conditioned faces and amygdala activity. *The Journal of Neuroscience: The Official Journal of the Society for Neuroscience, 28*(26), 6607–6615.

Phan, K. L., Fitzgerald, D. A., Cortese, B. M., Seraji-Bozorgzad, N., Tancer, M. E., & Moore, G. J. (2005). Anterior cingulate neurochemistry in social anxiety disorder: 1H-MRS at 4 Tesla. *Neuroreport, 16*(2), 183–186.

Phan, K. L., Fitzgerald, D. A., Nathan, P. J., & Tancer, M. E. (2006). Association between amygdala hyperactivity to harsh faces and severity of social anxiety in generalized social phobia. *Biological Psychiatry, 59*(5), 424–429.

Phan, K. L., Orlichenko, A., Boyd, E., Angstadt, M., Coccaro, E. F., Liberzon, I., & Arfanakis, K. (2009). Preliminary evidence of white matter abnormality in the uncinate fasciculus in generalized social anxiety disorder. *Biological Psychiatry, 66*(7), 691–694.

Phillips, A. C., Roseboom, T. J., Carroll, D., & de Rooij, S. R. (2012). Cardiovascular and cortisol reactions to acute psychological stress and adiposity: cross-sectional and prospective associations in the Dutch Famine Birth Cohort Study. *Psychosomatic Medicine, 74*(7), 699–710.

Pinkham, A. E., Penn, D. L., Green, M. F., Buck, B., Healey, K., & Harvey, P. D. (2014). The Social Cognition Psychometric Evaluation Study: Results of the Expert Survey and RAND Panel. *Schizophrenia Bulletin, 40*(4), 813–823.

Plana, I., Lavoie, M.-A., Battaglia, M., & Achim, A. M. (2014). A meta-analysis and scoping review of social cognition performance in social phobia, posttraumatic stress disorder and other anxiety disorders. *Journal of Anxiety Disorders, 28*(2), 169–177.

Pollack, M. H., Jensen, J. E., Simon, N. M., Kaufman, R. E., & Renshaw, P. F. (2008). High-field MRS study of GABA, glutamate and glutamine in social anxiety disorder: Response to treatment with levetiracetam. *Progress in Neuro-Psychopharmacology and Biological Psychiatry, 32*(3), 739–743.

Ponniah, K., & Hollon, S. D. (2008). Empirically supported psychological interventions for social phobia in adults: a qualitative review of randomized controlled trials. *Psychological Medicine, 38*(1), 3–14.

Potts, N. L., Davidson, J. R., Krishnan, K. R., Doraiswamy, P. M., & Ritchie, J. C. (1991). Levels of urinary free cortisol in social phobia. *The Journal of Clinical Psychiatry, 52 Suppl*, 41–42.

Prater, K. E., Hosanagar, A., Klumpp, H., Angstadt, M., & Phan, K. L. (2013). Aberrant amygdala-frontal cortex connectivity during perception of fearful faces and at rest in generalized social anxiety disorder. *Depression and Anxiety, 30*(3), 234–241.

Preston, S. D., Bechara, A., Damasio, H., Grabowski, T. J., Stansfield, R. B., Mehta, S., & Damasio, A. R. (2007). The neural substrates of cognitive empathy. *Social Neuroscience, 2*(3–4), 254–275.

Preston, S. D., & De Waal, F. B. (2002). Empathy: Its ultimate and proximate bases. *Behavioral and Brain Sciences, 25*(01), 1–20.

Pruessner, J. C., Kirschbaum, C., Meinlschmid, G., & Hellhammer, D. H. (2003). Two formulas for computation of the area under the curve represent measures of total hormone concentration versus time-dependent change. *Psychoneuroendocrinology, 28*(7), 916–931.

Quadflieg, S., Mohr, A., Mentzel, H.-J., Miltner, W. H. R., & Straube, T. (2008). Modulation of the neural network involved in the processing of anger prosody: The role of task-relevance and social phobia. *Biological Psychology, 78*(2), 129–137.

Radenbach, C., Reiter, A. M. F., Engert, V., Sjoerds, Z., Villringer, A., Heinze, H.-J., ... Schlagenhauf, F. (2015). The interaction of acute and chronic stress impairs model-based behavioral control. *Psychoneuroendocrinology, 53*, 268–280.

Radke, S., Roelofs, K., & de Bruijn, E. R. A. (2013). Acting on Anger: Social Anxiety Modulates Approach-Avoidance Tendencies After Oxytocin Administration. *Psychological Science, 24*(8), 1573–1578.

Raichle, M. E., & Snyder, A. Z. (2007). A default mode of brain function: a brief history of an evolving idea. *NeuroImage, 37*(4), 1083-1090-1099.

Ralevski, E., Sanislow, C. A., Grilo, C. M., Skodol, A. E., Gunderson, J. G., Tracie Shea, M., ... McGlashan, T. H. (2005). Avoidant personality disorder and social phobia: distinct enough to be separate disorders? *Acta Psychiatrica Scandinavica, 112*(3), 208–214.

Rapee, R. M., & Heimberg, R. G. (1997). A cognitive-behavioral model of anxiety in social phobia. *Behaviour Research and Therapy, 35*(8), 741–756.

Rapee, R. M., & Lim, L. (1992). Discrepancy between self- and observer ratings of performance in social phobics. *Journal of Abnormal Psychology, 101*(4), 728–731.

Rauch, S. L., Shin, L. M., & Wright, C. I. (2003). Neuroimaging studies of amygdala function in anxiety disorders. *Annals of the New York Academy of Sciences, 985*, 389–410.

Reich, J. (2009). Avoidant personality disorder and its relationship to social phobia. *Current Psychiatry Reports, 11*(1), 89–93.

Reinelt, E., Stopsack, M., Aldinger, M., John, U., Grabe, H. J., & Barnow, S. (2013). Testing the diathesis-stress model: 5-HTTLPR, childhood emotional maltreatment, and vulnerability to social anxiety disorder. *American Journal of Medical Genetics Part B: Neuropsychiatric Genetics, 162*(3), 253–261.

Repasky, E. A., Eng, J., & Hylander, B. L. (2015). Stress, metabolism and cancer: integrated pathways contributing to immune suppression. *Cancer Journal (Sudbury, Mass.), 21*(2), 97–103.

Rettew, D. C. (2000). Avoidant personality disorder, generalized social phobia, and shyness: putting the personality back into personality disorders. *Harvard Review of Psychiatry, 8*(6), 283–297.

Riggio, R. E. (1986). Assessment of basic social skills. *Journal of Personality and Social Psychology, 51*(3), 649.

Riggio, R. E. (1992). Social interaction skills and nonverbal behavior. In R. S. Feldman (Ed.), *Applications of nonverbal behavior: Theories and research* (pp. 3–30). Hillsdale, NJ: Lawrence Erlbaum.

Rivier, C., & Vale, W. (1983). Interaction of corticotropin-releasing factor and arginine vasopressin on adrenocorticotropin secretion in vivo. *Endocrinology, 113*(3), 939–942.

Robinson, R., Roberts, W. L., Strayer, J., & Koopman, R. (2007). Empathy and Emotional Responsiveness in Delinquent and Non-delinquent Adolescents. *Social Development, 16*(3), 555–579.

Roelofs, K., Elzinga, B. M., & Rotteveel, M. (2005). The effects of stress-induced cortisol responses on approach-avoidance behavior. *Psychoneuroendocrinology, 30*(7), 665–677.

Roelofs, K., van Peer, J., Berretty, E., Jong, P. de, Spinhoven, P., & Elzinga, B. M. (2009). Hypothalamus–Pituitary–Adrenal Axis Hyperresponsiveness Is Associated with Increased Social Avoidance Behavior in Social Phobia. *Biological Psychiatry, 65*(4), 336–343.

Rogosa, D. (1980). Comparing nonparallel regression lines. *Psychological Bulletin, 88*(2), 307–321.

Rohleder, N., & Kirschbaum, C. (2006). The hypothalamic-pituitary-adrenal (HPA) axis in habitual smokers. *International Journal of Psychophysiology: Official Journal of the International Organization of Psychophysiology, 59*(3), 236–243.

Rohleder, N., Kudielka, B. M., Hellhammer, D. H., Wolf, J. M., & Kirschbaum, C. (2002). Age and sex steroid-related changes in glucocorticoid sensitivity of pro-inflammatory cytokine production after psychosocial stress. *Journal of Neuroimmunology, 126*(1–2), 69–77.

Rohleder, N., Schommer, N. C., Hellhammer, D. H., Engel, R., & Kirschbaum, C. (2001). Sex differences in glucocorticoid sensitivity of proinflammatory cytokine production after psychosocial stress. *Psychosomatic Medicine, 63*(6), 966–972.

Rohleder, N., Wolf, J. M., Piel, M., & Kirschbaum, C. (2003). Impact of oral contraceptive use on glucocorticoid sensitivity of pro-inflammatory cytokine production after psychosocial stress. *Psychoneuroendocrinology, 28*(3), 261–273.

Romanczyk, R. G., White, S., & Gillis, J. M. (2005). Social skills versus skilled social behavior: A problematic distinction in autism spectrum disorders. *Journal of Early and Intensive Behavior Intervention, 2*(3), 177.

Root, J. C., Tuescher, O., Cunningham-Bussel, A., Pan, H., Epstein, J., Altemus, M., … Silbersweig, D. (2009). Frontolimbic function and cortisol reactivity in response to emotional stimuli. *Neuroreport, 20*(4), 429–434.

Ruscio, A. M., Brown, T. A., Chiu, W. T., Sareen, J., Stein, M. B., & Kessler, R. C. (2008). Social fears and social phobia in the USA: results from the National Comorbidity Survey Replication. *Psychological Medicine, 38*(1), 15–28.

Sabbagh, M. A. (2004). Understanding orbitofrontal contributions to theory-of-mind reasoning: Implications for autism. *Brain and Cognition, 55*(1), 209–219.

Salkovskis, P. M. (1991). The Importance of Behaviour in the Maintenance of Anxiety and Panic: A Cognitive Account. *Behavioural and Cognitive Psychotherapy, 19*(01), 6–19.

Sandi, C., & Haller, J. (2015). Stress and the social brain: behavioural effects and neurobiological mechanisms. *Nature Reviews Neuroscience, 16*(5), 290–304.

Sanfey, A. G. (2007). Social decision-making: insights from game theory and neuroscience. *Science (New York, N.Y.), 318*(5850), 598–602.

Sapolsky, R. M. (1990). Adrenocortical function, social rank, and personality among wild baboons. *Biological Psychiatry, 28*(10), 862–878.

Sapolsky, R. M., Alberts, S. C., & Altmann, J. (1997). Hypercortisolism associated with social subordinance or social isolation among wild baboons. *Archives of General Psychiatry, 54*(12), 1137–1143.

Sapolsky, R. M., Krey, L. C., & McEwen, B. S. (1986). The Neuroendocrinology of Stress and Aging: The Glucocorticoid Cascade Hypothesis. *Endocrine Reviews, 7*(3), 284–301.

Sapolsky, R. M., Romero, L. M., & Munck, A. U. (2000). How do glucocorticoids influence stress responses? Integrating permissive, suppressive, stimulatory, and preparative actions. *Endocrine Reviews, 21*(1), 55–89.

Sareen, J., Cox, B. J., Afifi, T. O., de Graaf, R., Asmundson, G. J. G., ten Have, M., & Stein, M. B. (2005). Anxiety disorders and risk for suicidal ideation and suicide attempts: a population-based longitudinal study of adults. *Archives of General Psychiatry, 62*(11), 1249–1257.

Saslow, L. R., McCoy, S., van der Löwe, I., Cosley, B., Vartan, A., Oveis, C., ... Epel, E. S. (2014). Speaking under pressure: Low linguistic complexity is linked to high physiological and emotional stress reactivity. *Psychophysiology, 51*(3), 257–266.

Sassenrath, E. N. (1970). Increased adrenal responsiveness related to social stress in rhesus monkeys. *Hormones and Behavior, 1*(4), 283–298.

Scaini, S., Belotti, R., & Ogliari, A. (2014). Genetic and environmental contributions to social anxiety across different ages: A meta-analytic approach to twin data. *Journal of Anxiety Disorders, 28*(7), 650–656.

Schmidt, K.-H., & Metzler, P. (1992). Wortschatztest. Beltz-Test.

Schneier, F. R., Abi-Dargham, A., Martinez, D., Slifstein, M., Hwang, D.-R., Liebowitz, M. R., & Laruelle, M. (2009). Dopamine transporters, D2 receptors, and dopamine release in generalized social anxiety disorder. *Depression and Anxiety, 26*(5), 411–418.

Schneier, F. R., Johnson, J., Hornig, C. D., Liebowitz, M. R., & Weissman, M. M. (1992). Social phobia. Comorbidity and morbidity in an epidemiologic sample. *Archives of General Psychiatry, 49*(4), 282–288.

Schneier, F. R., Liebowitz, M. R., Abi-Dargham, A., Zea-Ponce, Y., Lin, S.-H., & Laruelle, M. (2000). Low Dopamine D2 Receptor Binding Potential in Social Phobia. *American Journal of Psychiatry, 157*(3), 457–459.

Schulz, C., Mothes-Lasch, M., & Straube, T. (2013). Automatic neural processing of disorder-related stimuli in social anxiety disorder: faces and more. *Cognitive Science, 4*, 282.

Schulze, L., Lischke, A., Greif, J., Herpertz, S. C., Heinrichs, M., & Domes, G. (2011). Oxytocin increases recognition of masked emotional faces. *Psychoneuroendocrinology, 36*(9), 1378–1382.

Schurz, M., Radua, J., Aichhorn, M., Richlan, F., & Perner, J. (2014). Fractionating theory of mind: A meta-analysis of functional brain imaging studies. *Neuroscience & Biobehavioral Reviews, 42*, 9–34.

Schwabe, L., & Wolf, O. T. (2009). Stress Prompts Habit Behavior in Humans. *Journal of Neuroscience, 29*(22), 7191–7198.

Seefeldt, W. L., Krämer, M., Tuschen-Caffier, B., & Heinrichs, N. (2014). Hypervigilance and avoidance in visual attention in children with social phobia. *Journal of Behavior Therapy and Experimental Psychiatry, 45*(1), 105–112.

Seeman, T. E., Singer, B., Wilkinson, C. W., & McEwen, B. (2001). Gender differences in age-related changes in HPA axis reactivity. *Psychoneuroendocrinology, 26*(3), 225–240.

Segerstrom, S. C., & Miller, G. E. (2004). Psychological Stress and the Human Immune System: A Meta-Analytic Study of 30 Years of Inquiry. *Psychological Bulletin*, *130*(4), 601–630.

Segrin, C. (2000). Social skills deficits associated with depression. *Clinical Psychology Review*, *20*(3), 379–403.

Segrin, C. (2001). Social skills and negative life events: Testing the deficit stress generation hypothesis. *Current Psychology*, *20*(1), 19–35.

Segrin, C., & Flora, J. (2000). Poor social skills are a vulnerability factor in the development of psychosocial problems. *Human Communication Research*, *26*(3), 489–514.

Selye, H. (1936). A Syndrome produced by Diverse Nocuous Agents. *Nature*, *138*, 32–41.

Selye, H. (1950). Stress and the General Adaptation Syndrome. *British Medical Journal*, *1*(4667), 1383–1392.

Shamay-Tsoory, S. G. (2011). The Neural Bases for Empathy. *The Neuroscientist, 17*(1), 18–24.

Shamay-Tsoory, S. G., Tomer, R., Goldsher, D., Berger, B. D., & Aharon-Peretz, J. (2004). Impairment in cognitive and affective empathy in patients with brain lesions: anatomical and cognitive correlates. *Journal of Clinical and Experimental Neuropsychology, 26*(8), 1113–1127.

Shanafelt, T. D., West, C., Zhao, X., Novotny, P., Kolars, J., Habermann, T., & Sloan, J. (2005). Relationship Between Increased Personal Well-Being and Enhanced Empathy Among Internal Medicine Residents. *Journal of General Internal Medicine, 20*(7), 559–564.

Shea, M. T., Stout, R. L., Yen, S., Pagano, M. E., Skodol, A. E., Morey, L. C., ... Zanarini, M. C. (2004). Associations in the course of personality disorders and Axis I disorders over time. *Journal of Abnormal Psychology, 113*(4), 499–508.

Sheffer, C. E., Penn, D. L., & Cassisi, J. E. (2001). The effects of impression management demands on heart rate, self-reported social anxiety, and social competence in undergraduate males. *Journal of Anxiety Disorders, 15*(3), 171–182.

Shen, B. J., Wachowiak, P. S., & Brooks, L. G. (2005). Psychosocial factors and assessment in cardiac rehabilitation. *Europa Medicophysica, 41*(1), 75–91.

Sifneos, P. E. (1973). The prevalence of "alexithymic" characteristics in psychosomatic patients. *Psychotherapy and Psychosomatics, 22*(2), 255–262.

Singer, T. (2006). The neuronal basis and ontogeny of empathy and mind reading: Review of literature and implications for future research. *Neuroscience & Biobehavioral Reviews, 30*(6), 855–863.

Singer, T., & Lamm, C. (2009). The social neuroscience of empathy. *Annals of the New York Academy of Sciences, 1156*, 81–96.

Singer, T., Seymour, B., O'Doherty, J., Kaube, H., Dolan, R. J., & Frith, C. D. (2004). Empathy for pain involves the affective but not sensory components of pain. *Science (New York, N.Y.), 303*(5661), 1157–1162.

Sladky, R., Höflich, A., Küblböck, M., Kraus, C., Baldinger, P., Moser, E., ... Windischberger, C. (2015). Disrupted Effective Connectivity Between the Amygdala and Orbitofrontal Cortex in Social Anxiety Disorder During Emotion Discrimination Revealed by Dynamic Causal Modeling for fMRI. *Cerebral Cortex, 25*(4), 895–903.

Smeets, T., Dziobek, I., & Wolf, O. T. (2009). Social cognition under stress: differential effects of stress-induced cortisol elevations in healthy young men and women. *Hormones and Behavior, 55*(4), 507–513.

Smith, A. (2010). Cognitive empathy and emotional empathy in human behavior and evolution. *The Psychological Record, 56*(1), 1.

Smith, S. M., & Vale, W. W. (2006). The role of the hypothalamic-pituitary-adrenal axis in neuroendocrine responses to stress. *Dialogues in Clinical Neuroscience, 8*(4), 383–395.

Smyth, N., Thorn, L., Oskis, A., Hucklebridge, F., Evans, P., & Clow, A. (2015). Anxious attachment style predicts an enhanced cortisol response to group psychosocial stress. *Stress, 18*(2), 143–148.

Soares, J. M., Sampaio, A., Ferreira, L. M., Santos, N. C., Marques, P., Marques, F., ... Sousa, N. (2013). Stress Impact on Resting State Brain Networks. *PLoS ONE, 8*(6).

Solano-Castiella, E., Anwander, A., Lohmann, G., Weiss, M., Docherty, C., Geyer, S., ... Turner, R. (2010). Diffusion tensor imaging segments the human amygdala in vivo. *NeuroImage, 49*(4), 2958–2965.

Soma, K. K., Scotti, M.-A. L., Newman, A. E. M., Charlier, T. D., & Demas, G. E. (2008). Novel mechanisms for neuroendocrine regulation of aggression. *Frontiers in Neuroendocrinology, 29*(4), 476–489.

Sonnby-Borgström, M. (2002). [The facial expression says more than words. Is emotional "contagion" via facial expression the first step toward empathy?]. *Lakartidningen, 99*(13), 1438–1442.

Spielberger, C. D., Gorsuch, R. L., & Lushene, R. E. (1970). *Manual for the State-Trait Anxiety Inventory*. Palo Alto, CA: Consulting Psychologists Press,.

Spokas, M., Luterek, J. A., & Heimberg, R. G. (2009). Social anxiety and emotional suppression: The mediating role of beliefs. *Journal of Behavior Therapy and Experimental Psychiatry, 40*(2), 283–291.

Spurr, J. M., & Stopa, L. (2002). Self-focused attention in social phobia and social anxiety. *Clinical Psychology Review, 22*(7), 947–975.

Sripada, C. S., Angstadt, M., Banks, S., Nathan, P. J., Liberzon, I., & Phan, K. L. (2009). Functional neuroimaging of mentalizing during the trust game in social anxiety disorder: *NeuroReport, 20*(11), 984–989.

Stangier, U., & Heidenreich, T. (2005). Die Liebowitz Soziale Angst-Skala (LSAS). In CIPS (Ed.), *Internationale Skalen für Psychiatrie*. Göttingen: Hogrefe.

Stangier, U., Heidenreich, T., Berardi, A., Golbs, U., & Hoyer, J. (1999). Die Erfassung sozialer Phobie durch die Social Interaction Anxiety Scale (SIAS) und die Social Phobia Scale (SPS). *Zeitschrift Für Klinische Psychologie Und Psychotherapie, 28*(1), 28–36.

Stangier, U., Heidenreich, T., & Peitz, M. (2003). *Soziale Phobien: Ein kognitivverhaltenstherapeutisches Behandlungsmanual* (1st ed.). Weinheim: BeltzPVU.

Stangier, U., Schramm, E., Heidenreich, T., Berger, M., & Clark, D. M. (2011). Cognitive therapy vs interpersonal psychotherapy in social anxiety disorder: a randomized controlled trial. *Archives of General Psychiatry, 68*(7), 692–700.

Starcke, K., Polzer, C., Wolf, O. T., & Brand, M. (2011). Does stress alter everyday moral decision-making? *Psychoneuroendocrinology, 36*(2), 210–219.

Stein, D. J. (2009). Social anxiety disorder in the West and in the East. *Annals of Clinical Psychiatry: Official Journal of the American Academy of Clinical Psychiatrists, 21*(2), 109–117.

Stein, D. J., Ipser, J. C., & Balkom, A. J. (2004). Pharmacotherapy for social phobia. *The Cochrane Database of Systematic Reviews*, (4), CD001206.

Stein, M. B. (1998). Neurobiological perspectives on social phobia: from affiliation to zoology. *Biological Psychiatry, 44*(12), 1277–1285.

Stein, M. B., Chartier, M. J., Kozak, M. V., King, N., & Kennedy, J. L. (1998). Genetic linkage to the serotonin transporter protein and 5HT2A receptor genes excluded in generalized social phobia. *Psychiatry Research, 81*(3), 283–291.

Stein, M. B., Heuser, I. J., Juncos, J. L., & Uhde, T. W. (1990). Anxiety disorders in patients with Parkinson's disease. *The American Journal of Psychiatry, 147*(2), 217–220.

Stein, M. B., & Kean, Y. M. (2000). Disability and quality of life in social phobia: epidemiologic findings. *The American Journal of Psychiatry, 157*(10), 1606–1613.

Stein, M. B., & Stein, D. J. (2008). Social anxiety disorder. *The Lancet, 371*(9618), 1115–1125.

Steinbeis, N., Bernhardt, B. C., & Singer, T. (2012). Impulse control and underlying functions of the left DLPFC mediate age-related and age-independent individual differences in strategic social behavior. *Neuron, 73*(5), 1040–1051.

Steinbeis, N., Engert, V., Linz, R., & Singer, T. (2015). The effects of stress and affiliation on social decision-making: Investigating the tend-and-befriend pattern. *Psychoneuroendocrinology, 62*, 138–148.

Stephens, M. A. C., & Wand, G. (2012). Stress and the HPA Axis. *Alcohol Research : Current Reviews, 34*(4), 468–483.

Steptoe, A., & Wardle, J. (2005). Cardiovascular stress responsivity, body mass and abdominal adiposity. *International Journal of Obesity (2005), 29*(11), 1329–1337.

Stocks, E. L., Lishner, D. A., & Decker, S. K. (2009). Altruism or psychological escape: Why does empathy promote prosocial behavior? *European Journal of Social Psychology, 39*(5), 649–665.

Stopa, L., & Clark, D. M. (1993). Cognitive processes in social phobia. *Behaviour Research and Therapy, 31*(3), 255–267.

Stopa, L., & Clark, D. M. (2000). Social phobia and interpretation of social events. *Behaviour Research and Therapy, 38*(3), 273–283.

Strahler, J., Mueller, A., Rosenloecher, F., Kirschbaum, C., & Rohleder, N. (2010). Salivary alpha-amylase stress reactivity across different age groups. *Psychophysiology, 47*(3), 587–595.

Straub, E. (1990). Commentary on Part I. In N. Eisenberg (Ed.), *Empathy and its development* (pp. 103–115). Cambridge: England: Cambridge University Press.

Straube, T., Mentzel, H.-J., & Miltner, W. H. R. (2005). Common and distinct brain activation to threat and safety signals in social phobia. *Neuropsychobiology, 52*(3), 163–168.

Stravynski, A., & Greenberg, D. (1989). Behavioural Psychotherapy for Social Phobia and Dysfunction. *International Review of Psychiatry, 1*(3), 207–217.

Swaab, D. F., Nijveldt, F., & Pool, C. W. (1975). Distribution of oxytocin and vasopressin in the rat supraoptic and paraventricular nucleus. *The Journal of Endocrinology, 67*(3), 461–462.

Takahashi, T., Ikeda, K., & Hasegawa, H. (2007). Social evaluation-induced amylase elevation and economic decision-making in the dictator game in humans. *Neuro Endocrinology Letters, 28*(5), 662–665.

Talati, A., Pantazatos, S. P., Schneier, F. R., Weissman, M. M., & Hirsch, J. (2013). Grey Matter Abnormalities in Social Anxiety Disorder: Primary, Replication, and Specificity Studies. *Biological Psychiatry, 73*(1), 75–84.

Tamres, L. K., Janicki, D., & Helgeson, V. S. (2002). Sex differences in coping behavior: A meta-analytic review and an examination of relative coping. *Personality and Social Psychology Review, 6*(1), 2–30.

Taylor, C. T., & Alden, L. E. (2011). To see ourselves as others see us: an experimental integration of the intra and interpersonal consequences of self-protection in social anxiety disorder. *Journal of Abnormal Psychology, 120*(1), 129–141.

Taylor, S. (1996). Meta-analysis of cognitive-behavioral treatments for social phobia. *Journal of Behavior Therapy and Experimental Psychiatry, 27*(1), 1–9.

Taylor, S. (2006). Tend and Befriend: Biobehavioral Bases of Affiliation Under Stress. *Current Directions in Psychological Science*, *15*(6), 273–277.

Taylor, S., Gonzaga, G. C., Klein, L. C., Hu, P., Greendale, G. A., & Seeman, T. E. (2006). Relation of oxytocin to psychological stress responses and hypothalamic-pituitary-adrenocortical axis activity in older women. *Psychosomatic Medicine*, *68*(2), 238–245.

Taylor, S., Klein, L. C., Lewis, B. P., Gruenewald, T. L., Gurung, R. A. R., & Updegraff, J. A. (2000). Biobehavioral responses to stress in females: Tend-and-befriend, not fight-or-flight. *Psychological Review*, *107*(3), 411–429.

Teo, A. R., Lerrigo, R., & Rogers, M. A. M. (2013). The role of social isolation in social anxiety disorder: a systematic review and meta-analysis. *Journal of Anxiety Disorders*, *27*(4), 353–364.

Teruhisa, U., Ryoji, H., Taisuke, I., Tatsuya, S., Fumihiro, M., & Tatsuo, S. (1981). Use of saliva for monitoring unbound free cortisol levels in serum. *Clinica Chimica Acta*, *110*(2), 245–253.

Thomasson, P., & Psouni, E. (2010). Social anxiety and related social impairment are linked to self-efficacy and dysfunctional coping. *Scandinavian Journal of Psychology*, *51*(2), 171–178.

Thompson, S., & Rapee, R. M. (2002). The effect of situational structure on the social performance of socially anxious and non-anxious participants. *Journal of Behavior Therapy and Experimental Psychiatry*, *33*(2), 91–102.

Tibi-Elhanany, Y., & Shamay-Tsoory, S. G. (2011). Social cognition in social anxiety: first evidence for increased empathic abilities. *The Israel Journal of Psychiatry and Related Sciences*, *48*(2), 98–106.

Tickle-Degnen, L., & Rosenthal, R. (1990). The Nature of Rapport and Its Nonverbal Correlates. *Psychological Inquiry*, *1*(4), 285–293.

Tiihonen, J., Kuikka, J., Bergström, K., Lepola, U., Koponen, H., & Leinonen, E. (1997). Dopamine reuptake site densities in patients with social phobia. *The American Journal of Psychiatry*, *154*(2), 239–242.

Tillfors, M., Furmark, T., Marteinsdottir, I., & Fredrikson, M. (2002). Cerebral blood flow during anticipation of public speaking in social phobia: a PET study. *Biological Psychiatry*, *52*(11), 1113–1119.

Trower, P., Bryant, B., & Argyle, M. (1978). *Social skills and mental health*. University of Pittsburgh Press.

Tucker, J. S., & Anders, S. L. (1998). Adult Attachment Style and Nonverbal Closeness in Dating Couples. *Journal of Nonverbal Behavior*, *22*(2), 109–124.

Turecki, G., & Meaney, M. J. (2016). Effects of the Social Environment and Stress on Glucocorticoid Receptor Gene Methylation: A Systematic Review. *Biological Psychiatry*, *79*(2), 87–96.

Turner, S. M., Beidel, D. C., & Townsley, R. M. (1992). Social phobia: a comparison of specific and generalized subtypes and avoidant personality disorder. *Journal of Abnormal Psychology*, *101*(2), 326.

Twentyman, C. T., & McFall, R. M. (1975). Behavioral training of social skills in shy males. *Journal of Consulting and Clinical Psychology*, *43*(3), 384–395.

Tybout, A., Sternthal, B., Keppel, G., Verducci, J., Meyers-Levy, J., Barnes, J., ... Maxwell, S. (2001). Analysis of Variance. *Journal of Consumer Psychology*, *10*(1), 5–35.

Ugurbil, K. (2016). What is feasible with imaging human brain function and connectivity using functional magnetic resonance imaging. *Phil. Trans. R. Soc. B*, *371*(1705), 20150361.

Uhde, T. W., Tancer, M. E., Gelernter, C. S., & Vittone, B. J. (1994). Normal urinary free cortisol and postdexamethasone cortisol in social phobia: comparison to normal volunteers. *Journal of Affective Disorders, 30*(3), 155–161.

Ulrich-Lai, Y. M., & Herman, J. P. (2009). Neural regulation of endocrine and autonomic stress responses. *Nature Reviews Neuroscience, 10*(6), 397–409.

Uvnäs-Moberg, K., Ahlenius, S., Hillegaart, V., & Alster, P. (1994). High doses of oxytocin cause sedation and low doses cause an anxiolytic-like effect in male rats. *Pharmacology, Biochemistry, and Behavior, 49*(1), 101–106.

van der Linden, G. J., Stein, D. J., & van Balkom, A. J. (2000). The efficacy of the selective serotonin reuptake inhibitors for social anxiety disorder (social phobia): a meta-analysis of randomized controlled trials. *International Clinical Psychopharmacology, 15 Suppl 2*, S15-23.

van Honk, J., Bos, P. A., Terburg, D., Heany, S., & Stein, D. J. (2015). Neuroendocrine models of social anxiety disorder. *Dialogues in Clinical Neuroscience, 17*(3), 287–293.

Van Overwalle, F. (2009). Social cognition and the brain: a meta-analysis. *Human Brain Mapping, 30*(3), 829–858.

van Peer, J. M., Spinhoven, P., Dijk, J. G. van, & Roelofs, K. (2009). Cortisol-induced enhancement of emotional face processing in social phobia depends on symptom severity and motivational context. *Biological Psychology, 81*(2), 123–130.

van West, D., Claes, S., Sulon, J., & Deboutte, D. (2008). Hypothalamic-pituitary-adrenal reactivity in prepubertal children with social phobia. *Journal of Affective Disorders, 111*(2–3), 281–290.

Vassilopoulos, S. P. (2005). Social Anxiety and the Vigilance-Avoidance Pattern of Attentional Processing. *Behavioural and Cognitive Psychotherapy, 33*(1), 13–24.

von Dawans, B., Fischbacher, U., Kirschbaum, C., Fehr, E., & Heinrichs, M. (2012). The social dimension of stress reactivity: acute stress increases prosocial behavior in humans. *Psychological Science, 23*(6), 651–660.

von Dawans, B., Kirschbaum, C., & Heinrichs, M. (2011). The Trier Social Stress Test for Groups (TSST-G): A new research tool for controlled simultaneous social stress exposure in a group format. *Psychoneuroendocrinology, 36*(4), 514–522.

Voncken, M., Alden, L. E., Bögels, S. M., & Roelofs, J. (2008). Social rejection in social anxiety disorder: The role of performance deficits, evoked negative emotions and dissimilarity. *British Journal of Clinical Psychology, 47*(4), 439–450.

Voncken, M., & Bögels, S. M. (2008). Social performance deficits in social anxiety disorder: Reality during conversation and biased perception during speech. *Journal of Anxiety Disorders, 22*(8), 1384–1392.

Voncken, M., & Bögels, S. M. (2009). Physiological blushing in social anxiety disorder patients with and without blushing complaints: Two subtypes? *Biological Psychology, 81*(2), 86–94.

Voncken, M., Bögels, S. M., & de Vries, K. (2003). Interpretation and judgmental biases in social phobia. *Behaviour Research and Therapy, 41*(12), 1481–1488.

Voncken, M., & Dijk, K. F. L. (2013). Socially Anxious Individuals Get a Second Chance After Being Disliked at First Sight: The Role of Self-Disclosure in the Development of Likeability in Sequential Social Contact. *Cognitive Therapy and Research, 37*(1), 7–17.

Vriends, N., Bolt, O. C., & Kunz, S. M. (2014). Social anxiety disorder, a lifelong disorder? A review of the spontaneous remission and its predictors. *Acta Psychiatrica Scandinavica, 130*(2), 109–122.

Walter, H. (2012). Social Cognitive Neuroscience of Empathy: Concepts, Circuits, and Genes. *Emotion Review, 4*(1), 9–17.

Washburn, D., Wilson, G., Roes, M., Rnic, K., & Harkness, K. L. (2016). Theory of mind in social anxiety disorder, depression, and comorbid conditions. *Journal of Anxiety Disorders*, *37*, 71–77.

Weiner, K. S., & Zilles, K. (2016). The anatomical and functional specialization of the fusiform gyrus. *Neuropsychologia*, *83*, 48–62.

Wells, A., Clark, D. M., Salkovskis, P., Ludgate, J., Hackmann, A., & Gelder, M. (1995). Social phobia: The role of in-situation safety behaviors in maintaining anxiety and negative beliefs. *Behavior Therapy*, *26*(1), 153–161.

Werner, K. H., Goldin, P. R., Ball, T. M., Heimberg, R. G., & Gross, J. J. (2011). Assessing Emotion Regulation in Social Anxiety Disorder: The Emotion Regulation Interview. *Journal of Psychopathology and Behavioral Assessment*, *33*(3), 346–354.

Wersebe, H., Sijbrandij, M., & Cuijpers, P. (2013). Psychological group-treatments of social anxiety disorder: a meta-analysis. *PloS One*, *8*(11), e79034.

Windle, R. J., Shanks, N., Lightman, S. L., & Ingram, C. D. (1997). Central oxytocin administration reduces stress-induced corticosterone release and anxiety behavior in rats. *Endocrinology*, *138*(7), 2829–2834.

Wittchen, H.-U., & Fehm, L. (2003). Epidemiology and natural course of social fears and social phobia. *Acta Psychiatrica Scandinavica*, *108*, 4–18.

Wittchen, H.-U., Fuetsch, M., Sonntag, H., Müller, N., & Liebowitz, M. (2000). Disability and quality of life in pure and comorbid social phobia. Findings from a controlled study. *European Psychiatry*, *15*(1), 46–58.

Wittchen, H.-U., Zaudig, M., & Fydrich, T. (1997). *SKID Strukturiertes Klinisches Interview für DSM-IV Achse I und II*. Göttingen: Hogrefe.

Wolf, O. T., Schommer, N. C., Hellhammer, D. H., McEwen, B. S., & Kirschbaum, C. (2001). The relationship between stress induced cortisol levels and memory differs between men and women. *Psychoneuroendocrinology*, *26*(7), 711–720.

Wölwer, W., Frommann, N., Halfmann, S., Piaszek, A., Streit, M., & Gaebel, W. (2005). Remediation of impairments in facial affect recognition in schizophrenia: efficacy and specificity of a new training program. *Schizophrenia Research*, *80*(2–3), 295–303.

Wykes, T., Huddy, V., Cellard, C., McGurk, S. R., & Czobor, P. (2011). A meta-analysis of cognitive remediation for schizophrenia: methodology and effect sizes. *The American Journal of Psychiatry*, *168*(5), 472–485.

Yeganeh, R. (2005). *Social Phobia and Occupational Functioning*. (Doctoral Dissertation). University of Maryland, College Park.

Yehuda, R., Giller, E. L., Southwick, S. M., Lowy, M. T., & Mason, J. W. (1991). Hypothalamic-pituitary-adrenal dysfunction in posttraumatic stress disorder. *Biological Psychiatry*, *30*(10), 1031–1048.

Yoon, K. L., Fitzgerald, D. A., Angstadt, M., McCarron, R. A., & Phan, K. L. (2007). Amygdala reactivity to emotional faces at high and low intensity in generalized social phobia: a 4-Tesla functional MRI study. *Psychiatry Research*, *154*(1), 93–98.

Yoon, K. L., & Joormann, J. (2012). Stress reactivity in social anxiety disorder with and without comorbid depression. *Journal of Abnormal Psychology*, *121*(1), 250–255.

Youssef, F. F., Dookeeram, K., Basdeo, V., Francis, E., Doman, M., Mamed, D., ... Legall, G. (2012). Stress alters personal moral decision making. *Psychoneuroendocrinology*, *37*(4), 491–498.

Yuguero, O., Marsal, J. R., Esquerda, M., Vivanco, L., & Soler-González, J. (2016). Association between low empathy and high burnout among primary care physicians and nurses in Lleida, Spain. *European Journal of General Practice*, *0*(0), 1–7.

Yuguero Torres, O., Esquerda Aresté, M., Marsal Mora, J. R., & Soler-González, J. (2015). Association between Sick Leave Prescribing Practices and Physician Burnout and Empathy. *PLoS ONE, 10*(7).

Zahn-Waxler, C., & Radke-Yarrow, M. (1990). The origins of empathic concern. *Motivation and Emotion, 14*(2), 107–130.

Zak, P. J., Stanton, A. A., & Ahmadi, S. (2007). Oxytocin Increases Generosity in Humans. *PLOS ONE, 2*(11), e1128.

Zald, D. H. (2003). The human amygdala and the emotional evaluation of sensory stimuli. *Brain Research Reviews, 41*(1), 88–123.

Ziegler, C., Dannlowski, U., Bräuer, D., Stevens, S., Laeger, I., Wittmann, H., ... Domschke, K. (2015). Oxytocin receptor gene methylation: converging multilevel evidence for a role in social anxiety. *Neuropsychopharmacology, 40*(6), 1528–1538.

Ziv, M., Goldin, P. R., Jazaieri, H., Hahn, K. S., & Gross, J. J. (2013). Is there less to social anxiety than meets the eye? Behavioral and neural responses to three socio-emotional tasks. *Biology of Mood & Anxiety Disorders, 3*, 5.

Zorn, J. V., Schür, R. R., Boks, M. P., Kahn, R. S., Joëls, M., & Vinkers, C. H. (2016). Cortisol stress reactivity across psychiatric disorders: A systematic review and meta-analysis. *Psychoneuroendocrinology, 77*, 25–36.